WOMEN'S LIV
CLOTHES IN WW2

WOMEN'S LIVES AND CLOTHES IN WW2
READY FOR ACTION

LUCY ADLINGTON

PEN & SWORD
HISTORY

AN IMPRINT OF PEN & SWORD BOOKS LTD.
YORKSHIRE - PHILADELPHIA

First published in Great Britain in 2019 by
PEN AND SWORD HISTORY
an imprint of
Pen and Sword Books Ltd
Yorkshire – Philadelphia

Hardback ISBN 978 1 52671 234 9
Paperback ISBN 978 1 52676 646 5

Typeset in Times New Roman 11/13 by
Aura Technology and Software Services, India

Printed and bound in India by Replika Press Pvt. Ltd.

Pen & Sword Books Ltd incorporates the imprints of Pen & Sword
Archaeology, Atlas, Aviation, Battleground, Discovery,
Family History, History, Maritime, Military, Naval, Politics, Railways,
Select, Social History, Transport, True Crime, Claymore Press,
Frontline Books, Leo Cooper, Praetorian Press, Remember When,
Seaforth Publishing and Wharncliffe.

For a complete list of Pen & Sword titles please contact
PEN & SWORD BOOKS LIMITED
47 Church Street, Barnsley, South Yorkshire, S70 2AS, England
E-mail: enquiries@pen-and-sword.co.uk
Website: www.pen-and-sword.co.uk

Or
PEN AND SWORD BOOKS
1950 Lawrence Rd, Havertown, PA 19083, USA
E-mail: Uspen-and-sword@casematepublishers.com
Website: www.penandswordbooks.com

Contents

Acknowledgements

With extra special thanks to Denise Curran for beautiful studio photographs, and to the fabulous studio models Francesca Duvall, Lucy Taylor, Meridith Towne, Vee Taylor, Iris Hillery and Elsie Walton.

With thanks also to the many, many people who provided support, photographs, memories, tours, family history, and who donated 1940s clothing to the ever-expanding History Wardrobe collection

Rachel Adie-Rhodes, Ben and Lorna Adlington, Ann Allan, Rachael Applegate, Paula Arkley, Annie Ayling, Ann Ayres, Mary Baldwin, Mavis Ballinger, Sarah Bartlett, Bankfield Museum, Elsie Beesley, Hanni Begg, Pauline Bell, Avri Ben-Ze'Ev, Dorothy Blewitt, Warren Bone, Stephen Bourne, Judy Brown, Sandi Bullen Janet Bulman-Hawes, Maureen Burrell, Barbara Button, Janet Callender, Miriam Joan Campbell, Lorna Carr, Janet Carter, Jenny Cathcart, Eva Clarke, Jim and Jenny Clarke, Veronica Coatham, Stephanie Coghlan, Christine Cole, Marion Crofts, Richard and Jan Crouch, Bridget Cuthbertson, Lindsey Devey, Digital Images York, Wendy Doeser, Sheila Duncan, Jean Elliot, Enid Ellis, Norman Ellis, Elvington Air Museum, Barbara English, Eunice Fairless, Patricia Ferguson, Mary Firth, Evelyn Gibbs, Judith Gilbert, Cate Gillespie, Judith Gittus, Peggy Glassett, Helen Godson, Yann Golanski, Marilyn Greenwood, Anne Grete, Kris Grey, Ann Guiver, Joan Hackney, Lorna Hale, Dorothy Hanlan, Jenny Harris, Richard Henley, Judith Helsby, Barbara Hind, Valerie Hollinrake, Jean Hordich, Imperial War Museum Manchester, Lynn Ireland, Amy and Paul Kanka, Maureen Kelly, Naomi Kenney, Gillian Kirkham, Wynnith Laidlaw, Kay de Lautour Scott, Paul Lazell, Leicester County Council costume collection, Linda Levick, Val Lewis, Minnie Lindsell, Judith Lindsey, Eileen Little, Vanessa Lorenz, Brigid Lowe, M&S Archives Leeds, Barbara Malcolm, Lesley Manser, Maureen McNeil-Smith, Ann Miller, Elisa Milkes, Helen Mitchell, Roberto Molle, Pam Morgan, Jayne Morland, National Holocaust Centre Ollerton, Nell Nicholson, Sue Oliver, Eileen Orange, Graham Panico, Linda Peace, Chris Pine, Anne Pont, Alison and Robin Powell, Audrey Pratt, Marjorie Pugh, Ruth Pugh, Gaynor Rhodes, Elizabeth Roberts, Helen Rose, Elizabeth Rusby, Noriko Sato, Terry Saunders, Diane Saywell, Jill Scargall, Eva Schloss, Rosalind and Rob Schrimpff, Hildegard McCormick, Mary Sherrard, Patricia Shotton, J.H. Smith, Patricia Snaith, Thalia Soffair, Jo Statham, Christine Steer, Judy Stephens, Pat Swainby, Marjorie Taylor, Ann Tiffany, Liz Tonks,

Acknowledgements

Tullie House Museum, Annette Turner, Elizabeth Turner, Richard and Valerie Tyers, Marjorie Upson, Ulla Vaeretz, Stuart Waite, Elizabeth Walker, Doris Walters, Margaret Walton, Washburn Heritage Centre, Alex Wells, Helen Westmacott, West Yorkshire Archive Service, Peter and Ann Whatson, Liz Whelan, Susan Whitwam, Maxine Willett, Gwen Williams, Susan Wilkinson, Windrush Foundation, Mary Wray, Richard Yasuhara, Hiroko Yomogida.

Picture Credits

All images are from the History Wardrobe collection with the following exceptions: p. 10 WPC6, Jill Scargall; p. 11 Four generations, Jo Statham; p. 17 Norwegian housewife school, Anne Grete; p. 18 Rottenburg painting, Elizabeth Rusby; p. 26 WVS, Iris Hillery; p. 28 NARPAC, Vee Taylor; p. 32 Alice Frain, Elsie Walton; p. 33 Milicianas, Wikicommons; p. 34 Zoya Kosodemyanskaya, Wikicommons; p. 39 Major Adams, Wikicommons; p. 41 Mary Whitwam, Susan Whitwam; p. 42 Russian riflewomen, Stuart Waite; p. 50 Mary Wray, Liz Roberts; p. 51 Freshening Up advert, Meridith Towne; p. 60 Esther Bruce, Stephen Bourne; p. 66 Edith Walton, Elsie Walton; p. 69 Doris Bell, Jenny Cathcart; p. 74 Lee Miller, Wikicommons; p. 75 Czech fabric samples, Graham Panico; p. 84, Blue dress, Vee Taylor; p. 99 Tailor's shop, Janet Bulmer-Hawes; p. 104 US cotton picker, Wikicommons; p. 105 Norwegian farmers, Anne Grete; p. 115 Irene Nequest, Diane Saywell; p. 122 Lettice Curtiss, Yorkshire Air Museum; p. 125, Russian bomber crew, Wikicommons; p. 128 Beachball, Terry Saunders; p. 131 Vivian Bullwinkle, Australian War Memorial; p. 135 Annice Sharp, Ann Tiffany; p. 149 Pyjama pattern, Meridith Towne; p. 154 Silk map housecoat, Macclesfield Museums; p. 159 Sylvia Bailey, Jenny Cathcart; p. 165 Noor Inayat Khan, Wikicommons; p. 167 Party girls, Audrey Pratt; p. 170 Peggy Colbourne, Susan Wilkinson; p. 172 Hattie McDaniel, Wikicommons; p. 173 Elisabeth Welch, Stephen Bourne; pp. 173/175 Mildred Turner, Terry Saunders; p. 194 New Zealand bride, Elizabeth Rusby; p. 197 1940 wedding, Alex Wells; p. 198 Nancy wedding, Christine Cole; p. 222 Civil Defence uniform, Vee Taylor; p. 231 Stella Eves, Robin Powell; p. 243 SS guards, Wikicommons (Yad Vashem); p. 246 Marta Fuchs, Thalia Soffair.

Whilst every effort has been made to trace the owners of copyright material, the author would like to apologise for any omissions and will be pleased to incorporate missing acknowledgements in any future editions.

Introduction

ON THE MOVE

'War has at all times called for the fortitude of women. Even in other days when it was the affair of the fighting forces only. Now all this has changed. For we, no less than men, have real and vital work to do.'

Speech by Queen Elizabeth for Armistice Day, 11 November 1939

I visited Berlin one cold February a few years back. The city was overlaid with so many historical experiences, yet vibrant with modern energy and architecture. I sought out the usual mementoes of past conflict – the re-built Reichstag building, Checkpoint Charlie, chunks of Berlin Wall. Crows perched on the hauntingly beautiful grey slabs of the Holocaust memorial built above wartime bunkers.

Amid all this history, the story that stuck in my mind was a snippet recounted by a teacher I knew, whose mother had been in the *Bund Deutscher Mädel* (Nazi League of German Girls). On the day Berlin buzzed with the news of a near-miss assassination attempt of Hitler this young German came up the steps of the metro and all she could think about was that her shoe strap had broken. Little details such as this ground us amid more monumental events.

There are many shoes among my collection of antique and vintage clothing, including a fascinating range of styles from the 1940s. Silver dance shoes speak of bright nights out and music. Wooden-soled shoes show thrift in the face of leather shortages. There are wellington boots for mucking out cattle and hobnailed shoes for trudging. Japanese straw *geta* sandals, and tiny Chinese *lotus* shoes of frayed red silk. Polished service shoes suggest a smart turn-out on the parade square. Marabou fringed boudoir slippers entice to more seductive activities.

This book explores the lives of women around the world during the Second World

This home-made cloth doll in Ukrainian clothes is a modest object, but it represents daily life in home and fields, the prevalence of female sewing skills, and a child's comfort in troubled times.

9

Above left: *Annie Ashby, bus conductor in Northamptonshire, 1941 – one of millions of women doing their bit in work previously considered men only. She is dressed fit for purpose.*

Above right: *WPC Miriam Campbell, one of only nine policewomen in the Lincolnshire Constabulary, armed with a whistle and a tin helmet. She met her husband, a returning prisoner of the Japanese, while in the police force.*

War – the very same people who would have worn such shoes. I've chosen to focus on women's experiences as a contrast to the concept that war is a male world, taking place only on battlefields, or in high-powered strategy meetings. War isn't an isolated event, fought by a few select combatants according to definable parameters. War affects everyone. Women experienced perilous daily realities of war. They were also remarkably active participants at almost every level. In this book we'll encounter spies, generals, soldiers, sailors, pilots, farmers, machinists and doctors. We'll also meet less obvious heroes of everyday life – the housewives, mothers, volunteers, writers, singers, cooks and prisoners. The women who make the tea and sew on buttons and hundreds of other tasks that never earn them medals or monuments.

When writing about women's lives there are an inspiring number of sources to draw on, including personal testimonies, historical sites, archives, art and

Above left: *c. 1944. Four generations of a family. Jo is the little girl. Her great grandmother Emily is seated, wearing black in continual mourning for her youngest son, killed in 1919. Jo's mother Olive is in the long bridesmaid's dress. Her grandmother Rose (left), a talented seamstress who worked at Harrods, made all the outfits, including her own dusky-pink-and-rust dress.*

Above right: *My grandmother Ella Pugh. Dressmaker, mother, housewife, artist, and maker of supremely delicious steamed puddings.*

artefacts. I've been lucky to meet with many 'veterans' during my twenty years of touring the UK to give presentations about social history. Over cups of coffee and plates of biscuits we've talked about their wartime days and what happened afterwards. I've browsed their photograph albums and rustled in tissue paper for lovingly-stored mementoes. As the years roll on it is often women who outlive men, so now we turn to them to ask, 'What did you do during the war?' Mostly it's too late for questions. We are left with what remains. Words. Pictures. Film. Archaeology. And clothes.

'In Hong Kong, when we first heard the news that the war had broken out, a girl classmate in my dormitory started panicking. "What am I going to do? I have nothing appropriate to wear!" she cried'
    From the Ashes by Eileen Chang.
                                        Heaven and Earth Monthly, 5 February 1944

A portrait of classic American style and confidence, inscribed 'To the sweetest mother in the world.' Fashion defied war.

Objects tell stories. They give history a tactile dimension. I'm a dress historian, so for me 'material culture' means looking at people's lives through clothes, sewing and textiles. For too long there's been a misguided belief that clothes aren't important, or that they're only significant to women. This may be true of fashion in some respects, but clothes are crucial to everyone. As uniforms they give a sense of identity, and a loss of individuality to a greater cause. As protection they are essential, providing warmth, camouflage or a sunscreen. They are key to attraction, to expression of

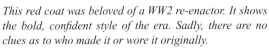

This red coat was beloved of a WW2 re-enactor. It shows the bold, confident style of the era. Sadly, there are no clues as to who made it or wore it originally.

personal flair and to textile artistry. They are a core component of human dignity and civilisation.

Clothes are sometimes all that survive when the people are gone. They are empty of life yet resonant with clues about the person who made, wore and stored the garment. Sweat stains, rips, darns, rank badges and couture labels, these are all details that humanise greater dramas. Throughout the book I've featured clothes from my own collection, many with personal histories. You'll see these modelled in studio shots, along with contemporary photographs. Aside from my own family treasures, some items have been donated by people who attend my 'History Wardrobe' presentations; some are gleaned from auction sites and car boot sales. There are few couture labels. These are everyday clothes and uniforms, worn by women to be ready for whatever they needed to do.

'When we were first married I didn't mind going without, or wearing the same dress all the time, and I would wash the same tablecloth every day and keep using it because I treasured every object, however small, in my possession'.

Gena Turgel, Holocaust survivor, *I Light a Candle*.

A Japanese dressmaking academy, circa 1948. Girls learned pattern drafting, cutting, making up and finishing. They made Western-style clothes in cotton, rayon and nylon.

Historians are adept at using a range of sources to seek out stories that may have stayed unseen. There is a lot more work to be done exploring the lives of women in the 1940s. I have, on the whole, been limited to sources available to me, translated into English. Because I'm based in England, this book has a strong British element. However, I also love to travel, so I have linked to stories and lives worldwide, gleaning histories and textiles from women on almost every continent. Of course this cannot

Above left: *In war or peace there are daily tasks to keep home, family and community working. This young Palestinian woman is no stranger to manual labour. Water had to be carried from the well by hand.*

Above right: *A girl from the Aleutian Islands, dressed for warmth and resilience while soldiers and ships gather to hold this strategic part of Alaska.*

Below: *Detail of a mid-twentieth century quilt. The pieces are taken from pyjamas, shirts and dresses – little bits of people's lives and memories stitched together.*

be a comprehensive account. The scope is, essentially, one billion women over ten years. Out of this number I've picked a tantalising selection of names, faces and incidents. There are some famous figures. Mostly they are women known only to their family, friends and colleagues. Do they deserve a place in a history book? Yes, if you believe that history is made up of myriad experiences, each a part of the whole.

In many cases there are glimpses only of non-Western non-European cultures. Too often women's experiences were considered inconsequential and left unrecorded, particularly when under colonial rule. It's necessary to search in the gaps and the silences. Fortunately, much

14

more work is now being done to amplify lost voices and give focus to those who've been invisible in mainstream remembrance. For those wanting to explore further, there is an extensive bibliography at the back of the book.

This book is an impressionistic history – a patchwork of lives. While each piece is individual, overall it is possible to see intriguing patterns. In my years of research I've been struck by the similarities of experiences as well as contrasts of allegiance or geography or culture. Women in war are connected by common fears, abilities, hopes and achievements. They experience high fashion and hard labour; motherhood and military service. I hope you enjoy this fresh perspective on the decade and that it leaves you with an appreciation for all the stories clothes can tell.

'War is first of all murder, and then hard work. And then simply ordinary life: singing, falling in love, putting your hair in curlers'.

Svetlana Alexievich, *The Unwomanly Face of War.*

www.historywardrobe.com
www.lucyadlington.com
@historywardrobe

Chapter 1

EVERYWHERE AT ONCE
Volunteers and everyday activities

'In this War, you don't have to be in uniform to be doing your bit for this is total War and everybody is in it. One of the most important parts to be played in this War is that of the housewife.'

British government propaganda card 'It All Depends on Me'.

'Without a doubt, the jobs the woman does in the house are innumerable: Cook, maid, seamstress, embroideress, mender, ironer, nurse, accountant, economist, teacher, hygienist!'

Medina magazine, Spain 1943.

The apron was a wartime uniform for many women worldwide. This is a British CC41 'Utility' apron, designed to be attractive yet serviceable with a cheery print to brighten dull jobs.

Wherever you go in the world there will be people quietly making things work – cleaning, clearing, mending, moving. They are rarely honoured and often overlooked. Some of the most undervalued work comes under the term 'housework' or 'homemaking'. It might seem strange to consider this in the context of a world war. Only recently has there been acknowledgement of the mundane repetitive tasks that enable bigger, bolder achievements.

The term 'maintenance activities' was coined by archaeologists and anthropologists to describe daily domestic work – the staple activities which cumulatively add up to a functioning society. Much of what cultures call women's work is in unpaid maintenance: provisioning, cooking, laundry, cleaning, childcare. This work doesn't stop when war starts. In fact, keeping families and communities functioning is made far harder during war. For women worldwide, a wartime 'uniform' meant an apron or pinafore, or simply their own dresses, sarongs, tunics, trousers or kimonos. They were heroines of everyday life.

Even during war, gendered divisions of work emphasised the domestic, nurturing role of women first and foremost. In 1942, Italian housewives were told, 'Now more than ever each Italian woman must take care of her home.' They were to be as stylish in their housework outfits as their streetwear, with pretty wash-frocks, aprons and wraps.[1] A student in Japan in the same year commented, 'They don't believe in educating girls here.

Trainees at a Norwegian housewife school, learning how to run efficient, hygienic homes.

Their education consists in them becoming good obedient '*yo-me-sans*' i.e., homemakers.[2] In Franco's Spain, the government-supported *Sección Feminina* (Women's Section) rebranded women's domestic work as essential to the functioning of a healthy state. Their 1942 declaration was, 'The true mission of the women is to give children to the Patria.'[3] In China, 1942 saw newspaper debates on the expectation that communist women were to support state enterprises *and* run the home, being criticised if they failed at either.[4] Not surprisingly, war was a catalyst for many women re-thinking their domestic labour. In December 1942, a Lancashire housewife wrote in her diary, 'I cannot see women settling to trivial ways – women who have done worthwhile things.'[5] Without the mundane duties there would be no home life, there would be no functioning society, no new generations, no actual country worth fighting for. The ordinary people doing ordinary jobs during war deserve recognition every bit as much as those who earned the right to parade at war memorial marches.

Doing the laundry might seem a trivial task compared with planning battle tactics, defending a besieged city or advancing into enemy territory, yet clean clothes are crucial for hygiene, well-being and morale. Home laundry in the 1940s was hard work, involving quite primitive equipment and a lot of lugging, particularly in buildings without running water. American and European washing was usually done indoors. Some European apartment blocks had communal laundries in the cellar, although underwear and delicate items would be washed in private. Labour could continue over several days. Iby Knill, born in Slovakia, remembers a washerwoman – Anna – coming to help with the big wash. Anna wore a full skirt, a white blouse,

Artist Kay Atkins painted this image of a typical scene in Rottenburg, Germany. The housewife sweeps, tends an allotment and child-minds while the washing dries on multiple lines.

a flowered apron and a big shawl crossed over in front and tied in the back. Anna's sleeves were soon rolled up as the soap shaving and water boiling began. Strength was essential for managing heavy-duty machines such as the mangle, and for lugging loads of wet washing.[6]

Wartime magazines aimed at women were full of cheery adverts for soap flakes and washing powders, all of which promised miracle cleaning without damaging precious textiles. *Lux* and *Persil* were familiar household names. As the war progressed the adverts are sometimes no more than nicely worded apologies that soap isn't available. A minor issue? Not when underwear, uniforms and nappies needed washing.

War also meant shortages of fuel for heating water; even ironing was limited if electricity supplies were erratic or non-existent. By 1944-5, German housewives despaired of finding soap for clothes; the government advised using ivy leaves to help clean dark-coloured clothing.[7] Living in countries with soap rationing in place often meant choosing between washing clothes and washing oneself.

Save Time, Toil and Temper on Wash Days !

K 2818 "Foldaway"
This new type "Fold-away" Wringer is ideal for the modern home. Well made and thoroughly reliable it is fitted with good quality 16-inch rubber rollers, easily adjustable by pressure screws, and has metal draining tank and removable running board. The frame is of selected wood finished a nice *Cream shade*, and the Wringer closes down to *table top size 23 x 16 ins. Full height 30 ins.* **£5/15/-** Or 16/5 Down.

K 2798 Ironing Board
Well-padded Ironing Board. The strong wooden folding frame is perfectly rigid when in use. Well made with all parts screwed instead of nailed, for extra security. The ironing surface is covered with a thick *Cream coloured woolly material*. Overall size of top, including asbestos iron-rest, 48 x 11 ins. **43/-** Or 6/2 Down.

For Stand or Table
K 2864—Wringer for fixing to Table or Stand. *Cream coloured metal frame with Cantilever pressure screw and adjustable handle.* Good rubber rollers, *size 16 ins. x 2¼ ins. diameter.* Self-lubricating drive. Compact and efficient **86/4** Or 12/4 Down.

K 2786—Metal Stand with tray, as shown...... **34/3** Or 4/11 Down. No tubing supplied.

WASHING BOILER
K 2808—Heavy Galvanized Washing Boiler with strong 10-gallon capacity copper pan well tinned. The Boiler stands on three die-cast Aluminium feet and has an outer casing of 24 gauge galvanized sheet steel. Fitted with hinged lid and knob, and having an 8-inch ring burner and nipple, with ¾-inch brass draw-off tap. A thoroughly reliable Boiler. *Height about 27 ins., diameter about 19 ins.* **66/3** Or 9/6 Down.

"KEYNOTE" WASHER
K 2836—This splendid Washer will halve your wash-day labours. It is hand operated—no electricity required—simple to use, and will wash anything from a handkerchief to a blanket easily and quickly without the slightest damage even to delicate fabrics. Strong, galvanized tank. Household Model as illustrated; 12 gallons capacity. Finished in attractive colours. **£7/14/10** Or 22/2 Down.

Latest Model "Mermaid"
K 2852—This new, improved "Mermaid" auto-lift table-top Wringer is a marvel of compactness and easy handling. The action of lifting the Wringer into position for use automatically brings the table-top to the rear where it acts as a tray to catch the finished washing. A simple release of the cocking handle brings it back to the table position. The frame of the Wringer is strongly constructed of cast-iron sprayed to a pleasing shade of *Green*; the 16 ins. x 2 ins. rubber rollers are specially prepared to give lasting wear and are easily adjusted by two pressure screws. All-metal draining tank with vitreous enamel top measuring 23 ins. x 14 ins. A simple and efficient Wringer specially designed for convenient use in the modern home...... **£7/7/6** Or 21/1 Down.

CEILING CLOTHES AIRER
K 2799—Strong, well-made Clothes Airer, *measuring 6 feet long*, and complete with pulleys, one single and one double wheel, also wood cleat, stout wood rods and metal brackets. Easy to fix. Provides a quick and most convenient method of airing clothes indoors. Length of Rope, 2/- extra. Complete **17/4**

USEFUL LONG BATH
K 2816—This useful Bath is made in extra stout gauge Zinc, with enclosed steel-framed top giving added strength. It measures *4 ft. long, by 20 ins. wide and 13½ ins. deep.* Fitted with two strong handles. Light in weight but exceptionally strong...... **29/9** Or 4/3 Down.

Oval Shape Bath
K 2827—Oval Bath made of heavy gauge sheet Steel, galvanized after manufacture for extra strength, and with double-seamed bottom. Two tubular steel handles firmly riveted to sides. A most useful *size; 24 ins. long, 9½ ins. deep* **16/3**

Non-Splash Dolly Tub
K 2843—Extra strong heavy galvanized Dolly Tub of full size, made with special non-splash rim and strengthened at the bottom with double hoops. A really serviceable Dolly Tub *measuring 18 ins. x 24 ins.* **27/6** Or 3/11 Down.

Clothes Boiling Set
K 2851—A most useful set for boiling and steeping clothes. The Washer is of 4½ gallon capacity, and is made from heavy gauge sheet steel, galvanized after manufacture for extra strength, and finished with double-seamed bottom, riveted handles, well-fitting lid and drainer. *Size 15 ins. diameter, 10 ins. deep.* The handy ladle is 9½ ins. diameter, and has a wooden handle and round beaded edge. The Set is completed by a pair of strong wooden clothes tongs...... The Set **26/11** Or 3/10 Down.

Sweeper with Self Cleaning Brush
K 2804—Very efficient Carpet Sweeper. Self-cleaning Spiral Brush. Japanned Dustpan released in an instant for emptying. Stout rubber furniture guards. Large rubber-tyred wheels. Complete with handle. **47/4** Or 6/9 Down.

5 and 3-Tread Steps with Side Bracket
K 2846—Safe and rigid! These most dependable five-tread Steps are extra strong in construction, yet light in weight for easy carrying, and are specially designed to take weight with perfect safety. A special side-bracket dispenses with the dangerous rope stay. Reliable Steps, built to last a lifetime. **33/6** Or 4/9 Down.

K 2784 As, K 2846 three-tread size...... **18/6**

OXENDALE & CO. LTD., GRANBY HOUSE, MANCHESTER 1

The Oxendales home shopping catalogue for 1949 shows surprisingly unsophisticated housework equipment, urging women to 'save time, toil and temper on wash days!' Basic kit includes a washer, boiler, scrubbing board, wringer, dolly tub and clothes-airer.

Household advice manuals and women's magazines were full of top tips on how to remove stains and wash clothes safely so they lasted longer – no small matter when textiles were in short supply and being thrifty was a necessity, not a fad. The range of stains to be removed is an evocative insight into a 1940s' lifestyle. They include ammonia, blood, butter, candle wax, car grease, chocolate, coffee, cream, glue, grass, ink, lipstick, mildew, mud, paint, paraffin, perspiration, rust, soot, tar and tea. Knitwear, mackintoshes, silks, corsets – all these needed specialist attention. Amateur dry cleaning involved heady concoctions of ammonia, benzine, methylated spirit, oxalic acid, turpentine and borax. And lots of rags.

Lucky the woman who had a semi-automatic washing machine to help with the hefty work. 'My new Canadian husband bought the latest model of washing machine which scared the daylights out of me,' recalled war bride Eileen Little. It proved a godsend as the family grew to include ten children.[8]

In Britain, communal laundries were suggested as a solution to the problem of each housewife struggling alone. Communal facilities were set up after bomb raids left families without equipment – or homes even. However, a 1943 survey of nearly 300 women resulted in a resounding 'no' to the general idea. The survey report concluded, 'We prefer to wash our dirty linen in private.'[9]

Not all cultures had this aversion to group work. Travelling by train to Delhi in 1945, performer Joyce Grenfell described 'eternal wash day' at a river bank outside Madras. Sheets, shirts and saris were whirled and pounded. The ground all around was carpeted

Shared washing was the norm in many cultures. Here Maori women take advantage of hot springs at Rotorua, New Zealand. Their only equipment is a bucket. Clothes are scrubbed by hand.

Apartments in Hong Kong, strung with lines of laundry in 1947. In more rural areas of China and Japan, bamboo poles were used to dry clothes. Around the world there would be washing drying on ropes, in the rafters of attics or strewn on bushes. In summer clothes bleached; in winter they froze to thin sheets of ice.

in grass dyed red, white, green and blue from non-fast sari dyes – 'like a patchwork quilt come to life on a grand scale,' she said.[10] Around the world there would be groups of women gathered around the nearest clear water source, scrubbing and rinsing. Often they carried the wash on their heads, and came with children in tow. Settled villages might build a wash-house, such as the Malayan palm-roofed atap huts where women could wash, chat and child-mind under shelter. This communal labour is still the norm in many countries now. Hiking travelling in Kenya not so many years ago I was struck by the scene of brightly-dressed women slapping cottons in concrete tanks by the street-side; in Kenya a variety of plastic buckets at the water spring was the only obvious clue that this was contemporary laundry, not washday from the 1940s.

'Some of them athletic but not one of them unattractive' – description of railway laundry workers in Colchester, servicing over eight million items per year for railway hotels, refreshment rooms and office. (Major, *Female Railway Workers of World War II*)

Body lice were a significant danger for military personnel and civilians, being vectors for transmitting potentially lethal diseases such as typhus and trench fever. They attach their eggs to clothes; loving seams and creases. Heavy duty washing was needed to keep clothes clean. Partisans in the Polish forest said their shirts would get up and walk away if they didn't pick the lice out daily.[11] In keeping with the notion that washing was 'women's work', it often fell to women to manage military laundries too. Maria Stepanova Detko spent the entire war washing Russian army gear by hand – padded jackets, army shirts, underwear, all infested with lice. In the first wash the water ran red with blood. The shirts had arms missing and holes in the chest. She said, 'you wash them with tears and rinse them with tears.' In winter the wash would be heavy with frozen blood.[12] When invading Russian troops reached Berlin, German women were forced into laundry work for soldiers, given minimal soap and sometimes just a hairbrush for scrubbing. Many of the textiles they ended up washing had been looted from German houses. Cold water was fetched from a street hydrant and heated in a kettle. Sexual harassment was common.[13] High in the Alsace mountains, journalist Lee Miller reported seeing village women washing for the French army, slapping khaki laundry in icy streams.[14]

Laundry is just one example of a humble maintenance activity. Women's labour was also a major contribution to systems of welfare in every nation at war. There were a myriad of women's welfare organisations, some local, some international. This was considered fitting work for women as it still tallied with a supportive, nurturing role. The work might be as seemingly simple as combining a day job as a charlady with knitting socks for the military in the evening, as in the case of young mother Maria Delley in Switzerland. She found the double shift exhausting, particularly after the birth of her first child. Before the war she said she was light-hearted and singing. After the war she never sang.[15]

If the apron was the uniform of the washerwoman, what of the millions of civilians who volunteered their time and talents outside of the home during the war? Their contributions were given a certain validity with the introduction of more obvious, formal uniforms. Putting volunteer workers in uniform was not without controversy. Some said it legitimised women's contributions to war work; others said it made them too masculine.

In New Zealand, the Women's War Service Auxiliary was established to take advantage of volunteer skills. Pakeha and Maori women gave up thousands of hours. Members were satirised as either glamour girls or frumpy battleaxes. There were concerns at the inevitable 'double shift' with one member asking, 'Does the

Young women in the Philippines are snapped by an American serviceman c. 1940. They wear everyday cotton frocks or skirts for the laundry work, sharing limited water and small washtubs. The steel tub in the foreground would be familiar to many Western housewives, known in England as a 'dolly tub'.

government believe that woman's work in the home is so unimportant that it can be left to take care of itself?'[16] The question of uniform was debated in *Woman's Weekly*, December 1940: 'If the uniforms are womanly, adequate and useful and the women wearing them are taking a serious part in the war effort of the nation, the effect of uniforms will surely be to emphasise collective effort.'

The American Women's Voluntary Services was one of many national organisations in the US. It trained and mobilised women for service as drivers, canteen workers, child care staff, and even for mending and repair work. They chose a military-style tunic as uniform with epaulets and fake brass buttons. The motto was *Unite and Serve*. Voluntary work did unite women, giving them a change from the isolation of domestic chores at home.[17]

Women in Japan were mobilised as state volunteers. Various patriotic associations merged to become the Greater Japan's Women's Association, 19 million members strong. Badges and sashes gave a visible sense of civic identity. Japanese culture placed great emphasis on women as protectors of the household. This somehow had to tally with other unpaid activities outside the home, including fire drill and neighbourhood self-defence teams.[18]

Germany boasted one of the most dedicated and politicised of all women's associations – the *Frauenschaft*, or Women's Bureau. National Socialist principles divided the public and private spheres into male and female, effectively eliminating women from politics in 1933 when the party came to power. Headed by the dedicated Gertrud Scholtz-Klink, the League nevertheless made the private home public business. Welfare workers were authorised to penetrate the domestic sphere both to support housewives and to monitor them. Social aid came with a hefty dose of political indoctrination, emphasising women's national destiny as breeders and companions. Sholtz-Klink in no way saw the domestic ethos as oppressive to German women, declaring 'Each of us has an unbreakable bond to the community.'[19] The Women's Labour Service demanded two years of *Deutches Frauenwerk* – obligatory female labour in nursing, childcare or agriculture, all dedicated to the Führer. Sholtz-Klink – usually dressed in an A-line skirt, hand-knit cardigan and sensible shoes – did not care for military-style uniforms, seeing them as too masculine. Essentially she wanted to improve the women's sphere rather than competing in the male world; leaving a legacy of women being a backdrop to mainstream history. One third of the female population of Germany was actively engaged in a Nazi party organisation, often in addition to paid labour and household duties. For better and worse the state could not have functioned without them.[20]

> 'Today they are justly proud of a magnificent record, and of the good-will and affection of the whole Army' – praise for the indefatigable work of the Women's Auxiliary Service (Burma), in jungle green uniform. (Priestley, *British Women Go To War*)

The benefits of welfare work were tremendous. The similarity of tasks worldwide is striking. Volunteers collected clothing for those in need; organised aid stations and first aid training. They ran mobile canteens for workers, and for war-weary soldiers not far from the front line. They oversaw evacuation of children from at-risk areas and helped house those made homeless. It was not glamorous or dramatic work. International groups such as the Women's Institute nevertheless contributed to a country's ability to keep functioning, and to wage total war if necessary. The Girl Guides and YWCA encouraged participation from younger women and girls. It was an immense collaboration.

Originating in Britain, the Women's Voluntary Service was established to provide structure and organisation to individuals wanting to do their bit. Outposts were found around the world, including in India, Nigeria and South Africa. Their work created mutual understanding between countries, and they also linked with the local and the international Red Cross. Their slogan was 'The WVS never says No'. At first, the British government underestimated what the women were

The Salvation Army – an international Christian welfare organisation dating back to the nineteenth century – branded itself as 'The army that serves on every front.' Their canteens, hostels and orphanages were life-savers. Sally Army women wore distinctive dark uniforms and old-fashioned bonnets. Mosques, synagogues and temples around the world also worked hard for the welfare of their communities.

capable of. After the Dunkirk evacuations in 1940, the WVS were initially only asked for darning needles. Despite early dismissive attitudes, the WVS went on to earn high praise from local authorities as they processed exhausted men being returned to England. It was one thing to mock women as fit only for knitting socks – a common attitude during all wars to this point – quite another to see women calmly conjuring up thousands of items of kit for men who'd lost everything. The WVS were spotted removing sodden socks from the feet of sleeping men, washing, drying and mending them, then returning them to their owners. This was in addition to providing canteens and endless cups of hot, sweet tea.[21]

Uniforms were a key part of WVS identity. Top London designer Digby Morton was asked to create a smart outfit that could be reproduced at industrial level. The grey-green was chosen so it wouldn't show dust, with claret red in the official jumper and beret to give a spot of brightness. It had no rank badges – the women all worked together without ostentation. Volunteers bought their own uniforms using their own ration coupons.

A core role for the WVS was the stocking and running of a national system of clothing depots. The first stores grew from cupboards and attics into super-efficient stock warehouses. Reclothing refugees and people who'd lost everything in a bomb raid was an important step in setting them up to start over. One happy side effect of the worldwide clothing collections were the links made between countries. Speakers toured, giving information about the overseas donors, spreading the word that women were united.

The WVS were familiar figures in communities around the world. The official greatcoat was designed to keep its shape so it could be slept in at night.

A wartime WVS group showing a mixture of official clothing and makeshift outfits. WVS skirts were plain to avoid the fuss of ironing. The sleeves were short. There was no need for collar or tie. The felt hat could be worn however the woman wished, to give a spot of individual flair.

'They do not flinch in facing and playing the foremost part in birth and death. They are not even afraid of assuming the most back-breaking of all burdens – the weight of routine.'

Lady Reading, founder of the WVS, praises women's endurance. (Graves, *Women in Green*)

Donations were not limited to clothes. Welfare societies also collected items for care packages. In addition to the usual chocolate, cigarette and soap, packages might contain pyjamas, socks and face flannels. These were simple items that felt like luxuries to prisoners of war, service personnel abroad or refugees. The tangible reminder that they were not forgotten was priceless. The Red Cross Supply stores sent out millions of parcels annually by 1944. Amongst those distributed in hospitals were parcels with plain grey suits for convalescent men. When queried if this was necessary in wartime, the Red Cross pointed out how quickly patients were rehabilitated when they felt they at least looked normal, rather than facing the world in pyjamas. Countless work parties produced the clothing for hospital aid packages, all volunteers. Stock cupboards supplied the tens of thousands of buttons and cotton reels and bales of cloths. Sewers converted them into bed jackets, surgical dressings, blood transfusion bags, and stump covers.

Traditional female roles of hospitality and nurture were expanded during war to encompass caring for evacuees, refugees and fugitives. One woman in Italy, who housed, fed and clothed those fleeing bombardment in nearby towns, called her war 'undramatic and unheroic' despite her daily efforts against the odds. Even so, she remembered individual moments of kindness among all the worry and fatigue – such as seeing a British fugitive PoW helping a peasant woman draw well water. In return, the Italian peasant mended his socks and knitted him a sweater. She even baked a cake for him on the day he left to continue along the escape route to Allied lines.[22] These small, shared moments were a powerful contrast to political ideologies which sought to emphasise divisions between nations and races.

'Whereas every country recognises and applauds its great war heroes, those responsible for death and destruction, no one builds monuments to the glory of the rescuers.'

Tzvetan Todorov, *Facing the Extreme*

War made great demands of everyone. As we'll see in following chapters, women worked hard to fulfil the range of their traditional roles as well as discovering they were capable of so much more. Women kept families intact and salvaged goods after destruction. They gave birth and raised children with absent fathers. They plotted fates via modern communication technology, flew endless air miles, built vessels of war – and were sunk in them. They armed fighters, fought alongside them, then took care of the broken bodies or buried the corpses. They entertained and wooed. They were imprisoned, executed. They were prison guards and torturers. They resisted and collaborated. They celebrated victories, lamented defeats and rebuilt in the aftermath. Although they did not initiate war or oversee its tactics, women truly did seem to be everywhere at once.

Welfare work was not limited to humans only. The National Air Raid Precautions Animal Committee was formed in Britain with the support of vets and animal welfare societies. Volunteers wore a distinguishing brassard. They were trained to log all pets so they could be tracked after air raids.

Chapter 2

TAKING AIM
Resistance, army auxiliaries and combat

'We fight with our spirits, and if we have no guns, we fight with our fists.'

Lo-Yin, Chinese silk shop owner in Lin Taiyi's 1943 novel *War Tide*

Women are no strangers to violence, in public spaces or in the supposed security of their homes. Years ago, working as a teacher in Andalucía, I read the poems of Federico Garcia Lorca including those written during the Spanish Civil War. They are saturated with tears and blood. As palm leaves from the Holy Week festival dried in the hot streets outside, I shared chocolate and *churros* with Spanish and English friends. Our talk turned to the silence around General Franco's oppressive regime. Then came whispers of more recent, more private violence. Stories of harassment and rape. Afterwards, in the cool of the evening, we went out to enjoy life and the stories were put away again.

The violence of war is often legitimised as protective – keeping homes, women and children safe. Traditional gender roles set men as protectors and women as vulnerable. Even now many modern societies are uneasy with the concept of women taking up arms and being violent. However, women have always fought, with or without weapons. During the wars of the 1930s and 1940s they were active in resistance roles, as army auxiliaries, Home Guard members, partisan fighters, infantry soldier and snipers. Women had equal incentive to defend their home, to show their patriotism and

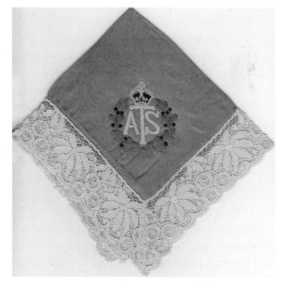

This lace-edged handkerchief embroidered with the ATS insignia is a small yet significant bit of textile evidence highlighting the ambiguous integration of women into a male world – they are army auxiliaries yet still comfortable expressing femininity.

even to avenge attacks on their nation. In 1944, the Allied Military Command's four types of resistance activity were listed as:

- Operations engaging enemy troops
- Military intelligence service
- Sabotage and seizure of enemy materiel
- Creation of civil disorder and passive resistance

Women were engaged in all four aspects. Clothes played their part.

Passive resistance helped civilians retain a sense of control and dignity in the face of overwhelming upheaval. Those in occupied countries or under oppressive regimes found ingenious ways to signal patriotism, including showing allegiance through clothes. This could be via the brown shirts of women in the early National Socialist movement of the 1920s and '30s, or the blue overalls of Spanish communist workers. Poles who supported the fascist invasion of their country showed their loyalty by wearing *Weisstrümpf* – knee-length white socks.[1]

Red, white and blue were symbolic of the British, Dutch and French flags. The colours were sported on jewellery, accessories and even theatre costumes to boost national feeling. In occupied Holland, one Dutch woman showed her defiance by hanging her washing out in the garden, come rain or shine. She always had three garments pegged next to each other, one red, one white, one blue. Flying the actual flag was strictly forbidden. Another Dutch woman knitted white socks for her 5-year-old daughter. Along the top of the socks she added fine bands of red, white and blue. As they passed a distinguished gentleman in the street he bowed and raised his hat to them saying, 'Madam, what delightful socks your daughter is wearing' and so the spirit of resistance was shared.[2] Norwegians who were anti-Hitler wore something red – a scarf, socks or jumper, anything to show their sentiment safely.[3]

Small acts of defiance concerning clothes and accessories always catch my attention, such as the teenage girls on Guernsey who spotted German soldiers swimming in the sea and deftly moved their piles of uniforms closer to the water so the tide would take them.[4] Or the angry French woman used her red lipstick to draw an enormous V sign on the windscreen of a German car.[5] Or the German seamstress who defied Nazi policies towards the Jews by *only* shopping at Jewish stores.[6]

Giving gifts and support could also be an act of resistance. Austrian Anna Strasser worked in an accounts office opposite the Mauthausen concentration camp station. During her lunch breaks she walked in the area, dropping small items that newly arriving prisoners could pick up. These included needles, thread and buttons. She was arrested and sent to a camp herself, but survived. Leopoldine Wagner, an Austrian interpreter at a factory employing slave labourers, gifted a bra-top to a prisoner who had no underwear. An SS officer warned her, 'If you have something to give then give it to a German.'[7]

Women used words as weapons too. Despite being a minority in all official governments, women spoke out. Two diverse examples: in Munich, student Sophie Scholl was executed along with co-conspirators in the 'White Rose' resistance group, for distributing anti-Nazi

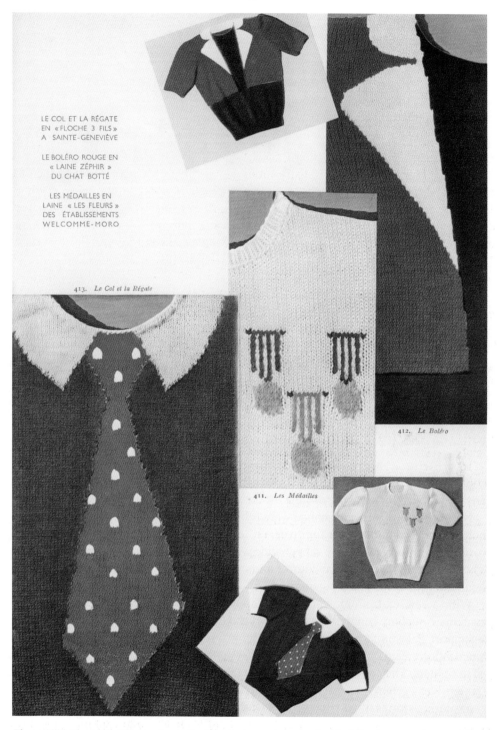

LE COL ET LA RÉGATE
EN «FLOCHE 3 FILS»
A SAINTE-GENEVIÈVE

LE BOLÉRO ROUGE EN
« LAINE ZÉPHIR »
DU CHAT BOTTÉ

LES MÉDAILLES EN
LAINE « LES FLEURS »
DES ÉTABLISSEMENTS
WELCOMME-MORO

413. *Le Col et la Régate*

412. *Le Boléro*

411. *Les Médailles*

These 1939 French knitting patterns for 'illusion' sweaters are clearly following a patriotic tricolour theme, and the military medals show support for French victory in the upcoming war.

No army can function without auxiliaries. Private Alice Frain (standing at the back) was an ATS cook. Her catering notebook details recipes for serving meals in multiples of one hundred.

propaganda; in India, Aruna Asaf Ali – part of a middle class elite, yet dressed in homespun saris – was jailed for speaking out against the war in public.[8]

Networks of wartime resistance were reliant on women in domestic auxiliary roles such as procuring clothes for fugitives, or, in the case of Eva Kløvstad, a leader of the Norwegian *Milorg* resistance movement, washing men's dirty underpants. Elisabeth Schweigaard was a resistance courier and coder who found herself doing dishes and vacuuming for British SOE agents.[9]

With a few exceptions, carrying weapons was considered a male prerogative, but female support supplying arms was valued. In 1947, Egyptian feminists vowed to support Palestinian women in preparations for war. In Jaffa, a secret women's organization called *Zahrat Al-uqhuwan* (Chrysanthemum Flowers) was formed, to give aid to fighters. They also dug trenches, smuggled weapons and there are references to a paramilitary group that did see combat action.[10]

Exploring stories of partisan groups worldwide, it soon becomes clear that women did engage in combat as partisans, as well as sabotage and other acts of resistance. Their aggressive roles were minimised post-war to highlight male heroism and to downplay 'unfeminine' action.

During the Spanish Civil War, communist women – supposedly fighting as equals with men – were primarily diverted away from actual combat to community roles such as running orphanages, kitchens and hospitals. However, the war temporarily broadened gender roles to include women on the frontline as well as the home front. Nearly a thousand of these *milicianas* fought. They were usually teenagers or in their twenties, with some older women. Some joined up assuming they'd serve as auxiliaries, sewing and cooking for men, then taking up weapons to avenge fallen comrades. A female combat group known as the Women's Battalion was stationed outside Madrid. They dressed the same as their male comrades, in dishevelled khaki uniforms. As the war progressed, attitudes shifted once again, and even communist newspapers returned to emphasising sweet, nurturing, supportive traits. Community equality, once represented by men and women wearing the workers' blue-trousered overalls, was quickly repressed under the winning fascist regime. Women were to have needles and cradles, not guns and hand grenades.[11]

'Fancy me, a weak woman, and now I can manage a gun with the ease that I used to wield a needle.'

Carmen, Spanish combat veteran (*Milicianas*)

Spanish milicianas – *military women – in a selection of military uniforms. Young women fighters stepped outside traditional roles in the home.*

In Ethiopia, women took up arms against Italian invaders and occupiers between 1935 and 1941, with the slogan, 'We the Women Will Fight'. This was in addition to the usual army auxiliary roles of nursing and provisioning. At a basic level they harassed enemy forces with avalanches of rocks from hilltops, as well as setting fire to enemy camps. In addition to guerrilla fighting, women fought in pitched battles. Kebedech Seyoum mobilised and commanded an army, fighting with them in men's uniform – while pregnant. Shewareged Gedle was called the Lion-hearted Woman, and the Ethiopian Joan of Arc. She mobilised a team of female patriots who vowed to fight the enemy until death.[12]

Veteran Zenebetch Woldeyes recalled, 'In battle, there was no gender distinction … We did not wear dresses; we wore trousers and jackets like the men and we were considered and treated each other as equals.'[13]

Greek women partisans – *Militini* – fought with the men against the Axis invasion of 1941 and the subsequent occupation. At this time women had virtually no citizenship rights. However, female fighters suffered the same punishments as their male comrades, such as the fighter from Mitillini, Elli Svorou, a former dressmaker, who was executed by firing squad. Other women were sent to concentration camps as punishment. They said it proved their equality when they could endure the same dangers with the same bravery as the men. Greek partisans generally wore the same kit as men – khaki shirts and trousers. One battle veteran, an Athenian girl called Thiella, had the distinction of wearing *lafira*. These were clothes taken from dead enemy soldiers. Even when her compatriots told her to fall in line with the rest of the uniform to look smarter she kept a pair of looted blue trousers because they'd seen her through so many battles.

Not all Greek partisans wore trousers. Fifteen-year-old Xeni was committed to fight after her sister was beaten to death by Germans. She always kept a handgun in her bag and wasn't afraid to use it. It didn't desensitise her to combat. At one time she saw her friends killed in the street and she used her skirt to cover their wounds. The trauma of having her friends' brains on her clothes stayed with her for decades.[14]

Resistance fighters in Polish cities wore what they'd got. Wearing any kind of Polish uniform would have got them shot. Dressed as civilians they were united in their struggle to overthrow occupying forces. Polish partisans often took to the woods to hide, plan and recuperate between sorties. Conditions were harsh. Any sort of clothing was hard to come by, let alone an official uniform. In general women were denied access to arms – these were confiscated by men – and they were put to domestic roles. Tailors and seamstresses worked in primitive conditions, sewing shirts from rough homespun linen.

Italian women also became accustomed to the hardships of living and fighting in rough conditions. Brigades under military command varied in their response to female volunteers. Some told them to stay home; others welcomed them as comrades. While political ideals motivated many female volunteers, some were simply caught up in the action. Maria Gaudino was just fetching water when she got caught in a street battle. She picked up a rifle and began to shoot, raging with anger at the years of hardship, bombings and trauma. She was only 17 years old. All told there were roughly 35,000 female partisan fighters in Italy, including all-female detachments commanded by women.[15]

'I am not here to find a lover. I am here to fight and I will remain here if I am given a weapon'

Elsa Oliva, joining an Italian armed brigade in May 1944.

In China, a few women were held up as role models of noble resistance, though their stories were often sanitised to fit an idealised image of feminine virtue. One of these heroes was Liu Hulan, a teenage member of the Women's National Salvation Association who fought Japanese forces attacking her village. She was beheaded in 1947 and effectively martyred by Mao Ze Dong's communist party. After her death she featured in dramas, comic books and even an opera, but with more emphasis put on her search for romance, rather than her warlike achievements.[17]

Like so many women, Ut Tich, a Vietnamese resistance fighter, took up arms to fight in place of her husband when he went off to war. She became head of the household, carried on the farm production and raised her children. The new communist party under Ho Chi Minh promised an end to inequalities if they could overthrow occupying forces. In 1946, it's estimated that women made up a fifth of all armed units.

Zoya Kosmodemyanskaya, a dedicated Russian partisan executed in 1941 for setting fire to stables of German horses. Although she was reviled by Russian women whose property she destroyed, after her hanging she was turned into a symbol of Soviet resistance.[16]

The first all-woman guerrilla unit was formed in 1945 by Ha Thi Que. The women wore woollen army uniforms, and they also wore the medals they earned with pride. Ho Thi Bi, from a poor farming family, became a guerrilla fighter against French colonials. She and other peasants fought with knives and bamboo sticks with poisoned tips.[18]

It was rare for women to have leadership over male guerrilla fighters. Rare, but not unknown. Ursula Graham-Bower was one of these remarkable wartime heroes. Visiting India as a photographer and anthropologist she fell in love with the area of the Naga Hills, bordering Burma. Local tribespeople came to see her as a kind of white queen. With the full support of the British administration and General Slim she mobilised Naga scouts against Japanese in the mountainous jungle. Her unit was known as 'Bower Force.' The Bower Force maintained trails from Burma to

W/268789 Pte Auld W.R.

FORM IN LIEU OF AFH. 1157.

LIST OF A.T.S. KIT.

Clothing	Kit Held	Necessaries	Kit Held
Anklets prs	1	Badges, cap	1
Blouses BD	1	Bags, kit	2 2
Boots, ~~Leather prs~~ R.K.	1	Bags, soiled linen	1
Caps	1	Belts, corset	2 2
Greatcoats	1	Belts, sanitary	1
Jackets, Serge	1	Brassieres	3 3
Jerkins	1	Discs, identity ~~with~~	
Overalls, Combination	2	cord set	1 2
Shoes, pairs	2 2	Dressings, field	1
Shoes, canvas, prs	1	~~Forks~~	
~~Skirts, serge~~	2 2	Gloves, knitted, drab prs	1
Slacks prs	1	Housewife	1
Sou'wester	1	Jersey woollen	1
~~Caps, P.T.~~	1	Knickers	3 3
		Knives, table	1
		Laces, boots spare prs	1
Cleaning & Toilet Articles.		" shoe "	1
		Lanyards	1
Brassos, cleaning	1	Panties	3 3
Brush, button brass	1	Pyjama Suits	2 2
" Hair	1	Shirts	4 4
" Shoe polishing	1	" collars	8 8
" Tooth	1	Socks worsted prs	4
" Clothes (20% of strength		Spoon	1
held on Unit Charge)		Stockings prs	4 4
Badges Formation 52 prs.		Studs	2
		Ties	3 3
Personal Equipment.		Titles prs	1 2
Bags Ration		Towels	2 2
Bottles water	1	Vests	3 3
Braces, web	1	Satchels	1
Carriers water bottle	1	Knickers PT	2
Whistles artillery	1	Shirts PT	2
Straps for above	1	Skirts Divided PT	1
Haversacks web	1	Cap Comforter	1
~~Helmets steel~~	1	Kerchiefs	3
~~Covers camouflage~~	1		
Rucksacks	1	Personal Equipment (cont.)	
Tins mess set	1	Mugs, drinking 1-pt	1
Dubbin, tins	1	" enamelled ½-pt	1
Sheets ground	1	Plates, steel rimmed	1
Blankets	1	~~Pint arrot A.B.~~	
Sheets	2	~~Resporator A.B. comp Pt~~	8
Pillow Slips	1		
~~Groundsheets~~	1		

It is regretted that items of kit (Deficient) have not been supplied as stores
are not available.

Signature of Auxiliary ...W.R.Auld.

Counter signature of Officer ....B. Helgin .....
Rt

.......Bangust 1945.
B.L.A.

A comprehensive ATS kit list from 1945, including clothes and personal care kit. The clothes included give an idea of possible work conditions: jerkin, sou'wester, greatboots, jersey and slacks.

India, aiding thousands of evacuees and escaped prisoners to reach safety. Bower herself carried a Sten gun, and even featured in a 1945 comic book.[19]

American and European governments were determined *not* to use women in combat. They were to be recruited as auxiliaries only. In Britain the ATS – Auxiliary Territorial Service – was formed as a branch of the British army. Members were on two-thirds of the pay of male soldiers and they were barred from combat. The ATS became the Women's Royal Army Corps in 1949. This official status was welcomed as it signified that women were an official part of the army, no longer camp followers. Their wartime uniform was a belted army-type jacket and skirt, in khaki. Flashes showed the trade, and there

ATS uniform jacket belonging to a 20-year-old corporal, who served in France, Belgium and Hamburg with General Montgomery's GCHQ. While in France she acquired some red velvet from a defunct dress shop. She had it made into a ballgown, then cut down to an evening cloak.

were many, from electricians and vehicle mechanics to switchboard operators and clerks. The kit was considered a perk of joining up – 'They *do* give you such *wizard* pyjamas!' exclaimed one recruiting officer.[20] Trainees weren't so enthusiastic about the khaki overalls: 'They felt so uncomfortable and degrading to wear, almost like we were prisoners.'[21]

There are a endless acronyms for official female military services worldwide. They almost all have one word in common – *auxiliary*. A male clerk was in the army. A female clerk was a needs-must add-on – valuable only for the duration. This is seen in so many countries. In Switzerland women's applications to join the army were dismissed outright – some put straight in the bin. One teacher, Berthe, decided to sign up and was put straight to sewing. She complained,

THEY'RE IN THE ARMY NOW! *SEE CENTRE PAGES*

HOME NOTES

3ᴰ

ON SALE SATURDAY, JUNE 12th, 1943 No. 1678

Jean Gillie in 'THE GENTLE SEX' *The Great Film about the A.T.S.*

Women of the British ATS wore adaptations of male army uniforms, including shirt and tie. This 1943 magazine cover portrays an orderly yet faminine figure – young, smart and with distinctive cosmetics. Hair stayed long, though kept clear of the collar.

This glamorous recruitment poster for American army auxiliaries shows a woman in battledress, with tin helmet as if for combat, but no weapons are carried and no fighting was permitted.

'I am no dressmaker; I liked nothing worse than needlework. It wasn't worth enrolling in the army to sew.' She eventually worked with refugees and stayed in the army post- war.[22]

Unusually, the US Women's Auxiliary Army Corps dropped the word 'auxiliary' to become the Women's Army Corps from 1943. At its peak there were over 4,000 African American women serving, (4.5 per cent of its total strength.)[23] They faced the double discrimination of being female and being black in a wartime environment that was white and mostly male. Lucia Mae Pitts put a voice to the sadness and anger this caused in her poem *A WAC speaks to a soldier* in which the young WAC has been told she has no place in the army, and that she should be at home waiting in a flimsy gown, 'Not in uniform like thousands of others.' The WAC speaks out saying she has swallowed the disapproval 'And joined up just the same.' There was a job to be done and women simply wanted to do it. Hazel L. Washington describes herself in the army – 'Brown like the khaki I wore.'[24]

Six hundred women from the West Indies volunteered to join the ATS. Of these, 200 were posted to the US and 100 served in Britain. They were all well-educated, yet still came up against racism – only white women were sent to America. The British War Office blustered over accepting non-white recruits, attempting to find subtle ways of turning down black women without being accused of colour prejudice. Connie Mark joined the ATS in Jamaica. Army pay gave her a new level of independence, but as a black recruit she came to feel bitter that she was paid less than white officers because of racial prejudice. Although she worked as a medical secretary it was still assumed that she would do cleaning work for English officers. Typing up medical reports of those injured by bombings or combat, gave her a powerful sense of the impact of war. VE day came as a huge relief – 'everyone was happy,' she recalled. 'Everyone just jumped up and down, and it meant that no more of our people would be killed.' Louise Osborne, serving with the ATS in England, found the winter weather bleak after her upbringing on St Lucia. She wore all her kit at once for warmth.[25]

New Zealanders were kitted out in men's uniforms when they first joined the army. This caused a lot of hilarity because sizing was so inappropriate for female figures, but also some embarrassment. Being seen in public in trousers was socially controversial.[26]

Major Charity Adams – the first African American female officer in the US army, inspects Women's Army Auxiliary Corp members stationed in England. Despite her rank and abilities she was once told, 'Don't let being an officer go to your head; you are still colored and I want you to remember that. You people have to stay in your place.' The US armed forces weren't desegregated until 1948. (Adams, *One Woman's Army: A Black Officer Remembers the WAC*)

Margaret McColl (right) joined the First Aid Nursing Yeomanry as a driver. FANY then amalgamated with the ATS. She spent five years maintaining and repairing vans and lorries, and driving them from docks to depots in convoy.

The lure of smart uniforms could be as much of a draw for women as men, as shown by this detail of a Canadian Women's Army Corp recruitment poster.

Women of the Women's Auxiliary Corps in India were formed from many communities – Bengali, Mongolian, Nepali, Anglo-Indian, British, Sikh. Whether in khaki suits or khaki saris, they served together as equals and were quick to pick up military procedures. One Nepali recruit was a Gurkha, considered one of the finest fighting races in the world. The WAC (India) was modelled on the British ATS. WAS (Burma) women supported the Burma Army.

'They go about their work secure in the knowledge that they are making a real contribution towards the enlightenment of India's womanhood which must come quickly if India is to assume her place as a world power.'

Women's Auxiliary Corps (India), from the
Illustrated Weekly of India, May 1945

One theory against women in combat was that it wasn't 'natural' for them to bear arms. Actually taking up a rifle was unusual for most women. This didn't mean they intended to stay defenceless. Enid Ellis, a teenager in England during the Blitz told me, 'You can't imagine what it felt like after Dunkirk. We felt so alone. Lots of girls bought a little knife that we kept sharp.' She packed an emergency haversack, ready to get on her bike and join guerrilla fighters in the Welsh hills or in Scotland if the German invasion was successful.[27]

As the war progressed, governments had to countenance arming women. Germany at the start of the war enjoyed the comfortable notion that brave women were virtuous and non-violent. Women operating anti-aircraft guns defending Germany against Allied invasion simply inherited the oversized uniforms left by male crews who'd been sent to the frontline. It blew apart the comfortable myth that men did all the defending while women stayed at home.[28]

When it comes to embracing the potential of women in combat, the Soviet

Lance Corporal Mary Whitwam trained as a teleprinter operator in the ATS. She had her uniforms tailor-made, as the kit issued was so awful. Her memories of D-Day preparations tell of tanks rumbling past, planes flying overhead and censored mail. Only in later years did she reveal that her job had been passing messages to Bletchley Park for decoding. She was an important cog in a vital wheel.

Union excelled, with 800,000 women in combat. German soldiers were disgusted at Russian military women, calling them 'dark and forbidding' in their uniforms and high boots.[29] The women themselves had to adjust. They went into the recruiting process wearing dresses and came out wearing trousers and an army shirt. It wasn't until a major revision of uniforms in 1943 that women got a proper khaki dress with box pleats. Supply issues meant they often had to do with male underwear.[30] They fought as machine gunners, tank crews, foot soldiers and snipers.

Russian infantrywomen display their rifles and their many medals. There's clearly pride and camaraderie within the unit. At least one rifle regiment raised in Moscow was all female. Other women fought alongside men as equals.

It is perhaps the Russian snipers who caught the public's imagination the most. Graduates of the Central Women's School for Snipers reputedly killed 12,000 Germans during the war, and they got widespread publicity for their achievements, as well as the highest military awards. Of roughly 2,000 female snipers, about 500 survived to peace.[31] One, Ludmila Pavlichenko, claimed to have 309 kills. She toured Britain and the US to raise awareness of Russia's needs, and was feted wherever she went, although one reporter reputedly said she looked fat in her uniform of thick brown blanket-weight wool with a tight red collar.[32] Corporal Maria Ivanova Morozova was awarded eleven combat decorations for seventy-five sniper kills. She could be up and dressed in five minutes, wearing boots that were one or two sizes too big, so no time would be lost getting into them. Footwraps were essential, to avoid frostbite while immobile. Sniper Sasha Shliakhova didn't dress so wisely – she made a visible target against white snow because she wore a red scarf. Germans were staggered when they caught her and realised it was a woman who'd been responsible for so many deaths.

Adapting to post-war life was difficult for those who'd seen combat, on physical and psychological levels. First Sergeant Klavdia Grigoryevna Krokhina – a veteran of seventy-five sniper kills – looked at skirts with horror when she was demobbed. She was used to trousers by then, drawn in tightly at the waist as rations thinned. They'd be washed at night and slept on – this counted as ironing. In the morning they'd freeze stiff if they weren't quite dry. 'How do you learn to walk in a skirt?' she asked a post-war interviewer. 'It was like my legs got tangled.'[33]

By 1943, after the heady rush of victories against China and the Americans had subsided, and the reality of potential defeat was sinking in, Japanese citizens were told, 'There can be no distinction now between the front line and the home front.' Women were to pick up a rifle bayonet, aim it at the enemy's chest and plunge it in. Once Okinawa was taken by US forces, a Voluntary Military Service Law of June 1945 drafted women aged between 17 and 40 into the National Volunteer Combat Corps.[34] Mary Kimoto Tomita, an American studying in Japan when war broke out, found the thought of invasion exciting in 1945. Her landlady, Mrs Nagata, had a butcher's knife ready to defend the house against Allied invasion.[35] Civilian women on Saipan and the mainland had already been told to train to fight with bamboo spears or farming tools. Grenades were issued to civilians, to be detonated in violent mass suicides as Americans approached. It's estimated that as many as 1,900 civilians may have died in this kamikaze fashion.[36] Japan did not countenance women as official troops.

Having grown up laughing at the fictional antics of the British Home Guard in the TV show *Dad's Army* I was surprised to discover there were female equivalents. I already knew the Women's Voluntary Service made Molotov cocktails, despite being forbidden to carry weapons or to fight: the Lindsey Group of WVS in Lincolnshire concocted 2,000 bombs over one weekend.[37] However I didn't know that female Home Guards paraded in khaki uniforms and forage caps – paying for all the kit themselves. In November 1944, the *Yorkshire Post* newspaper reported on a band of married women who held their own training courses, learning sniper skills and ju-jitsu. They became known as the Alverthorpe Guerrillas. [38]

One final splendid anecdote illustrates how, with or without conventional weapons, women did not intend to be passive in conflict. It concerns a Mrs Cardwell, WVS member in a Yorkshire village, who saw a German parachute down near some farm buildings. She armed herself with a pitchfork and rapidly disarmed the airman, telling him, 'You are my prisoner. In the meantime, I'm going to make you a cup of tea.' She subsequently submitted her WVS report: 'One German parachutist captured by me yesterday.'[39]

Chapter 3

OUT OF NOTHING
Thrift and home dressmaking

'Can you remember – it is already getting difficult to remember – what
things were like before the war? The stockings we bought cheap and
threw away to save the trouble of mending?'

Dorothy L. Sayers, 'Why Work?' from *Creed or Chaos*

In Madison, Wisconsin one spring, I browsed an antique mall looking for ephemera of
daily life in the 1940s. I found flour sack fabric and a book called *Watkins Household
Hints*. I browsed and read the following: 'Print on flour sacks – to Remove. Mix one
gallon hot water and one cup kerosene. Soak sacks in the liquid one hour. Rub print lightly.
Wash in hot water and Watkins Shredsoap.' Why would flour sacks need print removing?

Even in the 1940s, many areas of the US were still suffering from Depression-era
poverty. Feed, salt and flour sacks were the only textiles available to families with
no cash to spare. Poverty hit African American families hardest as their wages were
usually kept lower than white workers. Older African American women wore starched
cotton aprons from well-washed fertilizer sacks for daily chores, saving best clothes
for Church. It was a strategy of
defiance against poverty and despair.[1]

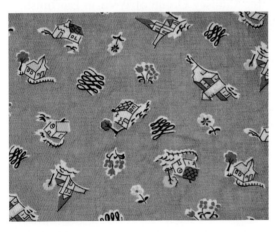

*Clever companies began producing calico sacks in
cheerful coloured prints as a form of promotion, knowing
they could be turned into sturdy yet attractive clothes.*

Such thrifty tactics were not
limited to North America. Across
the ocean in the Pacific Islands,
semi-subsistence was a norm. Island
stores sold calico and cotton threads,
but clothes were also made from
bleached flour bags, old pillow cases
and hessian bags softened by soaking.
'What can you do?' shrugged a
woman from Saibai island. 'You have
to cover up.'[2]

The pressure to make the most
of limited resources was universal;
the pressure was all the more acute

during the war, particularly for households sheltering refugees. Dutch woman Yfke de Gorter was in a house with ten people (some hiding undercover to avoid forced labour drafts) with no new clothes and no material. She acquired a spinning wheel and traded grain for wool from a friendly farmer. Iris Origo headed a large farm in Southern Tuscany. She clothed a constant stream of fugitives, using black market leather and goods bought second-hand from barrow-stalls in Florence markets. In India, many poor people only owned one or two saris, but there was no cloth available to replace them. There were gruesome rumours of grave-robbers taking shrouds for fabric. A Quaker Ambulance unit volunteer in Bengal wrote that those who couldn't replace worn out clothing stayed indoors rather than exposing themselves. 'Cases of suicide for want of clothing are frequently reported in the newspapers', stated a report from the Indian Censorship Control Department in summer 1945.[3]

Keeping up appearances was important for decency and also for morale. For occupied nations, being as well-dressed as possible was one sign of resistance to the invaders' policies of pauperisation of local people.[4]

'Although girls were taught home economics in school, there was no material available for us to sew, so we practised our first stitches on paper. Sometimes we were fortunate enough to get some sugar bags that we bleached.'
Catherine Bouwhuis, schoolgirl in Friesland, Holland. Home-sewing was traditionally considered a female task.

If thrift was a way of life for so many families worldwide, war would call for whole new levels of ingenuity and even coercion. In 1942, when the Australian Prime Minister announced, 'the darning needles is a weapon of war,' he knew full well that women's work of mending and renovating would be crucial as textile supplies were diverted to the military.

All wartime government policies to encourage 'make do and mend' bucked against a peacetime imperative to boost the economy through people shopping. Aldous Huxley recognised the power of consumerism in his dystopian novel *Brave New World*, in which citizens are brainwashed from birth with conditioning messages that tell them, 'old clothes are beastly. We always throw away old clothes. Ending is better than mending.' Huxley's fictional mantra 'I love new clothes, I love new clothes, I love new clothes…' was a reality of 1930s' commercialism.

It took strong state initiatives to promote new messages. In Japan, civilians were bombarded with slogans such as 'Luxury is the enemy.' Posters showed battalions of cotton-clad housewives with the banner 'Down with Luxury.' They demonised 'unpatriotic' women, depicted in expensive silk kimonos with brocade handbags, red nails and lace handkerchiefs, drenched in French perfume – 'the stuff of Western dependency.' Austerity was a new national god.

45

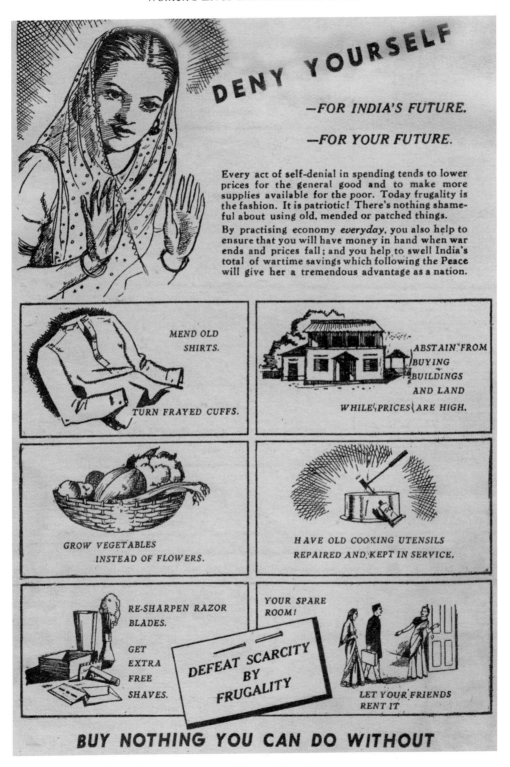

A 1945 magazine advert exhorts women to spend less and recycle more.

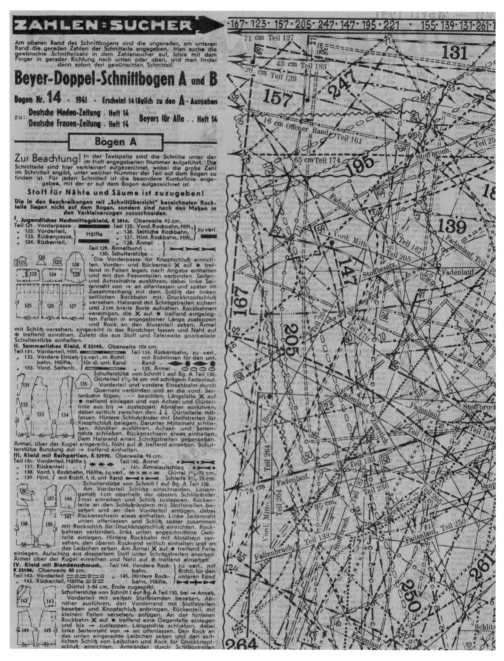

German dressmaking magazine pattern from 1941. Acute paper shortages necessitated the complex overlay of multiple garment patterns onto one tissue sheet.

Rationing could not be avoided. It was introduced as early as August 1939 in Germany. Food, clothing and footwear were to be strictly controlled by an insanely complex points system, using coupons called *Marken*. Official chits were necessary to buy new pairs of shoes. Anyone owning two pairs of shoes wasn't eligible for a

Above left: Even economy patterns – such as this British design for slips – required paper, which was increasingly in short supply. Experts suggested making patterns from old garments, by unpicking or tracing over seam edges.

Above right: American designs continued the 1930s trend for slender silhouettes and economic use of fabric.

new pair so of course everyone declared they only had one pair.[5] The Reich Clothing Office let people use their stamps to buy cloth pieces at 0.8m by 1m for repair, so some people made dresses by putting these small pieces together.[6] A German housewife lamented, 'Our clothing coupons are supposed to last till the end of the war. When will that be?'[7] By 1945, shops were usually empty regardless how many points a customer was allocated.

After the first US trade embargo on Japan in 1940, the Japanese Patriotic Women's Association encouraged members to donate clothing ration tickets for the cause of victory. Japanese housewives must have struggled to equate their strong patriotism with the awful reality of shortages, especially considering that by 1942 even a length of string or a washcloth would use up a whole textile coupon. Meanwhile, the United States resisted overt rationing, relying instead on a series of Limitation Orders to control production and consumption. Limitation Order 85 (L85) concerned clothing.

'When you are tired of your old clothes, remember that by making them do you are contributing some part of an aeroplane, a gun or a tank.'

Oliver Lyttleton, President of the Board of Trade, introducing clothes rationing in Britain, 1 June 1942.

Coupon systems were intended to prevent stockpiling by cash-rich customers, at the expense of poorer civilians, ensuring – in theory – that every civilian would be fairly dressed. Coupon values could be altered to allow for fluctuations in supply. In Britain, the Women's Voluntary Service were key to the scheme's logistical success. They addressed coupon books, marshalled queues and made tea for people waiting during serious hold ups. The poorest consumers simply couldn't afford to buy new clothes regardless of how many coupons they saved, so there was an illicit trade between those who had spare coupons and those with the cash to buy them. Coupon theft was unavoidable, and all such crimes were reported in local newspapers to deter others, as in the case of Florence Batley (35) who pleaded guilty to two charges of having stolen a clothing coupon book. Florence said she was sorry for what she had done. She was presumably even more sorry to be fined £2 and committed to prison for three months. Theft of clothing itself was an endemic problem.

The British Royal family were not exempt from coupon controls, but the queen did enjoy a generous 1,277 coupons per year. Mass Observation surveys suggested that 75 per cent of men and 43 per cent of women were in favour of rationing after a couple of months following its introduction. Clearly women felt the burden of sourcing clothing for themselves and their families more keenly.[8]

In addition to rationing, the British government introduced new controls in February 1942. The Consolidating Order *(Utility Apparel (Maximum Prices and Charges) Order)*

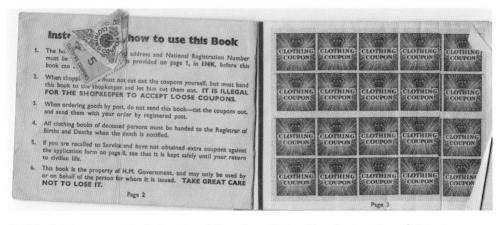

British clothing coupon book, introduced from June 1942, with a basic ration of sixty-six coupons per year, soon reduced to forty-four then a meagre thirty-six in 1945.

outlined homogenised designs and details for a clothing scheme popularly called Utility. Utility practices freed up factory space for the war effort and also made the most of limited textile stocks. Producers had detailed instructions about permitted numbers of buttons, pleats, or hem inches. Utility clothing was marked by a distinctive label: CC41. Historians still speculate whether this stands for Controlled Commodity or Civilian Clothing. The number 41 refers to the date of the scheme's creation, 1941.

The extensive wartime campaigns for household *Make Do and Mend* prove just how crucial this economy was on the Home Front. Almost everything was to be well-used, reused or repurposed; nothing could be wasted. First, worn or torn garments were to be mended. Strategies for freshening tired clothes were numerous. Flowers of yarn, embroidery silk or fabric applique could hide obvious clothing stains.

Repurposing was the next tactic after freshening and mending. In Britain, the International Wool Secretariat organised an exhibition to show the amazing ingenuity of the average housewife and mother. Among the items on display were a child's wool jersey made from the tops of brown stockings; slippers made from old felt hats, and jackets fashioned from blankets. Such skills may seem humble but they averted the danger of a population in rags and tatters.

Above left: *Mary Wray models a thrift competition dress, made by her accomplished Auntie Prim. The sign she holds originally read* Make Do and Mend.

Above right: *Darning skills were essential. Socks could be re-heeled and re-footed using a wooden darning mushroom. One little Dutch girl was so charmed by a red darning mushroom painted with white spots, she took it and 'planted' it in the garden, as a toadstool.* (Langford, *Written by Candlelight*)

A German brochure outlining essential mending techniques. Evening classes in both Allied and Axis countries were common, teaching darning and patching skills.

British freshening-up tactics from the wartime 'Clothes Doctor', in alliance with the government's 'Mrs Sew-and-Sew' icon to educate home stitchers.

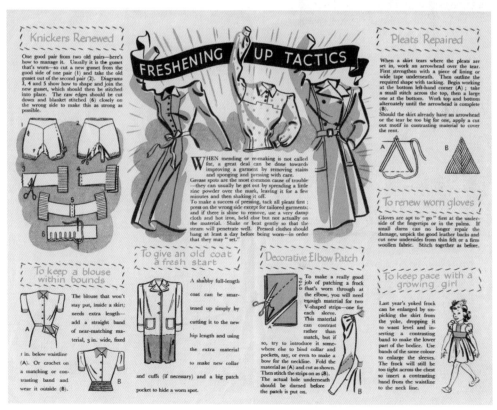

'Stay Gay! – Lay out your wardrobe and go through each piece to revamp and revitalise. Accept it as a challenge, something to call out every scrap of your ingenuity, capability, strategy and tactics.'

Weldon's Ladies Journal article, August 1944.

Women's magazines vied to share the most useful ideas. Jackets were to be turned into waistcoats; trousers into skirts. Two tired dresses were re-stitched into one 'new' frock. Shabby blouses were used as a half-lining for your winter dressing gown. Other tips included replacing worn panty gussets with new knitted ones; turning old mackintoshes into aprons, sponge bags, cot sheets, leggings, gloves for men on minesweepers in the Atlantic, or even a tennis racket cover. Making new clothes out of old was the most powerful defence against rising prices and clothing shortages.

It wasn't only old clothes which were repurposed. Bedspreads became dresses, as did dinghy sails, car seat covers, railway lavatory hand towels, and draughting linen from architects' offices. A German housewife sheltering evacuees from a bombed-

SIDE FRONT OF PATTERN CUT TO MAKE LOWER PART A POCKET WITH LINING MATERIAL UNDER IT. DOTTED LINES SHOW SEAM ALLOWANCE

A Jacket from a Man's Coat

Better Dressmaking *manual showed how to turn a man's coat into a woman's jacket... 'If you are sure he won't want it again after the war,' cautioned the British Board of Trade.*

out city was disgusted to see her guests had taken down the bedroom curtains to make into a dress. This was not an isolated incident of repurposing.

Not all renovations were innocent. A matron from a munition worker hostel in the north of England was caught stealing government-issue chamois leather window cleaning cloths. She stitched them into attractive gloves and flogged them for fancy prices in town. When confronted she defended her actions, saying her taxes helped finance the government, therefore she had a right to help herself.[9]

Every little scrap of fabric or yarn was to be saved in a rag bag and used for projects. To cover cold floors and cheer a wartime home, oddments of

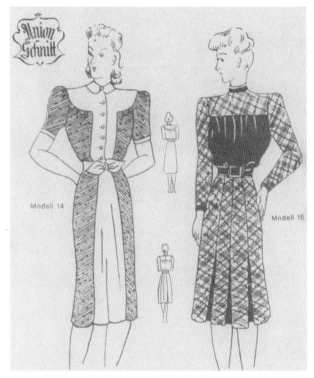

German dress patterns from Lutterloh's Union Schnitt system, showing how to use small sections of contrasting fabric – possibly from old garments – to create one two-tone dress.

cloth were hooked into rugs, using hessian, bran bags or old sandbags as a base. Plaited rugs were virtually indestructible.

Scraps made excellent toys for children. Untold numbers of women crafted toys to sell in fundraising drives. Elsie Walton, a child during the war, remembers a local dressmaker with the delightful name of Dolly Dibble. Miss Dibble transformed offcuts into clothes for Elsie's doll, inadvertently creating a miniature memorial to Elsie's grandmother's clothes, which Miss Dibble had just sewn, from pink silk underwear to a white-and-navy best dress.

By far the most popular use for fabric scraps was quilting – a traditionally thrifty method of crafting bed covers and cushions. Quilters in Canada were particularly prolific during the war, with outhouses becoming like small factories as volunteers cut and stitched fabric remnants. The Red Cross distributed many hundreds of such quilts to needy families in Canada and overseas, including people who'd been bombed out. Mary Miller in Ontario was a junior Women's Institute member. She said visitors were warned to hang onto their pants and skirts or they might find them in a quilt![10] The only reward for such intense endeavours was a thank-you badge from the Red Cross – and the knowledge that their handiwork brought comfort and warmth to those in need.

Stitch-craft magazines offered free embroidery transfers in order to beautify plain household linens.

This plain cotton summer dress from 1945 has a sash and hem embroidered with exquisite cottage-garden floral designs.

'An elderly woman is sitting on a little bench knitting a stocking during bursts of machine-gun fire and anti-aircraft guns firing away.'

Russian journalist Vasily Grossman notes a touch of domesticity in the middle of besieged Stalingrad. (Grossman, *A Writer at War*.)

The woman sitting knitting is an archetypal image. Before the First World War, staying home to knit for troops was considered a primary female role. In reality, knitters found time for their craft even after a double shift of factory work and family care. They knitted in committee meetings and at music concerts; on the bus and in bomb shelters. Women were even spotted knitting while walking mountain paths in Macedonia. It was both a national service and a soothing blackout hobby. Each stitch knitted while on down-time in hospitals, canteens, schools, and air raid defence posts was a stitch closer to the end of the war – or so the women hoped. Many a cardigan was completed waiting for the All Clear to sound.

'We got out our knitting, got on with the mechanics of our jobs, settled again to waiting through the grey days.'

Air Force women endure the long months of wartime service.[11]

Servicewomen stationed in lonely places were encouraged to knit; Japanese defence volunteers and transport workers were obliged to knit on their breaks, even as their male colleagues relaxed with newspapers. Knitting circles provided much needed community support for Spanish women rebuilding their lives after the trauma of civil war – and for New Zealand women feeling cut off from war, and wanting to 'do their bit'.

Much of the impetus for knitting undoubtedly came from the urgent need for service woollens. Governments simply could not supply the millions of articles needed, which is where volunteers stepped in. Around the world needles clicked, producing balaclava helmets, pullovers, mittens, flying gloves and flying jerseys, chest warmers, earmuffs, hoods and scarves. Sailors' mitts had string coverings, to keep them from freezing to ropes and gears on icy seas.

If women weren't knitting, they'd taken up a crochet hook, transforming yarn into blankets and shawls of many colours. Wool was often supplied by the indefatigable Red Cross, with knitting circles setting targets for how many items they could produce. The wool was precious and expensive. The price of a ball of wool in England shot up from 4*d* to 3*s* 6*d*; knitting a jumper cost about £3, roughly £75 in modern money.

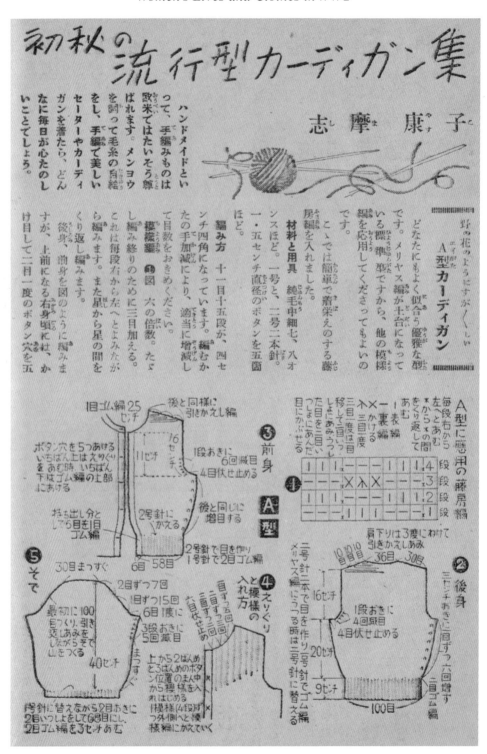

A late 1940s Japanese knitting pattern.

56

To make up shortfalls, children gleaned tufts of sheep wool from hedges; old woollen goods were unravelled and the wool washed, wound and knitted up into new garments. The Girl Guides of Jamaica, having no needles or yarn, taught new recruits to knit using pieces of wire and string, until wool and needles were available.[12]

Fay Timbers, reluctantly knitting as a child in Ottawa, says she was taught to knit socks for the troops while a Brownie. Progress was slow. 'The war will be over before you get one pair done,' sighed her mother.[13] When the war was finally over, the knitting continued; needles wouldn't fall silent until rising prosperity in the late twentieth century made it cheaper to wear shop-bought woollies rather than knitting one's own. Even then the craft persisted. Modern-day knitters are now re-discovering vintage patterns of the 1940s to re-create wartime styles.

Lady's service cardigan pattern, to be made up in the appropriate military hue – khaki, blue, green or brown.

A 1940s' Fair Isle waistcoat. Stripes and Fair Isle patterns were perfect for knitters in times of austerity, as they used leftover oddments of wool.

Chapter 4

AT THE MACHINES
Industrial work and the textile trade

'Come to Marks and Spencer's and see your smartly uniformed sisters
from Yorkshire's largest Royal Ordnance Factory demonstrating the
simplicity, safety and cleanliness of their BIG contribution towards
Humanity's struggle against barbarism.'

Wakefield Express 16 May 1942

My maternal grandmother Ella planned to train as a professional dressmaker. Then
she met handsome young Frederick, a bus driver, and had to give up her career plans:
their first child appeared rather too soon after the wedding. Ella continued to sew
family clothes as well as freelancing for local dress shops.

A Russian seamstress at work. The sewing machine was vital for domestic and military production.

The sewing machine is arguably the most significant mechanical invention in women's lives. It was a household staple from the 1860s onwards, whirring through long seams and tough layers which previously had been stitched by hand. By the 1940s, manual work in textile industries – a major part of many countries' economies – was overwhelmingly carried out by female labourers, from yarn treatment and spinning to garment making-up and finishing. Perhaps because of its gendered associations, the textile industry is almost considered an afterthought in histories of wartime production. In this chapter we'll see how women's industrial labour not only clothed millions but how women also worked in an unexpectedly diverse range of heavy-duty roles, from mining to munition making.

'One day my mother's sister, who made her own clothes, took me to a local market and made me choose a pattern. This was the first time I had seen patterns. I chose material, and when we got back to her house I was given a thorough grounding and actually made my first dress. After that I went on sewing and made - and later designed - my own clothes.'

Enid Ellis, born 1919[1]

The introduction to sewing machines began at an early age, with girls learning the basics on simple models working in chain stitch. They progressed to hand-cranked machines or those worked by a foot treadle. A few modern models worked directly from electricity. Segregated lessons at school – girls learning to sew and boys doing metal work and carpentry – reinforced gender roles. Professional sewing was one of the few respectable professions open to women. Historically it was poorly paid, labour-intensive work. It was, however, a living, whether at home or factory-based. This reliance on the sewing machine cannot be underestimated when looking at women's wartime lives.

Home sewers might visit households for weeks at a time to complete new orders, or they might run their own informal businesses. Labourers were also based in workshops or large factories. The results of their industry is evident in almost every photograph of wartime activity: soldiers, shoppers, generals, actresses – all wear clothes.

In some households, women produced the cloth and the thread that went into the clothes they made. The work had to be completed alongside housework and childcare, and often in additional to agricultural tasks. In China, for example, these sewers were so important that communist communities organised official sewing circles to improve production. The work must have seemed endless: Chinese-style cloth shoes took two days to stitch, but lasted only five or six months.[2] Collecting stories of seamstresses worldwide, I was struck by the common threads of their stories – training, hard work, low pay – regardless of whether they were in a rainy English town, or the sun-baked Middle East. A few examples give a sense of the diversity too.

Kathy Greaves was a tailor's apprentice in Halifax, West Yorkshire. The workroom was in a cellar lit by a coal fire. She bought her own fabric shears with her first wages, giving the rest to her mother. The bad-tempered tailor thwarted her career progression by refusing to teach her advanced skills.[3]

Rosa Parks, famous for her tireless contributions to the American Civil Rights movement, supported herself through professional sewing even before she became a figurehead for the cause in the 1950s. After childhood labour picking cotton she graduated to stitching it, at a denim factory.

Ilse Attar left her native Germany in 1938, aged 15, to escape persecution as a Jew. She began an apprenticeship as a seamstress in Tel Aviv then worked in various salons. In 1940, Ilse's sense of style accidentally saved her father's life. Ilse made him late for his regular bridge game, telling him to change out of a shirt she particularly hated (white with purple stripes). As he put on a fresh shirt the bridge club was bombed during an Italian raid, killing other players. Ilse later emigrated to the US, working in the New York Garment District.[4]

Working in a factory at least provided set hours and steady work, even if pay levels were universally lower than male wages and opportunities for management roles for women were limited. During peacetime,

Esther Bruce, pictured here at a 1949 family wedding, began work picking up pins, graduating to sophisticated dressmaking at Miss Mary Taylor's in Chelsea, whose clients included glamorous music hall star Elisabeth Welch. (Bourne, Aunt Esther's Story)

factory owners knew there was a reliable pool of female labour; wider wartime opportunities meant women were often tempted away for less monotonous and more lucrative jobs. Patriotic propaganda aimed to lure women into factories. Low wages were justified by the usually unproven claim that women could do less than men.

'It used to be a relief, you know, to come out at five o'clock and be able to clear the serge out of your nose. I found it difficult, just sort of sticking it out, you know, and it gave me an appreciation of people in jobs like that, factory jobs, very monotonous and grubby too.'

Joanna Hatton, New Zealand teacher doing vacation war work.[5]

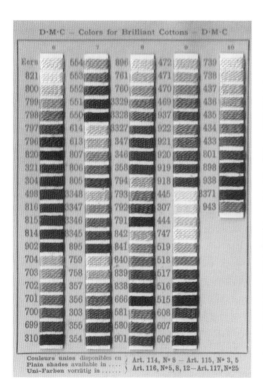 

Above left: *Dollfus Mieg et Cie cotton threads were exported globally. Palestinian outworkers used DMC threads to embroider elaborate designs onto commercial tunics and trousseau wear. Pattern sharing and communal stitching gave women a strong sense of identity and continuity. Sewers also earned money to ornament their own costumes and so become fashion leaders in their own right.*

Above right: *Detail of Palestinian embroidery on a Western-style dress made and sold in Jerusalem. Embroiderers gave stitches agricultural names such as 'ears of corn' for herringbone, 'sickles' for zigzag joining stitch and 'planting' for running stitch.*

The demand for military clothing was inevitably intense in every warring nation. Maori woman Ruku Arahanga worked alongside Pakeha women in a New Zealand factory, stitching parachutes and uniforms. Even though the war was seen as a Pakeha affair, it gave Maori people an opportunity to identify with a collaborative patriotism. Uniforms weren't easy work. Another New Zealander was in tears daily, trying to plough through mounds of heavy army overcoats, when she'd been used to making delicate ladies' fashions. In June 1940, as the Germans seemed set for total European domination, the New Zealand Minister of Labour described the making of men's battle-dress the most important war service that the women workers could render.[6]

Chinese village women grafted, sewing quilted cotton winter uniforms, stitching until sunset despite aching eyes and fingers. Bonus schemes offered incentives to boost production, with ever-rising targets.[7] Some rural communities in China had no tradition of home weaving until extended warfare created the need for all-hands-on-deck contributions, leading to the establishment of cooperatives to buy cotton and make cloth sales. This had amazing follow-on effects: with the collected profits, women could be better dressed and afford to buy animals to push heavy grindstones, which, in turn, led to increased maternal health and fewer miscarriages. Collective craftwork also saved money on heating and lighting. The benefits of interaction over isolation are incalculable. In the later 1940s, a more efficient factory system was organised, and it was difficult for country women to adapt to industrial methods.[8]

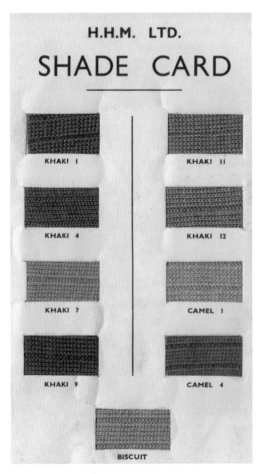

The fuzz from khaki wool fabric got up the nose, in the eyes and hair. Wool treatment chemicals rubbed off the material, leaving a green sheen on whatever came into contact.

Russian factory workers were often former peasants, co-opted to industrial work. Factories were dark, dirty and dangerous places. Amongst other items, textile workers made parachutes, army shirts, *portyanki* footwraps and camouflage netting, all in the desperate struggle to beat back Nazi invaders. Their days 'off' were spent digging trenches, labouring alongside German Prisoners of War.

As an imperial colony, Indian workers were put under immense pressure to produce millions of uniforms and leather boots for Britain. The demand for jute for khaki was huge, bringing increased prosperity to workshops and factories. The profits were not passed down to workers, and conditions were dire. In Bombay's textile mills workers were fined if they broke thread or tore cloth. Machines were ancient and outdated; industrial accidents frequent.[9]

'Sweat rolled down our cheeks as we sewed the deep crimson crosses onto the white uniforms. But the heat was no problem for us because our labour service to the nation gives expression to our boundless gratitude for the (nurse) warriors who wear the white uniform'.

Japanese school girls sewing during their summer vacation.

Photo Weekly Report, July 1939.

One of the worst military textile jobs was reconditioning used uniforms. The emotional impact was harrowing. Stains, holes and rips were evidence of wounds and fatalities. The bundles of old garments were usually filthy and infested. Jews in Nazi-occupied territories would be lumbered with the task of undoing seams, cleaning and patching. Gena Turgel, living in the Krakow ghetto in Poland, recalled, 'I often had to run out to the cloakroom, itching, and strip down to my underwear, shaking off insects from my clothes, skin and hair.'[10] Jewish women weren't the only ones enduring forced labour. When the Japanese occupied Korea, locals were bullied into factory jobs for the new overseers. Yun Turi was only 14 when she began work in the sewing department of a rubber factory, moving to Nishimura Garments – a Japanese company – for a heavy workload of uniform production. Her lowly status meant she had no protection from repeated assaults by her manager.[11]

Factory life wasn't all about monotony, graft and grit. The camaraderie of factory work could be a happy contrast to the isolation of housework. Workers also found their own way to connect with those who'd be wearing the uniforms: they might write letters and tuck them inside garments, much as stitchers had done a generation before in the Great War. Sadie Baty worked for John Barran Ltd in Gateshead, in the north of England. Barran's women became unofficial pen pals with servicemen via letters hidden in the lining of coats they made. One of Sadie's letters ended up in a greatcoat worn by an officer who'd been captured and made a prisoner of war in Germany. He in turn gave his coat to a mate, Bill, who was ill. Bill found the note in the coat and wrote to Sadie. Through her he was introduced to Sadie's sister Mary, who helped her handle the pen pal correspondence. When he was released from captivity, Bill came right back to England to marry Mary. Two baby boys quickly followed.[12]

Indigo cotton fabric detail from West Africa. Nigerian adire indigo cloths were particularly coveted at home and for export. Women painted and tie-dyed cloths with individual creative designs. Blue-stained mud was a familiar sight in the yards of Yorubaland.

There was far more to textile work than the cutting and sewing. Women were involved in every stage of the industrial process of turning raw materials into finished items. The work was tough, whether picking, treating, refining, carding, spinning, dyeing or weaving. The British government, amongst others, was keen to boost morale on the 'Cotton Front' as they called it. They produced a cigarette card which praised cotton workers: 'Spinning yarn, weaving cloth, bleaching and finishing is as essential today as building ships and planes and tanks, for the soldier cannot fight, the airman cannot fly, nor the sailor set to sea without equipment which is extensively made of cotton.' Cotton was needed for tents, tarpaulins, groundsheets, barrage balloons, lifebelts and mosquito nets in addition to clothing. Hospital bandages, bedding and towels were all cotton-based.

'The men and women in the cotton mills do not wear uniform, but they are front-line fighters all the same.'

British propaganda card - *It All Depends On Me.*

Worldwide trade linked so many countries and cultures. The network of connections shows the importance of international trade. Jute, linen, cotton, silk and wool were shipped in raw form to manufacturers, and then exported in turn as finished goods. Britain's 1939 export destinations read like a travel wish-list for those with wanderlust: China, India, Burma, Australia, South Africa, Norway, Argentina, Norway, Sweden, West Africa, Indonesia, the East Indies and Switzerland.

Values and volume of textile imports/exports in the late 1930s and 1940s are staggering. Nations depended on the free movement of goods to maintain the lucrative textile economies. Countries which couldn't produce raw materials relied on trade routes being safe and reliable. Of course war disrupted everything. Political unrest was a disaster for stock market values; military hostilities were destructive to goods en route. Some local economies thrived on an influx of service personnel; others were devastated by shifting allegiances and the physical destruction of combat.

Textile industries simply couldn't function without raw materials. As the usual natural fibres became scarce, industrialists vied to produce effective substitutes. Even in the 1930s, Germany, a nation of chemical innovators, was ahead of the field. Not only did they recycle existing fur, cotton, linen, wool and rayon, they also experimented with fibres from potato peels, corn husks, soybeans and wastewater from margarine production. Synthetic blend uniforms did not hold colour well, leaving German army privates stained green from their uniforms.[13] Ersatz clothing in Germany included artificial wool and fur, neither of which was as warm as the real thing. It's surprising to think of fake fur as a fashion in the 1940s. A reddish-brown fake fur coat in my collection was originally donated to a Coventry woman named Janet Paxton after her house was destroyed by the blast of a bombed ordnance factory nearby. Ironically she felt too guilty to wear it, as she felt others had suffered more than she had.[14]

Artificial silks such as viscose and cellulose acetate were already a key element in global markets, to the great concern of real silk specialists. Synthetic producers had their own headaches as the war caused loss of access to raw material imports such as coal tar. Textile specialists around the world reported with excitement on the American invention *nylon*, the first non-plant based synthetic. Its greatest impact would come after the war ended.

This beautifully stitched rain coat and hood was a gift from a British sapper in the Eighth Army to his sweetheart Ada in England. Ernest Arrowsmith fought his way from Monte Cassino to Rome, where he bought the coat. It is waterproof, pliable and semi-translucent, made of an as-yet unidentified plastic textile, similar to a British product advertised in 1939 as 'rain-tite Pliofilm', possibly a version of cellophane.

Edith Walton (top right) worked for Drake and Waters joiners in Yorkshire. Planks such as these were used to construct seventy-two armour-plated flat-bottomed landing craft used in the 1944 D-Day invasion – highly confidential work. Edith caused a stir locally wearing bib-and-brace trousered overalls outside of work.

Textile industries may have been core employers, but women also worked in a remarkable range of industrial roles worldwide. Not all of this work was in response to labour shortages as men were drafted for the military. Factory work could be an absolute financial necessity for women supporting a family, or a rite of passage for young women saving for a trousseau. In some countries, the only difference between 'women's work' and 'men's work' was that women did all the same jobs as men for far less pay – and in addition to their household and childcare duties.

How a nation portrays its female workers reveals a great deal about the culture. Countries such as Germany and Japan were keen to promote a national identity based on housework and motherhood, with fewer images of industrial labour. They were also keen to maintain the illusion of a placid home front, in which men were breadwinners and women curated the domestic sphere. Japanese women who also endured appalling industrial work condition were not feted in the press.

Both Japan and Germany resorted to the use of forced labour. In 1942, the Japanese Minister of Welfare said the government wouldn't follow the Western example of drafting women, 'out of consideration for the family system'.[15] They had no qualms about conning or kidnapping girls from Korea to work in Japanese factories. This was under the guise of a Women's Voluntary Labour Corps, and there was nothing voluntary about it. Kang Tŏkkyŏng joined the Corps from Korea in 1944, aged 15. She was hoping to study in Japan and earn money. Instead she worked cutting components in an aeroplane plant in Fukiko City, wearing a brown uniform and cap with a Women's Volunteer Corps badge. One girl who did not wear her cap caught her hair in the machine, and she was dragged in and killed. The Korean workers never received wages and food was minimal. Untold numbers were subsequently forced into military brothels as sex slaves.[16]

Oblivious to health-and-safety issues, this Scottish metal grinder works in her own short-sleeved woollen jumper and cotton overalls. Her hair is mostly covered by a turban – popular headgear for industrial women.

Across the Third Reich, non-Germans were rounded up for labour. A 1943 photo shows Ukrainian women loading bundles of belongings onto a freight train bound for Germany. They wear many layers, with headscarves, long plain dresses and thick stockings. Such foreign workers were heavily discriminated against, receiving reduced food and clothing rations. Slave labourers from concentration camps fared the worst. They could be hired out to local industries, with minimal wages being paid directly to the SS. There were no nice notions of the work being too tough for ladies when such workers were labelled 'subhuman'.

'We wore nothing but short shifts made of burlap, no shoes, no underwear. We used to collect the scraps of paper that were strewn about our workplace, especially the heavy cement bags that were thrown out. Even though it was strictly forbidden, we stuffed them under our shifts so that we would freeze a little less.'

Heda Margolius Kovaly, a Czech Jewish concentration camp prisoner put to work in a brick yard.[17]

Above left: *Working-class and lower-caste Indian women could expect no special treatment – or special clothing – as they laboured long days fulfilling war contracts in coal mines, in road mending or construction. Confounding ideas of feminine delicacy or weakness, this sari-clad brickie carries her load on her head.*

Above right: *Industrial work required industrial clothing, although safety gear wasn't always issued or used. This 1943 British welder, observed by a woman from the ATS, has goggles, gloves and a leather apron at least.*

Elsewhere, a need for large numbers of new recruits to the factories lead to widespread uplifting imagery of women at work. Unlike fashion photography, which showed decorative idealisations of femininity, wartime images were carefully posed to show factory labour in a positive light. This meant normalising rather unfeminine outfits such as boiler suits, overalls and outsize gloves. Contemporary photo captions still comment on the women's attractiveness and potential for marriage.

One of the most famous images of the war is the American poster of 'Rosie the Riveter', with her blue cotton sleeves rolled up to imply muscles and her hair tucked in a red spotted bandana that was typical headwear of the WOWs – Women Ordnance Workers. The bandana was designed in accordance with US Army specifications to be water repellent, washable and dustproof. It came to represent a spirit of strong 'can do' activity, and a picturesque compromise between gritty labour and feminine attractiveness.

Rosie the Riveter is a white woman: African Americans were not the visible face of the United States at war. Images of Black Americans working were celebrated only in publications with an African American readership. President Roosevelt's Executive

Order 8802 banned race discrimination in defence industries and civil service jobs from June 1941, but it was not well enforced.

Black women workers were 'last hired, first fired' in wartime America. They were often segregated from white workers, and invariably given the worst jobs. In March 1945, *Negro Story* magazine published a story called *Tar*, by Shirley Graham, in which a southern girl, Mary, comes to Harlem to work as a dressmaker. Mary's white customers are furious when she announces she's leaving the fashion trade to do war work, as if Mary has no right to be patriotic. Mary excels in sheet metal cutting, but because of her colour is rejected by employers. She eventually gets a job filling vats with tar. Hortense Johnson, a real-life munitions inspector in a New Jersey arsenal, struggled to buy heavy-duty workwear out of her pay. She was undaunted: 'Of course the work is hard and sometimes dangerous, but victory in this war isn't going to come the easy way. By doing my share today, I'm keeping a place for some brown woman tomorrow.'[18]

Many factory women seemed to embrace the new tough prettiness. In Canada, women in white turbans walked to work with purpose swinging big metal man-size lunch boxes.[19] One chemical worker from Huddersfield remembered a gang from Barnsley joining the firm 'big strapping girls, they could swear like the men and they could wheel barrows of concrete....'[20] Eventually they blended with the men. Women building the new Waterloo Bridge across the Thames in London wore flat caps, dungarees or overalls just like their male colleagues. The work included crane operations, brick-laying and welding. When the bridge was opened in 1945 there was praise for 'the men who built Waterloo Bridge' with no mention of the women. Perhaps they'd blended too well.[21]

Women taking on new industrial roles on the railways had to be dressed the part too. Platelayers on the Great Western Railway in Britain thought nothing of working in overcoats, trousers, sturdy shoes and turbans. Mary Woodfield, a GWR lineman's assistant was delighted with her bib and braces overalls: 'I felt the cat's whiskers in them.'[22]

Doris Bell of Newcastle was nearly 6 ft tall and sturdy with it. Her studio portrait shows a young woman in an unassuming buttoned frock. In fact, Doris broke away from a stereotypical role as home helper to work in the shipyards as a blacksmith's striker.

'Of course it's no film star's job. We've got no time for lipstick or powder, and we haven't got to be afraid of dirtying our hands or faces.'

Female railway worker, *Daily Mirror*, 25 September 1940

Of all war work, munition-making was the most contrary to a pre-war ideal of delicate, decorative, domestic women. Instead of creating life, munition workers engineered armaments to destroy it. It was, by its very nature, potentially highly dangerous work. In the stirring yet patronising pageant to women's labour *British Women Go To War*, a photo of a woman drilling a gas block on the barrel of a cannon gun has the comment: 'She might be baking a pie for the family, but she is not, she is helping to construct a weapon of war with which to defend the home she has had to leave.'

Protective clothing was crucial. Australian munition workers thought their workwear was 'ghastly'. They wore heavy woollen slacks made of wool for protection against fire and explosions, a belted jacket and a navy cap. Welted brogue shoes had wooden springs.[23] Factories didn't always provide workwear; if they did, it was often surplus men's clothing. A young English girl put to assembling Bren guns was issued leather gloves that were far too big for her. Pushing a spring in she got her

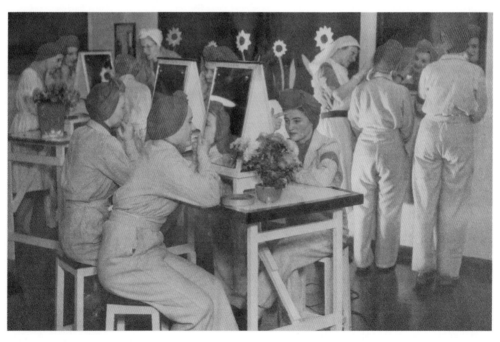

Munition workers put on make-up before a shift. Protective face cream and lip salve were vital to keep the skin form absorbing explosive powder.

gloves caught. The section of men facing her considered this free entertainment. She rallied when a woman worker showed her the knack.[24]

There was an important transition from 'dirty' to 'clean' clothing for those handling explosive chemicals. This meant taking off outer clothes and shoes in a 'shifting house' so that dirt and grit wouldn't contaminate the work area. The smallest spark could set off a devastating explosion so clothing with metal fastenings were strictly forbidden. Wedding rings had to be taped over. Workers wore rubber boots or footwear with no metal segs or nails. Inspectors checked for stray hairpins and other sundry contraband items such as needles, sweets or cigarettes. Hair was put up in fireproof turbans. Underclothes were covered in fire-resistant cotton overalls.

At times industrial workers felt empowered to strike in protest at low wages; others carried out acts of industrial sabotage to protest hostile regimes. For most women, working at the machines was a necessary evil, the monotony enlivened by workers' radio programmes and gossip networks. Yet taking industrial roles also created a sense of pride – they were living, sweating proof that women could do so-called 'men's work', and do it well.

Chapter 5

ALONG THE CATWALK
Haute couture and high street fashion

'How shocked one is, absolutely beautiful clothes, material, buttons,
beads. Everything non-utility.'[1]

Martha Gellhorn in Paris 1944

Strolling around central Vienna under Christmas lights, I admired the window displays
of Chanel, Ferragamo and Dior – all names from the 1940s still thriving in the modern
fashion world. Then I found the address I was actually looking for – 11 Kohlmarkt.
This was once the elegant shop of Jewish milliner Trudi Kanter, who was forced to
give up her business and the city she loved, due to brutal Nazi anti-Semitism. Kanter
escaped to England thanks to the help of her friend, the milliner Mitzi Lorenz. Once
safe, Kanter and Lorenz continued creating adorable
highly-coveted hats. They survived and thrived. Not
far from Kohlmarkt was the home of extraordinary
dress designer Emilie Flöge. Her dresses were
immortalised in the paintings of her friend Gustav
Klimt, most famously the portrait of Adele Bloch-
Bauer, the *Woman in Gold*. In 1945, Allied
bombs destroyed Flöge's apartment and all
the gowns and memorabilia inside.

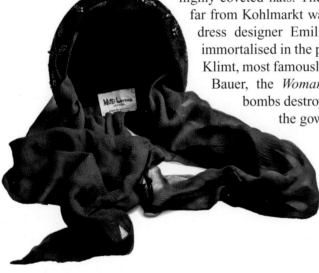

Fashion and war hardly
seem compatible, but their
stories are intertwined with
strange and sometimes
grotesque intimacy. High
fashion was a powerful
and lucrative industry.
Wartime governments
attempted to harness this
power to shape images
of national identity;
occupying forces swiftly

*A charming Mitzi Lorenz beaded toque hat with chiffon veil. Lorenz
and her family were notable millinery entrepreneurs who thrived in
post-war Britain. Their story would have been very different if they'd
stayed in Austria after the Anschluss.*

72

sought to profit from fashion's finances – and to wear the couture of captured cities. Caught up in conflict, designers, investors and makers all fought to keep the creative vision alive. Throughout long years of war, fashion defied shortages and the dominance of khaki. It offered escapism and indulgence to exclusive salon clients and high street shoppers alike.

The elite end of fashion was true haute couture – a select number of salons offering the most exquisite cut, embellishment and exclusivity. The *griffe*, or label, sewn into the back of the dress, gave couture clients a wonderful sense of confidence, whether the embroidered name was Worth, Balenciaga or Chanel.[2] The skills required to work in a couture salon took years to learn and hone. Designers had strong teams helping transform their sketches into actual garments. The whole

Late 1930s' chiffon tea gown with sweetheart neckline and short sleeves – features that would continue in popularity through the war years. Hems, however, were set to rise.

process took tremendous graft, from pattern-drafting and cutting, to making up, embellishing and fitting. Scale models could be crafted for wooden dolls; these were upscaled to live mannequins. The next stage was to sell to clients, and this was when the magic of fashion truly sparkled – at the fashion shows.

Salon décor tended to be luxuriant, with textile hangings, gilded chairs with silk upholstery and a general air of refinement. The front row was the most important seat, for the most influential magazine editors and the wealthiest clients. An actual fashion show followed an established sequence of casual wear, followed by town outfits, then glamorous evening gowns, then the finale of bridal wear. The mannequins were often young society girls, made up to look sophisticated and mature; taught to walk with their pelvis pushed forwards, shoulders back and chins tilted at a haughty angle. A mannequin needed poise, a good walk and the ability to carry clothes. She worked hard to earn her wages, not only along the catwalk, but also in the endless hours of preparation in the workrooms, where she was treated as a cross between a clothes-horse and a duchess.

When the orders came in it was back to the workroom and the army of specialists. Overheads were high even if textile-workers' wages were comparatively low. Every

Above left: *A portfolio page from Rhode Island School of Design student Ruth Bragdon, 1939. Talented designers needed the backing of fabric suppliers and the patronage of wealthy clients if they were to establish their name.*

Above right: *Lee Miller was a photographer, model and journalist – a woman of exceptional talent, drive and beauty. Her work was so compelling she was commissioned to be the war correspondent for* Vogue *magazine, combining an eye for fashion with insights into war-torn Europe.*

potential client had to be courted to ensure there would be profits in the account ledger. Fashion journalism played a key part in building brands and advertising haute couture innovations. Readers devoured photographs and illustrations showing the big names in the fashion world. *Vogue, Queen, Harper's Bazaar:* the very names of the magazines conjured up a world of affluence and pure quality. Journalists had access to the most renowned fashion collections, often wearing couture garments bought at special prices.

Key fashion centres at the start of the war were Paris – the heart of couture – London and Prague. Czech fashion had a renaissance in the inter-war years, with many fashion houses headed by women, such as Hanna Podolská's couture house. It began as a small seamstress' workshop and grew to be a formidable and award-winning enterprise, and a founding member of the influential Prague Fashion Society *Prazka Moda*.[3] Milena Jesenská was a prominent fashion journalist who wrote a regular column about style. Her preferred outfit was a well-cut English suit with plenty of pockets, sensible English shoes and a classic trench coat. After the German invasion of Czechoslovakia and the dismantling of the fashion industry, Jesenská was active in the underground resistance. She was arrested and sent to Ravensbrück concentration camp, where she died.[4]

Czech fabric samples for the international market, 1938. The great Prague fashion houses struggled to survive the fascist invasion, then the postwar communist regime.

AU SOLEIL
LES TISSUS ANTIFROISS

LE soleil, grand mangeur de couleurs, restera impuissant devant vos robes fraîches, si vous lui opposez la netteté, la parfaite résistance des tissus Antifroiss. La mer ne les attaquera pas davantage et vous pourrez sans inconvénient les porter à toute heure du jour. Les jeunes grand-mères elles-mêmes trouveront parmi les Antifroiss de larges dessins sur fonds blancs qui seront parfaits pour leur cure à Vichy ou à Contrexéville. Vente à notre Service de Commission aux prix imposés : Mouss Anti, 23 francs en 0 m. 98 ; Azur Anti, 19 fr. 50 en 0 m. 78.

31. *Petite robe en Antifroiss ; jupe à plis montants au-dessus de la taille. Poches au corsage. 3 m. 50 en 92.*
32. *Boléro en Azur Anti à larges fleurs, posé sur une jupe foncée. Métrage : 3 mètres 90 en 0 m. 80 de large.*
33. *Petite robe en Antifroiss, jupe en forme. Blouse : 1 mètre 50 en 0 m. 80. Robe : 3 m. 50 en 0 m. 80 de large.*
34. *Nos mères porteront cette robe d'après-midi nouée et froncée dans la ceinture. Métrage : 3 m.50 en 0 m.80.*

(Voir dos page 529.)

1939 magazines offered promises of fashions that will potentially seem from another world once war is declared. The French Jardin Des Modes *May issue promoted spring designs by Jean Patou, Lucien Lelong and Maggie Rouff amongst others. Lucien Lelong would be instrumental in negotiating protection of the Paris couture industry once the city was occupied.*

During the war there was an understandable craving for novelty and news that distracted readers from grim reality. This fashion publications could provide, along with up-to-date tips gleaned from the world of couture.

In 1939, *Chic Parisien* fashion journal showed exuberant spring fashions with tight bodices and full skirts. By winter, prominent couture colours were Royal Air Force blue, aeroplane grey and camouflage green. Already war was showing its influence.[5] The immediate effect of war came in trivial military-style trappings such as brass buttons, gold braid, epaulets and cockades. War also had a deeper impact on the apparel industry worldwide, putting French dressmaking dominance in jeopardy and affecting the actual clothes made, sold and worn.

As German military expansion swallowed up much of Europe, so German bureaucrats attempted to impose German taste on the fashion world. The swift occupation of Paris was shocking on many levels. It forced French fashion houses to decide whether to continue trading – safeguarding French jobs and prestige – or to shut up shop and flee. Those who did stay entered an uneasy collaboration with their new clients – Germans and those wealthy clients who still thrived under German rule. About two-thirds of haute couture houses remained open for business and roughly 12,000 jobs were saved because of functioning French salons.[6]

1939 fashion in America, influenced by military uniform. A Life *magazine article* 'War and Fashions' *stated,* 'its effect on women's styles is great but unpredictable'.

German dressmaking patterns from 1941.

'Whoever runs the world, Paris intends to go on making his wife's clothes'
Time magazine, 21 August 1939

Even if German economic experts said constantly changing fashion was problematic, diverting labour and money from the armaments industry, they were up against a very human desire for novelty and indulgence. Nazi propaganda pushed images of 'Gretchen' braids, flat heels and dirndl skirts; wives of high-ranking Nazi officials – such as Emmy Goering and Magda Goebbels – were stylishly and expensively dressed.[7] Despite Hitler's dislike of any change in appearance, his mistress Eva Braun loved new fashions. She was always tastefully dressed in elegant clothes from the best dressmakers. Hitler's favourite dress from her wardrobe was of black silk with a bell-shaped skirt and fabric roses at the deep neckline. Becoming Frau Hitler in April 1945, she wore this dress for the double suicide pact that followed, having first given away her favourite silver fox fur to Traudl Junge, one of Hitler's secretaries.[8]

Captain Molyneux closed his Parisian fashion house just in time to escape the 1941 invasion. He reopened in Grosvenor Street, London. This label is from an austere black crepe dress, enlivened only by the dramatic bow of a waist sash.

Whatever the fads of each season, a suit was always in fashion. This is a British wool suit from 1943, worn with a stylish 'plate' hat. Suits were an expensive investment, and were bought to give good service. Different blouses and accessories would add variety.

With Paris fashion houses isolated for the duration, other style centres faced a choice – either panic that they had no French guidance, or celebrate the lack of French tyranny and consolidate their own designs. If there was a sense of loss, it was quickly set aside in Britain and America.

Britain was famous for its tailoring. Out from the shadow of Paris, it could also boast designers with a flair for evening wear and day dresses. Digby Morton, Hardy Amies and Norman Hartnell were important figures. Less well known but equally deserving of admiration is Bianca Mosca, cousin of Elsa Schiaparelli. Mosca had worked for the house of Paquin in Paris. From 1939 she was head designer for Jacqmar. Her sense of fun is seen in a wartime silky blouse and hat, made in fabric printed with made-do-and-mend slogans. Mosca was one of the founding members of the Incorporated Society of London Fashion Designers – IncSoc - established in 1942 to promote British textiles and couture abroad – all a boost for the wartime economy. IncSoc members linked with the government to create 'Utility' designs for the general public.

In America, styles spanned high society ball gowns and fun leisurewear for the beach. The legacy of Depression-era poverty added an element of thrift to new designs which was perfectly in keeping with the patriotic mood once the US entered the war in December 1941. The clothing industry wanted designs which would translate into mass appeal and country-wide sales. Designers such as Claire McCardell and Vera Maxwell pioneered easy-to-wear wardrobes with jersey garments, layering and useful colour combinations. 'Wearability' was key, and the concept of the 'capsule' wardrobe

A 1943 schoolgirl's fashion designs, painted with watercolours in an exercise book. The lure of fashion was pervasive and creative.

was in the air. McCardell's signature 'pop-over' dress became a classic. She also helped launch the leotard as fashion wear. Meanwhile, Maxwell was designing jumpsuits that would be appreciated by civilians and industrial workers. Overall there was a sense of clothes contributing to well-being, and an active lifestyle. It was a clean modern style.[9]

Home dressmaking was a key feature in American households. Pattern companies translated high fashion into wearable styles with mass appeal. These mix-and-match outfits are from a 1945 Simplicity *pattern book.*

'All the pleasure I have had, I owe to my sewing. I enjoy it so much, I wish I were physically able to do all the work myself.'

Ann Lowe, highly successful African American designer and dressmaker working in Florida and Harlem. She dressed Olivia de Havilland for the Oscars in 1947, and later made Jacqueline Bouvier's wedding dress, for her marriage to John F. Kennedy.[10]

American fashion was happy to appropriate styles from every country and culture – Mexican embroidery, 'gypsy' aprons and Tyrolean dirndls. This was not unusual. One interesting twist in wartime fashion on both sides of the Atlantic was the popularity of peasant-style clothes. These added a touch of gaiety to outfits in America, England, France and Poland. Eastern European countries occupied by Russia had to be careful to adapt to communist ideals, which meant so-called peasant clothes were a wise choice. Fancy fabrics and frivolous embellishments could lead to accusations of bourgeois tastes; a potential trigger for a one-way ticket to Siberia. Dressing like a cleaning lady became a survival tactic.[11]

Non-Western cultures were by no means slaves to Paris, London or New York. While many countries adopted Western fashions, they still retained their own fashions, rooted

Italian designs for dresses suitable for afternoon and evening wear. The lace adds glamour to pared-back lines. Hems are just below the knee.

An elegant blue day dress with matching belt..The sleeves are short, the skirt is cut to give an illusion of fuller fabric. Printed designs such as these were hugely popular. They looked fresh and pretty, and sometimes disguised lack of quality in fabrics and dyes.

Practical styles dominated most wartime fashion collections. Fuel shortages meant cycling rather than driving, so divided skirts became popular. This is an Italian skirt and breeches combination from 1942.

in national heritage. An imaginary international catwalk of fashions around the world might see Japanese silk kimonos woven with gold thread; Xosa beaded collars, Kampala robes and Swazi tribal headdresses in Africa; jewel-coloured brocades or indigo cottons in Palestine with gauzy veils; chequered sarongs and straw hats in Indonesia. In the foothills of the Himalayas 'fashion' meant brightly-embroidered long gathered skirts and veils hung with coins; in Yemen, silver-embossed belts around striped silk gowns.

Trousers were commonplace in many Middle Eastern and Asian countries, but they were still one of the most controversial garments on the Western fashion scene. In 1942, a French poll for or against the wearing of trousers came down on the verdict of 'unforgiveable' and 'bad taste'. Nonetheless, many French women were heads of households, with their husbands prisoners of war. Ski trousers were popular among young people. The old-fashioned British tailoring establishment did concede that younger generations of women were likely to wear trousers and shorts, commenting that the modern woman 'usually knows what she wants and expects the maker to interpret her wishes to the letter.'[12]

This American woman is happy to be photographed in her stylish slacks and blouse – dated July 1940. The legs are generously flared. Most women's trousers fastened on the hip or at the back.

'Whether you run a home or have a career, the first thing to do is to have a good basic wardrobe so that you can be certain of having the right thing to wear for any occasion.'

Three 'musts' were a good suit, a coat and a black dress.

Everywoman magazine, March 1947.

French fashions from February 1945. Shoulders and waist are heavily emphasised, with statement hats. The flared skirts prefigure the post-war revolution in styles.

Simple crepe fabric draped nicely, hiding the minimal yardage in the dress pattern. Small details made up for austere lines – gathers, matching belt and embroidery. This dress has a long row of covered buttons at the back to add interest.

'It gave me a taste for life again. Never mind the dress: its sheer arrival was enough, carried by a man in uniform, in its enormous new cardboard box, surrounded by pounds of tissue paper. When I signed for it I felt everything was worthwhile, that life was exciting again. Thank you.'

Customer at Maison Balmain, after the liberation of Paris.[13]

After liberation in 1944, Paris was quick to assert its role as the heart of international couture, but salons looked a little dingy, and genteel clients were crowded out by hard, vulgar customers with black-market money, paying for the latest models with cash.[14] Couture would never quite regain the prestige it held in the first part of the twentieth century. Established names in America and Britain had no intention of deferring to France if they could help it.

Mass production and mass-market profits were powerful forces. Even couture houses recognised they would have to appeal to the less affluent customer, through perfumes and accessories. The *griffe* on haute couture that once denoted absolute quality and exclusivity would eventually be touted as a 'designer' label on any high-street garment.

Whatever the country or ruling regime, fashion's influence still reached from the top down, all the way through licensed couture copies in department stores, illegal copies, and aspirational imitations. The most exciting designs of the 1940s would take the world by storm from 1947 onwards, but that's a story for another chapter.

Chapter 6

IN THE QUEUE
Shopping and the black market

'We must, each of us, regulate, restrict, and confine our right to buy.
This does not mean that we must stop all buying, but that we must buy
with wisdom and discretion.'

Speech by Sir Samuel Hoare, *War Illustrated,* March 1940

One delight of travel is shopping. The acquisition of beautiful local goods as souvenirs, gifts or objects of pleasure. Alongside my own collection of antique costumes I have memory-rich textiles bought while exploring and researching – jade-green silk and indigo cottons from Japan; jewel-coloured cloth from Guatemala, woven on a backstrap loom; batik prints from Kenya; turquoise beads from Egypt. I've window-shopped in the fashion centres of the 1940s: New York, Rome, Paris and London. In every elegant arcade, or in small shops of back streets in Portugal, Poland, Holland, Tokyo and Geneva, I've wondered what it was like to shop during the war.

Wartime economies struggled to provide a full range of goods,

J.A. Davis *catalogue. Mail order catalogues were the twentieth century equivalent of internet shopping. Customers browsed styles and checked prices. Goods were ordered by letter or telephone, and could be altered at home or by the local dressmaker for a perfect fit. Furs were considered luxurious, but also essential for winter warmth.*

and many of the items produced had to be exported. Even so, a tour of shops worldwide in the 1940s gives a sense of how precious purchases could be, and how evocative of personal histories. It also highlights the incredible international trade connections for goods, and, indirectly, the sheer scope of the war. The daily experience of shopping was usually a female experience, either for household necessities, clothing or more luxury items. Whatever went on in the news, the task of re-stocking had to continue, often meaning extra duty for women already working at paid employment as well as the unpaid labour of housework and childcare.

It's clear that shopping was more of a chore than a pleasure when prices were high, stocks were limited and coupons needed counting. 'Quite unobtainable' and 'Take them while you can' were familiar phrases in Britain. Shop workers found their customers hard to please. Customers found assistants rude and unhelpful. Londoner Gladys Langford battled through crowds of highly perfumed and under-washed women at D.H. Evans' store in the West End. She complained, 'Assistants ignored my presence – the only one I questioned announced she was not a saleswoman, so I walked out.'[1] Jamaican Marjorie Griffiths came to England to

HOLD EVERYTHING! a useful shopping bag

MATERIALS: Some fine string or twine and a No. 10 crochet hook.
TENSION: 5 tr. to 1 inch. Original bag measured approx. 13 inches square.
Front, base and back in one: Make 123 chain, turn. 1ST ROW: Miss 3 ch., * 1 treble in next ch., repeat from * to end, turn with 1 ch. 2ND ROW: 1 d.c. in each tr. to end, turn with 3 ch. Repeat these 2 rows until work measures 13 inches; fasten off.
Sides: Make 51 ch., turn, and work in pattern as before for 3½ inches. Make another piece the same.
To make up: Fold main piece and sew in sides, making double pleats at top. Using string double, work 1 inch d.c. all round top (1 round consists of approx. 120 sts.). Finish off with 1 round s.c.
Handles: With dbl. string make 61 ch. and work 4 rows d.c. Place several lengths of string down centre, roll over and sew up.

Queuing for purchases with a collection of bags was a familiar experience to housewives during the war. Shop shelves were frequently so bare the philosophy was, whatever was for sale once you reached the front of the queue – buy it.

serve in the ATS. She found her colour counted against her in the shop queue: 'If you went into a shop to buy anything, people would pretend they didn't see you. Although you would stand right in front of them they would call for people standing behind you.'[2]

'Do not comment loudly on the dress of customers. They may look as though they have dressed hurriedly in the dark, but we can't all be style conscious.' Shabby was the new chic.

Staff magazine note from Lewis's department store, Leeds.

Wealthy shoppers, such as this fur-clad lady arriving at Liberty's in London, were accustomed to excellent service pre-war. Standards inevitably dropped, as did levels of spending money.

Monica Baldwin, emerging into wartime England from three decades cloistered as a nun, was staggered by the democratisation of shopping. Obsequious shop assistants had been replaced: 'a few rather disdainful elderly women and scornful blondes in their teens had taken over.' Shopping meant purchasing a fantastically high-priced substitute for what was actually wanted. Later, dining at the Dorchester Hotel, a diamond-speckled, champagne-drinking woman was pointed out to Miss Baldwin – a black marketeer whose old clothes shop on the Mile End Road in London was making her a fortune thanks to burgeoning second-hand trade in clothes, and the appetite for garments without coupons.[3]

More humble operators in the black market system traded illegally in clothing coupons. These were usually acquired from women who'd no money to buy clothes anyway, regardless of how many coupons they were issued. Market traders sometimes accepted margarine coupons in exchange for fabric. The temptation for young people was strong. Many of them had money to spend thanks to war work and they craved the coupons to go shopping. Those 'in the know' cultivated relationships with dealers. They weren't all loud 'spivs' with painted ties and slouch hats. Housewives bought from bus conductors, who traded nylon stockings to passengers; or even parsons swapping eggs to obtain silk stockings and marmalade.[4]

Barter became the common form of trade on the British Channel Islands during the German occupation. A 'Barter Song' was written to celebrate the phenomenon, with an exuberant finale of 'Swopity, swopity, swop!' Another cheeky song was Under the Counter. Barter trade was advertised in local newspapers. The addition of the phrase 'or what' after a description of goods signified there were non-regulation items in the deal.[5]

In itself, second-hand trading wasn't illegal, it was a necessity. The Women's Voluntary Service had an international network of clothing exchanges. It was difficult to collect used clothes for the initial stock, as so few people had clothes to give away. Creative alterations converted depressing rejects into attractive garments. Rather like modern charity shop workers, WVS staff had to use firmness as well as tact when dealing with dreadful donations: some things simply couldn't be salvaged. Nearly 400 WVS exchanges helped raise the standard of clothing in poorer homes, as well as offering advice on how to renovate dilapidated garments.[6]

Window-shopping was advised, to pick up ideas and seek out the best prices. This was all hard on shoes and feet. Sensible footwear was essential, yet one of the hardest things to find in the war. Shops put customers on a waiting list for when new stock arrived.

Shoppers in general were offered endless advice on how to shop wisely during war. Savvy home dressmakers bought the pattern first, then looked for fabrics. Those tempted by remnants were reminded not to buy on the never-never, as this could lead to stockpiles of fabric for unspecified projects that never actually got used. 'Beware of sales bargains' was the Number One tip, closely followed by stern warnings not to follow clothing trends too closely as they'd soon go out of fashion 'ruining any claim to chic dressing,' according to one advice manual.[7]

Those serving abroad had to get used to living out of a kitbag. They also had wonderful opportunities for shopping experiences far different from their hometown stores. During the war, Cairo embraced a mass influx of military, medical and civilian personnel. For the well-monied it was business as usual at department stores such as

Hats were not rationed in Britain, so shopping for a new hat could be a much-needed pick-me-up. Novelty was still important despite the hard graft of war. This powder-blue crepe hat has silk velvet flowers and a cheerful bow at the back – perfect for a wartime wedding.

Cicurel's, Chemla's and Le Salon Vert. Tired shoppers could then refresh themselves with roasted coffee and fresh pastries at Groppi's café. Brits in Cairo lived in an unreal world, far from the Blitz back home. Cairo's shops stocked for British tastes – sensible clothes and chintz fabrics. Cottons and imported silks were quickly made up into fashionable clothes by Greek or Levantine dressmakers. Once Americans arrived in Egypt prices soared – Americans felt comparatively affluent and tended to pay whatever prices

were asked without haggling. It was a glorious boom-time for traders, and a problematic slump when Western armies pulled out of Egypt after the war.[8]

These pink leather sandals were bought in a Cairo souk in 1945, by Maureen Symington, wife of a civil servant stationed there. Joyce Grenfell, touring North Africa with ENSA found Cairo shops deceptively alluring – in her opinion, swags of bright colours hid shoddy quality.[9]

Entertainer Joyce Grenfell adored the souks of Syria. She coveted Kurdish boots in yellow leather with blue silk tassels, and red boots. She commissioned a pink corded silk bolero for herself and actually watched the fabric being woven at a silk loom shop. Her only comment on Syrian shoppers was to note the women were swathed in black. Continuing to Persia she noted women in coloured *abbas*, cut on the cross in pale pinks, green and mauves. Bargaining over dress lengths was fast-paced and intense.[10] Lewis Hulls of the Royal Corps of Signals found the Persian hospitality quite overwhelming. He learned to seek out genuine local products rather than trashy imported tourist goods.[11]

Closer to the equator, visitors to East Africa marvelled at the lively markets, with their colourful blend of local textiles and imported Indian silks. One Polish refugee arriving in Tanzania was struck by the women shopping, wearing beautiful beaded collars and golden rings around their necks.[12] Eslanda Goode Robeson, an African American anthropologist touring the continent with her husband, actor Paul Robeson, noted the German and Indian influences of Dar-es-Salaam markets. She happily shopped for an Assam silk bathrobe for Paul, a tussore silk coat for herself, pongee silk summer suits for both of them and silk nightwear. Everything was made to measure by hand, and delivered the next day to their lodgings on the island of Zanzibar. The Robesons also admired entrepreneurs selling crafts from their house porches.[13]

Mary Jane Russell was sent this tooled leather purse by an admirer serving in Egypt. It is clearly manufactured for a tourist market. The gift was bittersweet as Mary was in love with another man, who she eventually married.

American servicemen serving in the Pacific sent home souvenir carved wooden sandals, featuring novelty scenes such as palm trees and thatched huts. They were colourful and surprisingly comfortable to wear.

Even further south, Europeans in Durban were spoiled by shops filled with seemingly unlimited supplies of shoes, handbags, powder and lipstick.

Crossing to the Americas, those with money generally found the shops well stocked, particularly in major cities. In the US, Manhattan's Fifth Avenue was the go-to place for browsing. Sharry Traver Underwood was a professional dancer, used to wearing leotards and tap shoes. She took a break to window-shop in New York: 'I did not have things or fashionable clothes, so I mentally purchased whatever struck my fancy and did not owe a cent.'[14] Army dietician Caroline Morrison Garrett indulged dreams of owning the glamorous gowns on display in Fifth Avenue stores, but actually splurged in the Army Surplus Store for new uniform items.[15] As ever, the shopping experience could be tainted where race was concerned. *Negro Story* magazine published a true-to-life tale by Grace W. Tompkins called *Justice Wears Dark Glasses,* in which a black woman is accused of theft and arrested while trying on clothes in a store. The dress she wore was priced at $3.99 in the sale. The victim of this racial framing was sentenced to thirty days in jail, with a $35 lawyer's fee.[16]

The effects of the Depression were compounded by disruption to international trade in wartime. Shoppers weren't always understanding – one Canadian woman got angry because hairnets were no longer being imported from China.[17] Local shops survived because they were a focus of town and rural communities.

European shops suffered multiple crises. Countries with precarious economies, or those under siege, resorted to a barter system for basic goods. It is humbling to appreciate how little many people owned, and the hardship of replacing worn-out goods. One young woman in Macedonia was determined to leave home to join the resistance against German occupation. Her mother had to trade olive oil for footwear. These were *chokara* clogs made of wood and leather, not fancy shoes. Another young resistance fighter on Crete managed to get crude boots in return for wheat.[18]

The 'Wanted' and 'For Sale' columns in local newspapers give an insight into the needs of people in war-torn countries. In Krakow, Poland, for example, the *Krakow Messenger* classified ads included many fur coats and collars, Singer sewing machines, carpets, bedsheets and used clothing. Some were goods being shed by Jewish people destined for the ghetto or deportation; some were plundered from Jews who'd already been taken.[19] On a larger scale, the Nazi policy of plunder ensured a glut of luxury items in auction houses such as the Dorotheum in Vienna.

Impoverished families in Austria weren't shopping at the Dorotheum for high-end furs or paintings – they needed all their acquisitive skills to keep fed and clothed. Anne Dreer's family

Wartime magazines were produced on poor quality paper with limited ink ranges. Shoppers were still enticed by colourful adverts for goods, such as this promotion for Mexican fabrics.

were Germans in Croatia, forced to trek to Austria in 1944 where they found shops empty of clothes and fabrics due to Allied bombing raids. Anne's mother traded with former concentration camp inmates waiting to emigrate. Local farmers were also glad to trade food to get textiles. The Dreers made winter coats from army blankets, and underwear from army sheets.[20] This was a far cry from the indulgence of Viennese shopping in 1939, when luxury department stores bulged with expensive goods.

Often it wasn't a case of shopping *for* clothes, rather selling clothes themselves. As textiles became scarce hard-to-find items, good quality items were in demand. To avoid detection, some black-market dealers would move their stock by wearing it. A Jewish Polish family in hiding were visited in secret by a young cousin who looked unusually stout – he'd arrived layered with nightgowns, slips, stockings, brassieres and corsets salvaged from their former home. Even when he'd undressed, there were more clothes hidden in pockets. The hidden family later sold an imported English wool coat with an Astrakhan collar. Pre-war it had been worth a fortune. In desperate times it got enough to eat for a week.[21] In Communist countries there were heavy penalties for capitalistic trade, so the black market was particularly dangerous. There were still many covert deals for food, fuel, clothes, underwear and cosmetics.[22]

Trading in rural Spain meant miles of walking, with a donkey for heavy loads. Sturdy footwear was essential. This photograph was sold to German tourists on holiday cruises in the late 1930s.

'…We were sitting waiting our turn and heard the dressmaker talking to her customer inside the fitting room. The customer was very determined to have things just right. "It would look better with larger shoulder pads," we could hear her saying in an authoritative tone of voice, "and the hemline should be just a little higher, don't you think?" I was flabbergasted when the curtains were drawn back and there was Anne…'

Eva Schloss recalls her stylish friend Anne Frank shopping, before the Franks were forced into hiding.[23]

The anti-Semitic policies of the Nazi regime caused particular hardship for Jewish shops. Those that survived state-organised violence were usually forced to close as Nazi Brown Shirts put pressure on customers not to buy there. Other Jewish shops were appropriated by Aryan owners under new laws designed to strip Jews of their businesses. This included the 'Harrods' of Berlin – the KaDeWe department store. New laws limited the hours that Jews could shop; Jewish people received minimal clothing coupons. A courageous minority of shoppers defied the on-going boycott of Jewish shops. It was risky. German housewife Wilhelmina Haferkampf was furious to see the discrimination against Jewish shops, but was denounced by a neighbour for buying shoes from one.[24]

In the later years of war almost everyone in Germany suffered the hardship of a collapsing economy and the prospect of inevitable military defeat. Sewing needles and balls of thread were ranked as luxury goods. A Wehrmacht soldier taking a few days leave over Christmas 1942 saw that the Nuremberg shops showed nude mannequins – there were no clothes to display. Across Germany there were long queues outside the few shops that remained open.[25] By 1945, women took camp stools to queue from 7am onwards. 'There is no point in even trying,' said one disillusioned housewife. She later bartered walking boots for fuel, and some army boots for an electric stove.[26]

This was a stark contrast to the experience of Wehrmacht soldiers and German civil service women shopping in occupied Paris. After the 1940 invasion, Germans crowded the famous Galeries Lafayette department store, scrupulously paying for items which couldn't be found at home – stockings, shoes and perfume.[27] Prices were cheap for the invaders, and export restrictions were lifted on Germans buying furs, jewellery, silks and luxury goods in occupied territories. Soldiers buying for their sweethearts back home requested their sizes for underwear and blouses, and preferences for fabric colours. By 1941, the military postal services were handling over three million parcels of foreign goods being sent back to the Fatherland. The French, stripped of goods they desperately needed themselves, called the German troops 'potato beetles' because they were so heavily loaded. Ukrainians called them 'hyenas'.[28]

While Germans bought silks in France, the French were sourcing woollens and footwear. Flea markets and unofficial clothing exchanges proliferated. Truly indulgent shopping was limited to those who profited from black market food trading – known as BOF, or *boeuf-oeufs-fromages* – and to women of negotiable virtue who cleverly used their German admirers to fund their extravagances.In Vichy France, mistresses bought the most obscenely expensive items available, to show their new status. This gave rise to a fashion for matching crocodile bags, shoes and even wardrobe trunks.[29]

'Cigarettes Wanted – Warm Jumper in Exchange'; 'Soap Offered in Exchange for Food'

Noticeboard for prisoner barter at Frontstalag 142 civilian internment camp, France.

'Let's refrain from ostentatious shopping!' This plea came from the Japanese Women's Patriotic Association. In Tokyo's upmarket Ginza district, women handed out notes to shoppers considered flashy or fancily-dressed. This didn't dampen the vibrancy of commerce. The streets were crowded with young students, housewives in colourful kimonos, and girls with perms and painted faces wearing short American-style dresses. As the expense of war affected home markets in Japan there was a noticeable diminishing of courtesy from shop assistants, who would previously have bowed to customers and thanked them for honouring the shop with purchases. By 1941, it was the customer who had to thank the clerk for the honour of buying precious goods. It wouldn't be long before the beautiful silk kimonos were traded for rice on the illegal black market.[30]

Parts of China under occupation by Japanese forces struggled to sell home-produced silks, as shops were soon filled with Japanese fabrics. 'Who will come in now to buy good silk when there is cheap artificial silk as cheap as paper and just as thin?' lamented one Chinese shop owner. The shop was eventually looted – 'the silks were all torn down from the shelves and lay in heaps on the ground'.[31] Shanghai shoppers could browse neon-lit window displays on the Avenue Joffre. Wooden mannequins were adorned with slanted hats and Western suits; in contrast with the traditional Chinese style of clothing which was rapidly being consigned to the past. Chinese families who couldn't afford to shop in stores exchanged home-grown food for textiles. There was brisk bargaining around the fences of internment camps in Shanghai, where prisoners gave up precious items of clothing from dwindling stocks, in return for much needed eggs and fruit.[32]

Perhaps the most famous fictional story of internment is Nevil Shute's novel *A Town Like Alice*, inspired in part by the hardships suffered by Dutch women on Sumatra after the 1942 Japanese invasion. Shute transferred the action to a British colony. His story of Englishwoman Jean Paget offers rare glimpses of shopping in Malaya, with descriptions of itinerant sellers, small shops selling clothes, sweets, cigarettes and fruit, and cloth dealers bartering for European jewellery.

A mid-twentieth century embroidered silk skirt from southern China, to be worn over trousers and leggings. The waistband is of cotton, to keep the skirt from slipping down.

Detail of a silk dressing gown bought in Singapore by Joe Lonsdale, for his sister Anne. Joe was in the Argyll and Sutherland Highlanders. He was captured by the Japanese in Singapore. While in captivity in Changi gaol, then working as a slave labourer on the notorious Burma-Siam railway of death, Joe risked torture to protect his uniform cap and badge. Joe survived the war. His comrades did not.

My grandfather Charlie was a naval medic stationed in Hong Kong in 1947. He sent this dress to my grandmother Margaret. It is Chinese silk made in a Western style.

The tailor's shop in Singapore where Joe Lonsdale and friends shopped for gifts to send home to England. Fabric and patterns were chosen to be made up into garments. There are also items of Western used clothing for sale.

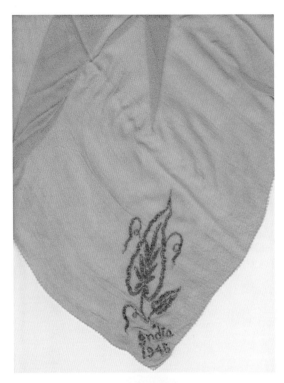

Service personnel from abroad stationed in India filled the Red Cross Duty Free Parcel depot with their purchases, including dress materials, buttons and hankies for family back home. This embroidered handkerchief was sent to Phyllis Clark in England by her father in 1943.

Long after the war was over, souvenirs of shopping trips abroad were saved. Precious clothes were packed in tissue paper to be kept 'for best'. This blue cotton dressing gown has amazing embroidery, including the wearer's initials A.A on the pocket. It was bought in India for Anne Abbott by her future husband.

India's booths, bazaars and boutiques offered local and imported wares. Goods were transported by railway, by donkeys, and by women loaded with baskets. Those with the money to shop could order clothes to be made up by tailors on ancient hand-cranked Singer sewing machines. The range of fabrics was intoxicating – chiffons, georgettes and ninons made gorgeous nightgowns and lingerie.[33] What was cheap to foreign shoppers was often unobtainable to local people. Government controls of cloth shops meant police pickets when crowds gathered to fight for much-needed fabric. In Calcutta, an Indian was appointed inspector of prices, to stop over-inflation.[34]

In many cases, it was shops reopening and re-stocking that gave reassuring signs of a return to some kind of normality. As the British Eighth Army moved south to north in Italy, pushing back German forces, it was clear how much local life had suffered, yet even as the volcano Vesuvius erupted near Naples, shop windows had displays of gloves, stockings and silks. Allied forces in Naples soon found the best trade was on the rampant black market – where a lot of their own pilfered kit ended up.[35]

Chapter 7

ON THE LAND
Agricultural work

'Boy, these farmers in this country really work. They get out in the
rice fields and work in the mud bare-footed. From sunrise to sunset
too. They are tough! The women are so strong! They surely are the
backbone of Japan.'[1]

Mary Kimoto Tomika

Above left: *Women on the island of Malta work the dry soil barefoot, wearing plain clothes and a headscarf.
Sourcing seeds and bringing a crop safely to harvest were tough when under siege and bombed intensively.*

Above right: *Abundant agricultural land was a deliberate target for invading forces. During the 1941-42
advance into Russia, a German Wehrmacht soldier took this photo of a summer field worker wearing light
cotton clothes, holding aloft a sheaf of wheat and an iconic sickle.*

Watching a recent Hollywood film about heroism and combat on the Japanese island of Okinawa I was struck by a scene of a palm-thatched building going up in flames. That building had once been someone's home – a farmstead, perhaps. A little imagination turns the shell-pocked, corpse-packed mud around the building back into fertile fields of sugarcane, beans, onions, radishes, and abundant rice paddies.[2] When the real battles subsided, civilian survivors – if there were any – would emerge to bury the dead, clear the debris and begin life again.

On a farming theme, other images of war might show tanks advancing across a grain harvest or dead cattle bloating on battlefield pastureland. War can destroy, in an instant, what takes months or years to cultivate, yet people must eat. Food is crucial for military success. Starvation is a weapon of war. Women were a vital part of the fight against hunger.

'The grass and crops had been stomped into the ground by thousands of feet. Chimneys were all that was left of the villages burnt down by the retreating Nazis. Everything was broken.'

A Soviet general looks out over former farmland In Kursk.[3]

Farm workers populated the wartime landscape of every nation. In many countries it was the norm to see women on the land. Women in black pyjama trousers and straw hats tilled the soil in Vietnam, carrying surplus food to local markets.[4] In Syria, Alawitin girls hoed stony soil in bright dresses. In Iraq, the date groves of Kerbela were tangled with pomegranates and oranges, carried to market by women in black scarves and burqas.[5] Burmese tea-pickers brightened the green bushes with multi-coloured saris. Mothers in Tanzania worked their crops with babies tied to their backs. Some were subsistence farmers, living from one meagre meal to the next; others built up lives of relative prosperity. Regardless of how hard they worked, few women were able to own land, due to patriarchal cultures and gendered inheritance laws.

Monpe *trousers such as these were typical agricultural wear in Japan. Quite simple to construct, they tie at each side of the waist.* Monpe *became synonymous with the working poor. Women and girls wore* monpe *to pick rice, or even to pull ploughs when draft animals were requisitioned by the military.*

103

A notebook of haiku poems and jottings has been turned into a sample book of Japanese woven cotton cloths, showing a range of patterns available to workers.

The long-reaching legacy of slavery in the southern states of America meant particularly tough conditions and low pay for African-American workers, despite the smiles of this 1940s cotton picker. Field work was harsh on people and clothes.

Nevil Shute's popular novel *A Town Like Alice* tells the story of a group of Western women trapped in Malaya by occupying Japanese forces. They are considered 'useless mouths'. After months of minimal rations and suffering, the white women wonder if they could stay in a village to plant rice for their keep. One of the older English women is appalled at such a drop in standards – the Malay women sensibly stripped down to minimal covering to work in the mud and water of the paddies.

The usual graft of tilling, sowing, weeding, feeding and harvesting was made far harder during war. It wasn't just the devastation of land or plunder of stock. Male conscription deprived farms of sturdy workers, leaving children, elderly people and women to pick up the slack. Government land requisitions uprooted families who'd worked the land for generations; policies of internment for so-called enemy aliens also cost families their livelihood, such as Japanese-descent American farm workers in the US.

In Western countries, women on farms were usually considered helpers rather than actual farmers: the farmer's wife's work was sometimes overlooked, or dismissed as merely supportive, when in fact any farm relies on all members contributing. A war-bride arriving in Calgary, Western Canada, noted that she'd joined a happy farming community where the women baked, sewed, stoked wheat alongside the men, and had babies. They did all this 'in colourful cotton dresses and a few bad hats'.[6]

In addition to their farm duties, women took an active role in resistance, helping to hide and feed fugitives. Farmers also made covert links with town households in occupied territories, to bring them much-needed food. Belgian farm traders had special pockets sewn into their coats to smuggle food past checkpoints and into a house. These would be filled with grains, peas, beans and barley, then shaken out over a sheet on the floor.[7] The town-country symbiosis worked well for both sides. In Germany, the bartering of household goods with farmers for food was known as hamstering. Women struggling to feed their families in town would swap extra clothing coupons with farmers in need of clothes from the city.[8]

Farming life was tough, particularly when men were drafted away from the farm. Elsa Diserens was a peasant farmer in Switzerland when she found herself alone on a farm with young children, and

Farming couple from the Schei farm Stadsbygd, Norway. The woman wears a cotton frock and apron, compared to the man's trousers. Showing elements of a matriarchy, the oldest woman on the farm was known as Mother and she was the boss. During the war the Schei family generously fed hungry town visitors, who then 'paid' with clothing.

ill from morning sickness with a new pregnancy. She had no choice but to learn to milk and to mow grass herself, in addition to mucking out cattle, feeding pigs, rabbits and chickens, cooking and managing the laundry. She gave birth in 1940 and still found time to make cheese to send to her husband in the army.[9] Although magazines might show picturesque images of rural women, most peasants' daily wear was dark-coloured cotton skirts with dark shawls and thick boots.

'It just wasn't done, like wearing slacks, you see. You felt you've got to do it, I'm important, I'm doing a man's job. What are they growling about?'

A female herd-tester dismisses prejudice against her trousers and her job, New Zealand.[10]

Governments in North America, Australia, New Zealand and Britain were anxious to make farm work seem more attractive. Schemes such as the Farmerette Brigade and the Women's Land Army encouraged women to sign up for farm labour in order to free men to fight. Recruitment images showed happy, hearty girls riding tractors in sunny fields, or feeding lambs on hay bales. The reality was far more arduous. Land Army work was a genuine national service.

Being dressed for the job was important to instil a sense of patriotic pride when doing less-than-glamorous tasks. A British Land Army leaflet explained, 'The purpose

Tough tasks required sturdy shoes. These land worker shoes have metal cleats hammered into the soles to help the leather last longer.

There could be quite a gulf between born-and-bred farmers and their new recruits. This cartoon shows a woman dressed for town, complete with fur stole and feathered hat. She announces that she is the new rat catcher.

of the uniform is that all Land Army members should be dressed suitably and alike. Do not try to add to or alter your uniform or to set a new fashion in wearing it.' The uniform also gave a sense of shared purpose – a group identity for young women in particular, who formed life-long friendships during their service. Perhaps donning a uniform helped new recruits overcome the shock of transition from their usual pattern of work, to outdoor farming. New members were also advised to treat their uniform with respect

Audrey Robson in WLA gear, 1944. She found hard manual labour a bit of a shock, but it didn't stop her flirting with handsome Italian prisoners of war. British corduroy breeches were sometimes known as 'whistling cord' because of the noise made when the fabric rubbed – and perhaps because of street whistles at the wearers.

and not to wear anything that would catch in moving parts. Worn-out uniform items would, in theory, be replaced. In actuality, there was much scrubbing and mending of stained uniforms, and re-soling of shoes. Uniform was, essentially, work gear first and foremost. Sturdy trousers and boots made sense on a farm; fashionable frocks did not.

'By the end of the day we were bloodied and dirty, looking far from elegant with our hair jammed up under grubby hats trimmed with fly veils.'

Betty Trowse, after sheep castration and tailing in South Australia.[11]

Uniforms were issued as and when they became available. The colour scheme was usually green and khaki, although the Australian government refused to release green dye, because it was reserved for fighting forces, so their Land Army wore khaki only. Australian women put their hand to sheep shearing and slaughtering, rock clearing, timber felling, crop picking, and tractor driving, all in their jodhpurs and shirts. Isolation, primitive billets, home sickness and taunts that they couldn't handle the work were all hardships to be faced.

'I wanted a uniform really so I ended up in the Land Army. I remember pulling turnips. It was cold and wet and I cried.'

Hilda Booth, WLA, *Washburn Heritage Centre, Yorkshire.*

In pre-war Britain there were fewer than 200 women in timber production, and these only in lighter aspects of the work. In 1942, the Women's Timber Corps – affectionately known as Lumber Jills – was established. Tree-felling was essential war work. Without wood there were no pit props; without mines there was no coal; without coal industry ground to a halt. Recruits were former hairdressers, shop assistants and typists. They were advised to bring heavy shoes and suitable heavy clothes. This was no easy task in the middle of clothing shortages and rationing. Lumber Jills begged for official ties and WTC shoulder tabs, so that locals wouldn't call them 'Farmer's Boy'.[12] Mavis Williams joined the Timber Corps because she didn't want to spend the war stuck in the office. Her excitement at the arrival of her uniform deflated somewhat when she tried it on. The knee-length breeches came down to her ankles – she wasn't quite 5 ft high. Luckily her father was a master tailor and alterations were soon underway. She said the girls' breeches attracted a fair bit of attention when they turned up at local dances.[13]

British women had distinctive khaki and green outfits, with breeches or dungarees, and green woollen pullovers. An added military element came from the arm brassards, with triangles denoting years of service. Gumboots such as these – 1944 government issue – were rare and highly prized.

Above: *A gang of Women's Timber Corps Lumber Jills in a motley collection of uniform items and civvies for summer logging. Many Timber Corps and Land Army memoirs bear witness to the camaraderie of outdoor work, where high spirits kept hard work bearable.*

Left: *Doris Walters (right) met her lovely husband Walter while working in the Land Army. He was a PoW farm labourer, formerly of the German Kriegsmarine. That took some explaining to Doris's dad and big brothers in Hull, a city that had been pounded by German bombs.*

Right: *The popular press in Japan showed idealistic images of post-war farm life, such as this fresh-faced worker in shirt and dungarees.*

Below left: *Mary Gale was a town girl who took to Land Army life and found she loved the country. After the war, deserted by her husband, she lived alone in a tiny cottage.*

Below right: *Palestine offered a contentious haven to Jewish people who survived the Holocaust in Europe. Rosa Steinkeller, a 17-year-old former inmate of Buchenwald and Belsen concentration camps, began a new life on a farm settlement in the Jordan Valley, needing only shirt, shorts and boots for kibbutz work.*

Women who didn't receive their full uniform quota – or who didn't like the quality – might have been tempted by adverts for made-to-measure breeches, and additional items such as rain coats and boots. Magazines also pushed adverts for beauty products, to achieve 'true loveliness' despite exposure to all elements. Number Seven preparations claimed to be 'as effective in the rustic billet as they were in the well-appointed boudoir.'[14] Lard made a cheap alternative for use on chapped skin.

The end of the war was by no means the end of Land Army work. Crops still had to be harvested while men waited to be demobbed. Some former Land Girls felt snubbed after the war, as if they'd only been wanted 'for the duration'. There were limited openings for women on the land and many missed the outdoor life. They also had happy memories of jolly hostel life with other young women.

For women in countries where farming was considered women's work anyway, the long days continued as usual, with the added burden of recovering damaged land and replanting crops. Refugees found fresh post-war opportunities farming in new lands, hoping for an escape from conflict. The regrowth was literal and emotional.

Chapter 8

SKIES ABOVE
Aviation

'Good show Worrals. You girls will be winning the war without
us if we don't watch it.'

Worrals Carries On, Captain W.E. Johns, 1942

In a two-seater glider above green fields in North Yorkshire the pilot asked if I'd like to take control. 'You'll remember the basics from your days in the Air Training Corps,' he said confidently. Yes, I remembered teenage days in the ATC – flying lessons over the Firth of Forth, and freezing Lincolnshire airfields; flared trousers, or, worse, skirts with 'bamboo' coloured tights. My one-time knowledge of the principles of flight had long since deserted me, however. What remained was a profound respect for anyone who flies, in peacetime or in war. I am still awestruck by the mighty noise of a Lancaster bomber engine as it taxis to the runway, or how small and nifty wartime fighter planes are.

Women have taken to the skies from the first – ascending in hot air balloons, or descending as performance parachutists in the eighteenth and nineteenth centuries. Excluded from Great War flight roles, women nevertheless flew post-war in the 1920s and 1930s. Flying was an elite sport, requiring money and talent. Early pioneers had to adapt civilian clothing for open-cockpit flying conditions. Some, in the 1930s, launched their own fashion collection inspired by aviation wear. Women such as Jean Batten, Amy Johnson, Amelia Earhart and Jacqueline Cochran set or broke distance, altitudes and speed records. They were not alone. In Russia female aviators reached legendary status in the 1930s. Despite the fact that there were qualified, experienced aviators worldwide – including in China, Australia, Egypt, Iran, India, Turkey and Czechoslovakia, women were turned down by most Air Ministries when offered their flying services for the Second World War.[1] It was a familiar problem: the inability to see beyond a stereotypical image of women to their actual skills and abilities. The war both expanded women's roles in aviation and consolidated the epic images of male flying heroes.

In Britain, recruitment first focused on the concept of 'free a man to fly'. Roles were to be auxiliary, and the service was named accordingly – Women's Auxiliary Air Force. This pattern played out across Allied services. This in no way diminishes the need or the importance of the roles first on offer. Typist, clerks and telephonists were a crucial part of air force communications, without which no planes could fly sorties,

Audrey Pratt, WAAF Radar operator – 'We were taken by lorry from Brixham for each watch and after a while we WAAFs were issued with battledress as it was difficult climbing on to a lorry in a skirt. Battledress consisted of slacks and a blouson jacket.'

or be intercepted. Radar work, fundamental to British defence, was highly skilled, requiring focus and good computational abilities.

WAAF memoirs describe the strain of being witnesses to major military events via radar screens or telephone exchanges. WAAF women were on duty during Dunkirk, the Coventry bombings and the Battle of Britain. WAAFs picked up the flight of Reich vice-chancellor Rudolph Hess when he made his strange landfall in England. During the famous Dambuster raid on Germany in May 1943, one woman typed the Operation Order and was on duty at the switchboard all night. She recalled, 'I was also in the Signals Section when they had to send out fifty-six telegrams for all the aircrew who were missing on that raid.'[2] WAAFs such as radar operator Audrey Pratt, working on the south coast of England, were keenly aware of Allied sea vessels going up the channel before the 1944 D-Day invasion of Occupied France.

Ann Pont had worked as a General Post Office telephonist in York before joining the air force aged 17½, partly to get away from home. She was trained at the radar school at RAF Cranwell and eventually posted to Scotland, on the Moray Firth, where she plotted local aircraft movements and loved the work. She plotted the sinking of the *Tirpitz* in northern Norway, 1944 – a significant loss for the German navy, though she didn't know it at the time. She worked on Chain Home Low, an early system of radar, right on top of a cliff. Her keenest memories of uniform concern the endless efforts to keep warm. When it inevitably snowed, the women were issued with wellingtons and seaboot socks. Ann's greatcoat fitted too nicely and looked far too chic, so she was pressured to get a larger one. This came in handy for sleeping in at night – it was so cold that hot water bottles were frozen by morning. She got added chills thanks to a wool allergy, which meant she couldn't wear woollen underwear. Even so, in her eighth decade Ann still declares 'I wouldn't have missed it for the world.'[3]

Eileen Younghusband worked as a filter officer, interpreting information provided by plotters. She wrote in her autobiography, 'I seemed destined to be on duty at times of special significance.' These included giving the first announcement of a V2 flying bomb over London. When Belgium was liberated she was sent there to pinpoint V2 mobile launch sites, making calculations on the rocket launch curves in a tense six-minute window, using only pencil, paper and a slide rule. The information was passed onto Mosquito bombers, which then attacked the launch trailers. A statue of Younghusband now graces the replica filter room at the Battle of Britain Museum in Stanmore.[4]

Men were flying the Mosquito bombers, but women were building them. As civilian shop assistants, housemaids, hairdressers and dressmakers, these women would have individual clothing styles. As machinists in the air industry all classes and backgrounds mingled in unifying overalls, producing world-famous aircraft such as Spitfires, Hurricanes, Lancasters and Halifaxes.

'Surely nothing is stranger in this strange war than the fact that these gigantic instruments of destruction, which drop their two-ton bombs far away in Central Europe, have been largely put together by girls who, a year or two ago, were handling silks or typewriters or manicure sets.' (Priestley, *British Women Go To War*.)

At first, WAAF fitters were a rare breed, and they faced prejudice from pilots who sometimes refused to take up planes which had airframes, engines and electrics solely fitted by women. Those who did fly the planes gave good reports.[5] Since sewing was considered a female task, many air force women became fabric workers. A WAAF recruitment leaflet asked, 'If there is a hole in a barrage balloon it is your job to patch it. Are you used to a sewing machine? And handy with a pot of glue?'

Fabric workers not only made and repaired barrage balloons, they also stitched the fabric components of aircraft. Unbleached Irish linen was the standard covering, being light, strong and durable. The linen was doped to stop water penetration – a heady job. Holes could be darned; rips were repaired in a herringbone stitch, using doubled, waxed linen thread, five stitches per inch. Fabric was secured to the trailing edge of the wings using lockstitch. The work was quite a step up from dressmaking. Repair work also highlighted how vulnerable the aircraft were – targets for enemy fighters, anti-aircraft guns and shrapnel.

Irene Nequest in 1942, civilian instrument fitter for Tiger Moths and other wartime aeroplanes at Brough airfield near Hull. Her husband ferried heavy bombers across the Atlantic as part of Air Transport Command.

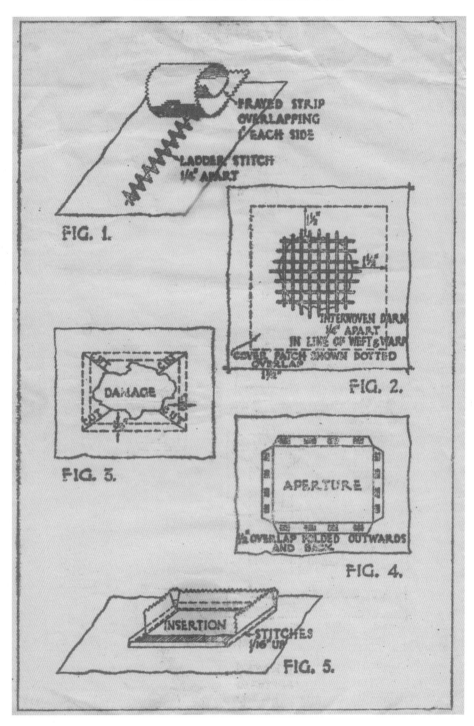

It is rather surreal to think that great Wellington bombers could quite literally be darned when damaged, just like a worn sock. This is a page from a fabric worker's book belonging to Aircraftwoman Irene Nellie Hall, detailing repair techniques.

Fabric workers were responsible for camouflage on aircraft. The temperate land scheme was dark earth and dark green; the Middle East land scheme used mid stone and dark earth colours; temperate sea scheme was dark slate grey and extra dark sea grey. Perhaps the fabric painters would never get to travel beyond their air base, but with a little imagination the paint colours conjured up different theatres of war.

One enterprising duo of seamstresses were charged with making a cover for one of the newly invented American Sikorsky helicopters. They weren't allowed in the hangar to see it, so had to reverse engineer their design from an existing cover. They used a fine, soft fabric called Medapolin. The biggest problems came from the many heavy zips, some of which had to be sewn into a circle. It was an immense task, and entirely successful. As a reward the two women were granted the privilege of seeing the uncovered helicopter – a rare glimpse of cutting edge aviation technology at that time.[6]

Parachute sewing and packing was not glamorous work but it had plenty of perks. On one level there was the knowledge that parachutes saved hundreds of lives. Packer Olive Houghton remembered a young Polish airman coming to the Parachute Section where she worked and shaking her hand for saving his life. In this way there was a

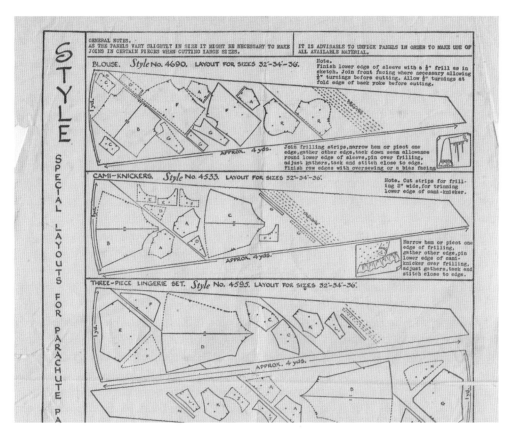

Detail of a 1940s parachute dressmaking pattern, gratis with a fashion magazine. With ingenuity several garment pieces could be cut from the triangular sections, including underwear and wedding dresses.

vital bond between the airmen and the auxiliaries. Some airmen followed a tradition of forwarding 10 shillings to the WAAF each time they had a successful parachute use, with the money used to fund dances. Packers also received little silver wings after eight successful dropped parachutes.[7]

The other bonus for parachute workers was the fabric itself. At the start of the war silk was the dominant fabric for parachutes, whether for human use or for dropped flares and parachute mines. The silk was highly coveted, as was the nylon of later parachutes. In Russia, female aviators stole the silk to make underwear, because they were only issued with male undies. There were harsh penalties. Two women were sentenced to ten years' imprisonment on the charge of destroying military equipment. They were allowed to stay on their regiment to complete wartime service. One was killed; one was heavily decorated.[8]

Black West Indian and black British women found the RAF generally more sympathetic to recruiting non-whites, but they still endured bigoted notions about keeping people of colour 'in their place', in addition to the usual gender discrimination which pushed many women straight into domestic roles. Lilian Bader was a British mixed-race pioneer, pushing against such barriers. Racial prejudice surfaced as she was interviewed for a Naafi canteen worker position. Bader held her ground and was accepted for work at Catterick Camp. She called it 'a world of our own' and was proud of her blue uniform and cap. Racial prejudice forced a series of moves across Yorkshire until Bader was eventually accepted into the WAAF and kitted out with the full WAAF uniform from overcoat, tunic and cardigan, down to knickers and suspender belt. Later she received a helmet and gas mask. Bader broke out of a domestic cleaning role to be trained as an instrument repairer. When she was promoted to acting corporal she couldn't wait to sew her new stripes on: 'I felt I had achieved something which, although it seems small now, was a lot to me then.'[9]

Air force women off-base saw their fair share of adventure. A South African reporter described meeting two transport drivers – 'dressed as neatly as an ad in *Vogue*' – who worked across the road networks of East Africa, narrowly escaping sexual assault and murder on several occasions. The reporter was impressed, commenting, 'You don't have to trail far to hear *blokes* talk about the Battle of Britain, Dunkirk, Tobruk and El Alamain, but it's not usual to hear a Jane shoot a line on that theme.'[10]

Whatever the rank and role within the air force, transitioning from civilian clothes to uniform was always a significant rite of passage. Kit was collected from the clothes store as and when it was available. Male uniforms took priority and in 1939 'air force blue' fabric was in heavy demand. Until they got full kit, air force women wore a medley of civilian and military clothing. Shortages of uniform even caused a hiatus in recruitment in the early months of war. By 1940, the situation was so desperate that selected WAAF women were sent on a tour of West End shops and wholesale warehouses, searching for alternatives.[12] For some it was a joy to receive complete outfits of new clothes. Others were horrified at the styles: 'underwear was so ancient that it might have seemed out-of-date even in the First World War.' Not realising the kit was government property, aircraftwoman Beryl Nicoll sent all the awful underwear home to her mother who put them in a jumble sale.[13]

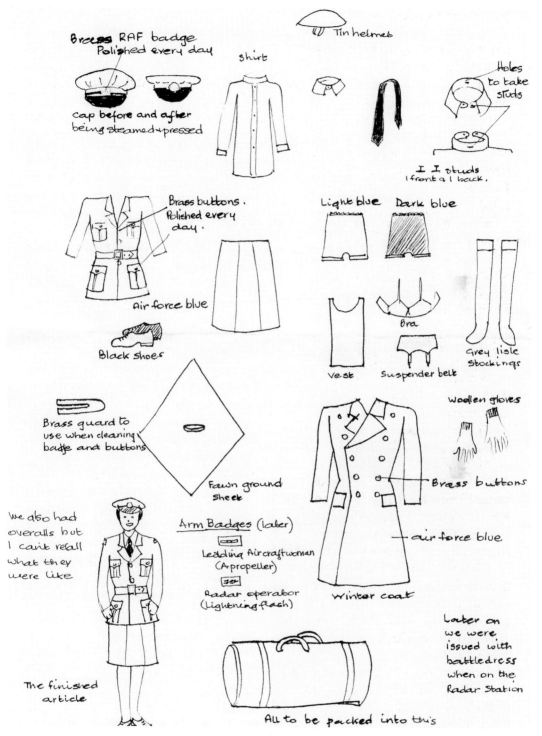

Full WAAF kit, drawn by Audrey Pratt: 'The day we got our uniform was very exciting and our civilian clothes were packed up and sent home.'[11]

119

'I was then handed something that made my eyelids flicker. Was it Grandmother's left-offs? No! My winter knickers!'

Cherry Symonds, WAAF. (Escott, *Our Wartime Days*)

Socialite Mary Lee Settle sailed from the US to join the British air force, with 'a year's supply of toilet paper, can after can of fruit juice, and evening clothes.' She turned up at the recruitment office in a Harris Tweed suit, hoping not to stand out. She soon found herself among recruits from London's East End, with hard, unkempt pompadour hairstyles. 'We were no longer undefined flotsam at the depot,' Settle wrote when uniforms were issued. She hated the hard shoes, 'as if I were being asked to walk across England with my feet in stone.' Incessant polishing of shoes and buttons at least staved off any thoughts of home sickness and despondency.[14]

Not everyone took to the rules that came with uniform. Joan Bell, working at RAF Cranwell, resented the fact that as a junior rank she had to salute young male trainee officers, so she used to take her cap off to avoid saluting at all. Twice she was spotted and put on charge. The second time her punishments included being given a large bundle of officers' unwashed football socks to darn.[16]

Sometimes uniform protected from sexual harassment, sometimes not. And while there was a residue of hostility to women in uniform, it could also open the door to kindness from strangers, who saw that women were dressed to do their bit.

Women were usually disqualified from air force flying on basis of gender alone. The employment of female Air Transport Auxiliary pilots was controversial. These were pilots to deliver planes between airfields. In Britain, the first contingent started small, with eight women ferrying Tiger Moth biplanes. The women's ATA expanded rapidly in terms of numbers and in the scope of craft they were permitted to fly, until they were ferrying the latest

Taking her break from washing her 'smalls', Eileen Little wrote home from a WAAF training camp, detailing the bewildering rules regarding uniform, 'such as wearing our overalls for breakfast, not wearing plimsolls around camp, wearing our caps always – except when in buildings or going to the cookhouse – rolling our sleeves up when not wearing tunics and as for saluting…!'[15]

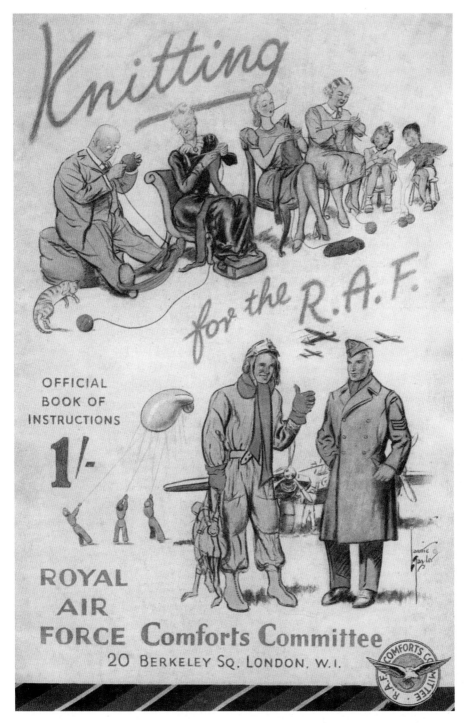

This Knitting for the RAF booklet shows women only in civilian roles, but WAAFs wore the woollies too. Warmth and protection were key, whether wrestling with barrage balloons in winter or simply surviving unheated work rooms.

fighter planes and heavy bombers. ATA pilots had diverse backgrounds including sheep farmer, ballet dancer, actress and ski instructor. The ATA were resourceful, under-paid and under-appreciated, often flying damaged aircraft, and in dire weather conditions. The first eight women were issued with sheepskin Irving jackets and trousers issued to RAF operational pilots. The jackets in particular were definitely a status symbol.[17] Since most women did not own a pair of slacks, they often flew in skirts.

Media images liked to show the contrast between pilots with nice hairstyles and lipstick, and the great machines they flew. In the air gender was no issue – the pilot did her job and did it well. The American ferry pilots, eventually known as WASPS – Women's Auxiliary Ferrying Pilots – were accepted for war service in 1942, thanks to lobbying by outstanding aviators Nancy Love and Jacqueline Cochran. WASP Shirley Slae was shown on the cover of *Life* magazine. She was in practical overalls, but with a bow on the end of her long plaited hair. The persistent valuing of female appearance over abilities was part of a broad social pattern, in which femininity was associated with vanity and frivolity, while masculinity equated to competence and strength. Regardless of how well they flew, women were denied a wider role in military aviation. This in turn impacted on post-war status. In the US, female ferry pilots were not given military status until 1977, when they finally gained privileges due to former combatants.[18] In Britain, the ATA was disbanded in 1945 with male pilots given preference in future flying roles, regardless of comparative skills or experience.

During her five years' ATA service Lettice Curtis delivered nearly 400 four-engined aircraft, 150 Mosquitos, and handled over 50 different types of plane. Not liking the Sidcot flying suit, she wore a teddy-bear cloth coat for warmth, tightly belted at the waist.

The prejudice was worldwide. French female ferry pilots were given a brief stint of service then told to go home and knit.[19] Maryse Bastié, a record-breaking long distance pilot refused to be put off, joining the French Military Air Transport Organisation in 1944, rising to the rank of flight lieutenant and commander of the Legion of Honour for 'exceptional conduct and acts of resistance in war.'[20] South African pilot Rosamund Everard Steenkamp flew to Teheran in a bold attempt to join the Russian Air Service, since she couldn't fly at home.[21]

In Germany, there was a strong resistance to women maintaining aircraft until severe labour shortages eroded this position in 1945. A few German women found the Third Reich supported their flying ambitions. These included the exceptional Luftwaffe test pilot Hanna Reitsch, who was the first female helicopter pilot. Dedicated to a Nazi victory she outlined a plan for human kamikaze V1 rocket missions, stating 'We loved our country and knew that this was the only way left to us to save it.'[22] Reitsch was one of Hitler's personal pilots, even visiting him in the Berlin bunker shortly before his suicide, but she told other young women to follow more feminine roles. Also in Germany, Lisel Bach maintained her own aircraft and designed her own aviatrix outfit, stitched with her initials for PR purposes. Her achievements were exploited for Nazi propaganda objectives, and she was permitted to fly in a ferry squadron, one of only a few. Countess Melitta von Stauffenberg was a highly decorated military test pilot and engineer, specialising in dive bomber test flights. Being the granddaughter of a Jew put her life at risk, but her aeronautic research gave her powerful contacts in the Nazi high command. She secretly supported her brother-in-law Claus' assassination attempt on Hitler in 1944.[23]

The nation which embraced the potential of female aviators the most was undoubtedly the Soviet Union. Communism in its ideal form had no gender distinctions. Reality was more complex – a society still built with a patriarchal framework that gave women dual roles as workers and mothers, without extra support. From 1943, there was new segregation in primary schools with girls learning domestic duties and boys taking military classes. Set in this context, the achievements of Russian female aircrews are even more laudable.

The first woman in aerial combat wasn't a Russian, however. This honour goes to Sabiha Gökçen, head of Türkkusu Flying School in Turkey, and first military female pilot in the world. However, the Russians pioneered all-female regiments as well as mixed-combat regiments during the war. It may have been a temporary expansion of gender roles, but Soviet women fighter and bomber crews were chosen for their abilities, not because there was a shortage of male pilots, or to fulfil empty propaganda roles.

Soviet airwomen fought on the front lines and beyond their country borders: they defended their nation and took the fight to the enemy. They were in Berlin in 1945, scrawling victorious graffiti on the walls of the ruined Reichstag building. Russian women were pilots, navigators, armourers, mechanics and commanding officers.

The 46th Guards Night Bomber Aviation Regiment was entirely female. They clocked up to fourteen missions a night during the long winter darkness, in secret competition with men flying the same Po2 aircraft. The bomber planes were so basic they earned the nicknames 'flying coffins' or 'flying broomsticks'. The Germans were said to call the bombers *Nachthexen* or Night Witches, and the name stuck. The bombers adopted Russian witch Baba Yaga as their mascot. Thick furs were essential in winter in open cockpits. Aircrews and mechanics layered up against the cold with calico shirts for underwear, footwraps and overcoats. The planes got so cold armourers' fingers froze to them as they attempted to load fresh bombs. Each young woman lifted 3 tons of bombs each on nights of maximum activity. One mechanic of armament was sent pink silk ladies gloves to protect her hands from cold metal.[24]

One legendary officer of the Night Witches was Marina Raskova who sent her crews into battle with the words, 'Stand in the ranks of the warriors for freedom!' She watched new recruits transition from a civilian mentality into being combat veterans. Part of this conditioning involved clothes and appearance. Raskova ordered hair braids cut off and all female clothes to be sent back home. One captain said they were sorry to be parted from dresses and high-heeled shoes. Fashion, femininity, even emotions were to be set aside. 'Clench your hearts like fists,' Raskova told her regiment when there were losses.[25]

In spite of – or perhaps because of – lower gender expectations, these female aircrews pushed to over achieve, to prove they had the skills, bravery, endurance and ferocity expected of the men. The numbers of missions flown are staggering – many tens of thousands. Patriotism was another fundamental motivator. Recruits were interviewed and selected at the Zhukovskii Air Force Engineering Academy, and there were crowds of applicants who would be expected to cram three years' flying training into six months, as well as tailoring their new blue uniforms. Inevitably there were supply issues. The Red Army was not prepared for women and not particularly interested in their needs: in the first few years of the war, women were issued male kit, including male boots, even if this meant they were too big to walk in, or that recruits did parachute jumps barefoot because their too-big boots would fall off. Women adapted as best they could. One had replacement boots made from an old tarpaulin.

The desire to outperform men went alongside attempts to look feminine in a masculine world. One girl who'd been a hairdresser before the war used a metal gun-cleaning rod heated in the oven to curl her hair.

This section of doped and painted linen was salvaged from a Russian Po2 open cockpit biplane, as flown by women of a Russian Bomber Aviation regiment.

'We were young girls and wanted to look womanlike. All of us liked to knit and do embroidery, except for one girl called Belova. We joked that if she started sewing the war would soon be over – and that's exactly what happened.'

Sgt Mariya Kaloshina, mechanic of armament. (Alexievich, *The Unwomanly Face of War*)

Four members of the famous 'Night Witches' bomber regiment, two in padded flying suits with fur-lined caps.

Fighter crews also balanced their military prowess with a determination not to set aside the boost that feminine identity could give. Lilya Litviak was a superb fighter pilot. With feminine bravura in the face of immense danger, she flew wearing a scarf sewn from painted segments of parachute silk stitched together to cover her hydrogen peroxide bleached hair, and her airplane wings were strewn with flowers before she took off. These touches were part of her signature style although she was no mere poster girl. She stated clearly that she was completely absorbed in combat life: 'I can't seem to think of anything but the fighting.' Nicknamed the 'Rose of Stalingrad' due to her combat successes over this beleaguered city, she became the first woman in history to shoot down an enemy aircraft. Litviak was killed in action in August 1943, aged only 22. At her death she was credited with a total of fifteen kills.[26]

At the end of the war, even the highly decorated Russian women were ejected from flying roles, thanks to new policies of promoting the role of motherhood and repopulation. Patriotic stories focused on male roles in combat; 'normal' roles were to be re-established.

Sometimes only a few clues remain of a woman's wartime role. In 2000, one family sorting through the belongings of their recently deceased Aunt Gladys were surprised to discover a special tablecloth among her belongings. It was embroidered with autographs from Gladys' wartime years. At that time the family were unaware that Gladys had been discharged from the WAAF in 1946 due to pregnancy. The baby girl – Mary – was put up for adoption. In 2006, Mary traced her birth family and made contact. She was given the autographed tablecloth as an heirloom and is now tracing the names on it, uncovering new stories.[27]

Women and men of the air forces found the return to civilian life difficult. Lilian Bader, the black British instrument fitter, was discharged from the WAAF in 1944 following her marriage and pregnancy. She missed the camaraderie of barrack life and struggled to cope with rationing. In a drapery shop she told the assistant she was setting up home as a young mother. He said they only had army blankets. She replied they'd have to do and mentioned that she was just out of the WAAF. The assistant quietly went upstairs and came down with two lovely white blankets. She kept them for years afterwards, a reminder of kindness and respect.[28]

Chapter 9

ALL AT SEA
Maritime travels

Semper Paratus – Always Ready

Motto of the Women's Reserve of the US Coast Guard

When my grandmother Margaret died in 2007 there was a small yet stalwart Wren Guard of Honour at the funeral. They were elderly yet so very smart. I felt saddened that I hadn't ever thought to ask my grandmother more about her naval service. Now it was too late. Perhaps it's why I now gather so many stories from history, because there's a sense of people's lives slipping away unrecorded. It's easy to forget that our own families are part of history too.

Margaret Tyers, formerly Leading Wren Griffiths, was typical of her generation. She simply got on with things. No obvious dwelling on the past, no talking about achievements. I wish she had. I have gleanings – that she loved her time as a medical secretary in the Women's Royal Navy; that she met her husband Charlie while both of them were serving in Scotland; that she was proud of her service and pleased when another family member excelled during her time with the modern navy.

In many ways we don't associate women with the sea, despite their ties to coastal work, to pleasure sailing, maritime exploration and even occasional piracy. In the West there was a superstition that women on board ships brought bad luck. Women were excluded from most ships' piloting crews and naval services. They certainly saw service during the Great War

WRN Margaret Griffiths in a typical wartime studio shot.

Above left: *Leading Wren Griffiths (back right) with colleagues, in smart double-breasted uniform jackets, shirt and tie, skirts and dark stockings – a fusion of male and female clothing to create a professional naval appearance. Their caps simply state HMS. For reasons of secrecy no ships are named.*

Above right: *In 1939, Mildred Turner posed for a photograph that would become a well-known post-war British Railways poster advertising holidays on the Isle of Man. For many people, 'sea' meant seaside, not serious work. The war would expand that view.*

and they were keen civilian sailors. By the 1940s, women were at sea as passengers and civilian crew members. Women's war work was also enmeshed with naval endeavours – cutting lumber for D-Day landing craft, giving up little ships for Dunkirk, plotting shipping, and sending coastguards a radar fix on downed aircraft.

Sea voyages were a staple of world travel in the mid-twentieth century. Taking a North Sea ferry from Hull to Bruges for a spot of wartime research in 2018 I was struck by the difference between my night-time crossing and the potential experiences of those going to sea during war. In a cabin listening to engine noise, or outside looking over the grey sea, there would be the ever-present worry about lurking submarines or aerial bombardment. No ocean was safe. Sea-faring women of the Torres Straits north of Australia got a shock when a submarine surfaced near their rowing boat. Local Straits' women had such excellent boat-handling skills and such familiarity with reefs and currents they were recruited for civilian pilot service. Because they weren't white or male they were not then invited to join the navy.

For many women worldwide the sea was home. This boat-woman in Shanghai works preparing shellfish. The boat is shelter, workshop, storeroom, laundry and crèche.

Overseas postings meant ocean voyages for service personnel in all branches of the military. Winifred Phillips travelled to Malta then Port Said with the ATS. Once on ship she was handed a blanket and told that should she die at sea she'd be sewn into it and tossed overboard. It was known as the 'death blanket'. The news made her feel excited rather than terrified. She was young. She hadn't been in a shipwreck, and luckily wouldn't experience a maritime catastrophe.[1]

The danger was real enough. Ships usually travelled in convoys, but they were still immensely vulnerable to attack by sea or air. Passengers being evacuated from Europe and Britain to North America often travelled with children. Englishwoman Nora Brown and her newborn daughter Judith spent two weeks zigzagging the Atlantic in a Cunard cruise liner that had been converted to a troop ship. A German U-boat was sighted. Nora strapped her 5-week-old baby into a lifebelt, waiting for the signal to throw Judith into the water, as was the drill. Luckily, the signal was never given and the crisis passed. On arrival in New York, other ships blasted their horns as welcome.

Mary Kimoto Tomita boarded the SS *Tatsuta Maru* to return home to America after a visit to Japan. On 8 December 1941, passengers heard the news that Japan had bombed Pearl Harbor – unbelievable news at the time – and had subsequently

129

Maritime themes were popular with civilian clothes, from sailor collars on frocks, to anchors on bathing suits. This is a wartime crochet pattern for a jaunty cap and mittens.

declared war on the United States. Life preservers were dusted off. Everyone slept with shoes and clothes on, expecting to be torpedoed at any moment.[2]

Refugees often endured terrifying conditions to escape to safety. When Norway was occupied by the German army, supported by a rogue Norwegian government, whole families joined 'escaping clubs'. At a given time they would travel in secrecy to a rendezvous, usually in polar darkness to avoid being seen. Boats and ships were waiting to take them to safer shores. Immensely courageous fishermen and naval men ran what became known as the 'Shetland Bus' route between the Norwegian coast and the Shetland Isles. Congestion on the ships was terrible, with people crowded below decks, damp and dark, often in heavy seas. The 'seamen' working the Shetland Bus route were haunted by tragedies, such as the sinking of a ship called the *Blia*, with the loss of all on board. Voyages were so tough, one seaman concluded that the true nature of war was 'innumerable personal tragedies, of grief, waste and sacrifice.' A surviving photograph of Norwegian refugees coming ashore at Scalloway shows women loaded with hand luggage, looking tired and stunned. They are dressed in heavy coats, thick wool stockings, fur collars, woolly sweaters and head scarves – wearing and carrying what they could to start a new life away from home among strangers.[3]

On a smaller scale was the daring voyage of a small group of Dutch people escaping from Amsterdam in an open fishing boat. Among them was 13-year-old Josephine Klein. None of the people in the boat had sailing skills. They hoped to be picked up by British ships searching for Dutch refugees. Unfortunately the sea was rough and they drifted towards enemy-occupied coast. As days passed without rescue they began to starve. The only way to get drinking water was through dropping a sewing thimble attached to a thread into the small hole of a water tank. They were eventually found drifting in the English Channel, barely conscious.[4]

German families were among the many thousands of civilians who died when the transport ship *Wilhelm Gustloff* was sunk near the port of Danzig in January 1945. It was evacuating refugees from across Europe threatened by the advancing Russian army. Back in the 1930s German workers would have worn their holiday clothes to enjoy cruises on the very same ship, in Nazi 'Strength through Joy' voyages around the Mediterranean. Life jackets were issued for the 1945 evacuation of the *Wilhelm Gustloff*. It was so hot and overcrowded on board some passengers wouldn't wear them. Stowaways didn't have the option. No matter how many layers of clothing they wore, the water was so cold those who didn't drown froze to death. Among the dead were 300 female German naval auxiliaries, billeted below decks in a drained swimming pool, where they could once have worn swimming suits not lifebelts. [5]

Naval auxiliaries, as with the army and air force, played a vital role supporting the service. New recruits to the navy may well have had some childhood experience of boats. Undeterred by the 'men only' attitude of the peacetime navy, girls were able to train as Sea Rangers in Britain. They proved their worth helping the River Emergency Service on the Thames. These were pleasure craft converted to ambulance ships to rescue casualties from vessels that had been bombed while anchored.[6] Adults owning boats along the southern stretches of English coastline volunteered their vessels – or had them commandeered – when Allied troops needed urgent

Sister Vivian Bullwinkle of the Royal Australian Nursing Corps was among a group of nurses and civilians evacuating Singapore as Japanese forces advanced. Their ship, the Vyner Brooke, *was sunk by Japanese aircraft. Survivors making landfall on Banka Island were then gunned down on the beach. Bullwinkle escaped the massacre but was captured and interned for three and a half years.*

evacuation from the beaches of northern France in 1940. However, even experienced female sailors – including powerboat racer Joe Carstairs (Marion Barbara 'Joe' Carstairs) – were turned down when they offered their services as crew. Vera Brittain recorded one girl cursing, 'Blast my sex!' when she was told men alone were eligible to go to Dunkirk in the rescue ships. Who knows if she made her way there incognito?[7]

The first women drafted into the British navy in 1938 were there for domestic and administrative duties. At first it was assumed they wouldn't need a uniform. This attitude changed when it became clear that women would be insiders, not just wives and volunteers giving a helping hand. The Women's Royal Naval Service motto from the Great War was 'Never At Sea'. At first it seemed this would ring true in the Second World War too, if they weren't allowed to serve at sea[8]. Their uniforms were updated versions of the super smart Great War outfits. One significant distinction between male and female members: men had gold braid insignia; women only had blue. There was a typical shortage of the blue serge uniform as the WRNS – or Wrens – expanded to release more men for service on board ships. Some worked with just a WRNS brassard until uniforms could be sourced.[9] Over in Canada, new recruits to the Women's Royal Canadian Naval Service stationed in Nova Scotia waded through heavy mud at their base, wearing black stockings and shoes, while men wore big rubber boots. Their thoughts on only receiving four-fifths of the pay of men are not recorded.[10]

Women manage naval clothing stores for the United States Marine Corps. The Marine Corps had women's reserves from 1943, supporting air squadrons. The WAVES – Women Accepted for Volunteer Emergency Service – was popular with recruits. By 1944, there were 63,000 Waves in service with the US Navy.[12]

Roxane Houston was warned off joining the WRNS because of the clumping shoes and thick black stockings. Undeterred she signed up for the service in summer 1940. The factory making Wren uniforms had just been bombed, so new recruits had to drill in summer dresses. Houston noticed that recruits from poorer families hardly had a single change of clothing. Sympathetic Wrens in the naval stores managed to wangle underwear and nightwear for the most needy. One such impoverished girl was 18-year-old Ada. Her new companions gave her a complete makeover, donating scented soap, toothbrush and paste, hair brush and a haircut. It was a confidence-boosting transformation. Of course, the women all felt self-conscious marching in civilian sandals and frocks, so they were excited when uniforms were issued that October. Suddenly distinctions in wealth and background were erased. Houston said they all gained 'a sense of belonging to a great and powerful institution, a Royal service in which they too could play a part, however insignificant.'[11]

In Britain, Queen Elizabeth approved the style of Wren hats, and King George approved the skirts with their slight bell-bottomed effect. New recruits didn't necessarily approve of either, calling the rating's hat a 'wilting, gabardine monstrosity' and 'an offence to womanhood'.[13] English Wren Patricia Mordue and her friend thought the uniforms were very badly fitting, so they set to work altering the skirt and jacket, and were subsequently told off for tampering with government property.[14] One of the most awkward deficiencies of the new uniform was a lack of big pockets and a ban on handbags. Male sailors had 'ditty boxes' for personal effects. Women stuffed needful items into their gas masks. Only after a frank appeal from the Wren hierarchy – presumably mentioning such items as sanitary towels – were compact navy blue shoulder bags issued.

'At first the Royal Navy was a little suspicious, perhaps a little jealous at the prospect of handing over to women jobs which men had done for years. But now there is complete harmony, and an admiration that is in no way grudging.'

HMSO *Life in the Wrens* leaflet.

Images of naval women in the war show them undertaking an impressive range of duties, with a varied range of clothes – dispatch riders are in duffle coats and peaked caps; mechanics in overalls with leather gloves; welders with face guards and dungarees. Photographer Lee Miller was commissioned to record the service of British Wrens. Her pictures tell the stories. Qualified ordnance workers stripped, cleaned, greased and reassembled guns for torpedomen; repair workers welded and repaired D-Day landing craft returning to the beaches; blacksmiths cast gears in a furnace at a submarine repair depot; supply assistants doled out kit judging size and shape by eye.[15] Naval women were crucial for communication networks, meteorology,

Above left: *Active duties required clothes fit for purpose. Wrens could be issued with the square-necked white sailor top and distinctive bell-bottomed trousers. This is 'Taffy', posing in a studio – her full name and background sadly unknown. The inscription on the back reads, 'The fleet's in port again! Lots of Love Taffski' December 1945.*

Above right: *Margaret Curry shows off her Wren uniform in the back garden, July 1944. Aged 18, having already endured the 1942 bomb raids on her home town of York, she joined the Fleet Air Arm as an air mechanic, working on Seafires, Hurricanes and Corsairs. On civvy street she was a costume curator at York's Castle Museum, a job she took up again post-war.*

computing and ciphering. However, the only women in the wartime British services to be paid the same rates as men were navy doctors.[16]

The question of whether Wrens could serve on ships was raised fairly regularly. It was accepted that they were already 'freeing men for the fleet'. Could they join them *in* the fleet? They did serve on converted passenger liners – the new troop transport ships – but they had to have guarded sleeping areas. Fears over sexual assaults meant the women were to be segregated, even though it was male behaviour that was potentially at fault.[17] Wrens did make up boat crews in coastal waters from 1941, in tugboats and harbour launches. They wore the distinctive 'white front' male vests, bell bottoms and plimsolls. They were also issued heavy woollen stockings, blue woolly drawers – and a seaman's knife.

Annice Sharp joined the WRNS in 1943 from the fashion department of Mansfield Cooperative Society. She swapped civilian jersey frocks for the naval uniform and an up-do. A government recruitment leaflet speculated that there might be a peacetime role for women in the navy, but that 'others look forward to the day when they can return to their chosen vocation.'

Wrens provided boat crews to collect stores or laundry or 'liberty men' – sailors going on leave. One boat crew found they were transporting four blindfolded captured German generals, complete with suitcases – this was a strange cargo.[18] Some Wrens took ships across the English Channel on D-Day and towed damaged vessels back to the shore, where Wren mechanics would fix them.[19] Boat crews found the work exhilarating. It bought a sense of freedom. Rozelle Raynes joined the navy in August 1943. She became a tug-boat stoker in the Portsmouth Command. She said it was 'the ultimate peak of happiness in all my 18 years'. She was devastated to be demobbed and would not give up going to sea, exploring European coasts and the Baltic, mostly sailing single-handed.[20]

There were 100,000 British wartime Wrens, and many more naval women worldwide. On VE Day, the British Admiralty announced their high appreciation of the Women's Royal Naval Service. Only a few women were kept on the payroll. The rest joined other demobbed service personnel finding their feet on civvy street. It would be many decades before navies around the world integrated women as full seafaring members, serving with honour on battleships and submarines.

'The Wren Torpedoman after the war, still has the valuable ability to repair electrical appliances; the Ship Mechanic will know how to weld patches and fittings to her prefab post-war house. Cooks, stewards and housekeepers will have well-run homes.'

Miller, *Wrens In Camera.*

Found among my grandmother's belongings after her death – her uniform buttons and identity tag. We also discovered a naval sewing kit complete with needle and threads, and a navy blue wool life belt. Small yet significant mementoes of service.

Chapter 10

BEHIND CLOSED DOORS
Underwear

'Our big joy was getting hold of a parachute – beautiful silk and
beautiful undies!'

WAAF nurse Mary Firth

Items of underwear hold stories of our most private moments. Their intimacy contrasts
with visible fashions and the bold display of military uniforms. As the final layer when
undressing, underwear can also represent vulnerability, or tell tales of sexuality.

While it may seem frivolous to write of lingerie or nightgowns in a book about war,
even these ordinary garments can be pick-me-ups during daily drudgery, or a powerful
contrast to war's trauma. For example, Helen Ernst, a French political prisoner held at
Ravensbrück concentration camp for four years secretly crocheted underwear using
threads stolen from the camp supply room. These clandestine clothes were more for
dignity than hygiene, and they helped keep her sane in a disorderly world.[1]

So what were the key undergarments of the 1940s, and how did women 'gird their
loins' in wartime?

In 1941, Monica Baldwin left the closed-order convent she had first joined as
a teenager during the Great War. She found a new war raging, and a whole new
world of clothing. Gone were her familiar neck-high combinations and the ankle-
length petticoats; gone were severely boned stays. Instead she was faced with 1940s
underwear, including a modern bra: 'Its purpose was to emphasise contours, which, in
my girlhood, were always decorously concealed,' she mused.[2]

As Monica Baldwin wiggled into her first girdle, it was clear there had been big
changes in foundation garments during her twenty-eight years of seclusion. Not only
had the fashionable silhouette changed entirely, the underlying structures shaping the
body had altered almost beyond recognition. New ideas of streamlining, simplification
and even seduction shaped a Western woman's underwear choices. Science had impact
too: by the 1940s new technologies popularised artificial silks and rubberised elastic.
DuPont's nylon fabrics were slowly making their way into the civilian market. These
modern fabrics were far less trouble than old cotton styles. A mother visiting young
army recruits in an American dorm was shocked to see they did not iron their undies.
She was told 'No one in our dorm spent valuable time ironing rayon panties and silk
slips. We just tolerated the wrinkles.'[3]

Directoire knickers with elastic above the knees and camiknickers, on sale in the UK, 1942. Lighter, looser 'French' knickers were far more appealing to the wearer and potential admirers.

Although reduced in number from the Edwardian age, there were still many different undergarments to contend with in the 1940s, as discovered by hapless CID officers investigating deaths in wartime London. Morgue secretary Molly Lefebure described detectives undressing female victims of crime in the mortuary, noting the clothes as they are removed: stockings, slip, panties vest, bra. 'These caused no trouble,' she noted. She calmly identified the scrap of fabric with ribbon straps for the men – a camisole. A puzzling new item was dangled. Lefebure confirmed it was a boned, strapless brassiere that had slipped down to 'a very funny place'. One staple of the 1940s wardrobe was recognised at once: 'Camiknicks!' CID officers chorused. Camiknickers were a nifty combination of knickers and camisole with dainty buttons to unfasten between the legs.[4]

'21 November 1945 – A parcel and two letters from M. The parcel contained some ghastly undies, mainly camiknickers and slips. The material is parachute silk – extremely nice but the garments were obviously produced with a buxom Fräulein in mind. It is almost impossible to obtain underclothes at present other than khaki knickers with elastic in the legs!'

Mary Morris receives a gift from her fiancé posted in Germany. (Morris, *A Very Private Diary*)

Lingerie adverts of the era show the glamorous, aspirational element of underwear. In reality, most was chosen for practical purposes, as an easily-washable buffer between the body and rougher outer layers. As already seen above, police reports on clothing at time of death are a stark record of what women actually wore. When a young woman named Dagmar was murdered by a lorry driver in England, 1946, it was found that her underwear was all from the local market, or home-made. She had a pink woolly vest, light green woolly knickers, home-crocheted combinations and a silk slip with a frilled hem. Nothing matched. Nothing was glamorous. Her assault has added poignancy when it's noted that she also wore a flannel belt for her towelling menstruation pad.[5]

Wartime shortages meant higher prices for shop-bought underwear and an even greater need for sturdy home-sewn items. Pattern books and leaflets included designs for full knitted underwear sets, including a knitted bra which looks too flimsy to be fit for purpose. One English dressmaking manual lamented, 'Gone are the days when any of us have either the money or the space to possess six of everything in our undies drawer. But you should try to have three of everything, one set on your back, one in the wash, and one clean and ready for any emergency that may crop up.'[6] Key staples were knickers, corsets or girdles, bras and stockings.

When German forces invaded the British Channel Isles, surrender was marked in one home by the waving of an old pair of knickers on a broomstick stuck out of a window. The voluminous style of pants known as *Directoire* would have been fit

Women's magazines offered patterns for embroidery motifs to embellish home-made underwear.

for this dramatic purpose. They were held with elastic at waist and knee, giving rise to the nickname *Harvest Festivals* – because 'all is safely gathered in'. A catalogue of fashions for spring 1944 advertised *Directoires* with 'extra-large gussets'. Sports versions had the intriguingly titled 'athletic gussets', suggesting extra sturdy protection. *Directoires* might be worn over flimsier knickers for a double layer of warmth and decency. They were invariably the styles issued to servicewomen. British WAAFs had dark blue knickers for winter and lighter blue for summer, also known as 'Blackouts' and 'Twilights'. Kit, including knickers, could be replaced at Clothing Exchange Parades. Airwomen recall being embarrassed by RAF personnel examining their returned knickers and enquiring loudly, 'Is this fair wear and tear?' WAAF Joan Bell used to take her loathed RAF issue knickers and vests home to her mother, who'd use them herself, swapping them for silk ones, which Joan far preferred. When the kit-issue ones were worn out, her mother gave them back to Joan to have them replaced.[7]

It's interesting to note that the British 1943 *Elastic (Control of Use) Order* (1943, No. 90) prohibited the use of elastic in all garments *except* women's corsets and knickers. Clearly underwear had to be taken seriously, despite the shortages of rubber for elastic caused by the fall of Malaya to Japanese troops, and the difficulties of shipping rubber from South America. Women's figures (and by extension, their virtue)

140

Above: *Camiknickers were a more alluring alternative to knickers and camisole, or knickers and vest. Cut on the bias, they were usually in slinky fabrics and pretty colours. These were a honeymoon gift to a bride marrying a sailor – note the anchor motif.*

Below: *A sensible CC41 'Utility' boned cotton corset with laces, worn by a housewife named Janet, who'd grown up knowing the long-line constriction of Edwardian stays. Peach and tea rose pink were popular colours for foundation garments. White showed the dirt and looked a little too clinical for 1940s' tastes.*

Woollen combinations were a warm base layer for outdoor work and during fuel shortages.

A trained fitter from firms such as Spirella or Twilfit could visit the home or measure a client instore, for the perfect shape and size of corset. Panels flattened the stomach and smoothed the hips. Suspenders help keep up stockings.

had to be well-controlled. Roll-on girdles were best suited to an average figure; larger women found structure and support from boned corsets. Going without a corset or girdle was not common for western women. It simply wasn't respectable, even for young women.

One of the government's splendid Make Do and Mend booklets rallied women to the cause of making their wartime corset last that little bit longer, declaring 'Now that rubber is so scarce your corset is one of your most precious possessions'. Corsets and girdles were worn over a vest or camisole, to protect them from grease and perspiration. They could be gently washed in light soap flakes only and there were to be absolutely no lazy quick-fixes with safety pins. Professional renovation services were available for worn-out corsets, at a fee of 12*s* 6*d*.

'We feel that what this country needs is a compulsorily good brassiere. The British busts that are bolsters when they ought to be impertinent twins is only outdone, in our opinions, by the posteriors that should be put into strait jackets.'

Nice Girls Don't Chase Men article by Maureen Wibberley
Woman's Fair March 1940.

Going bra-less may have been a statement of protest for some protestors in the 1960s and '70s but in the 1940s untethered bosoms were considered uncomfortable and indecent. This was such a strong mindset that even the toughest wartime scenarios could not break it. Chaja, a Polish partisan fighting and hiding in the forest in 1943, remembers a Jewish grandmother escaping from the Lida ghetto with a 2-year-old child. The older woman found subsistence in the wild too difficult, saying she couldn't live without a bra. Chaja's husband screamed at her, 'How can you think a brassiere at this time!' The grandmother and child returned to the ghetto. Both were murdered during the Holocaust.[8]

Bras also came in handy for carrying valuables as well as smuggling information and materials for sabotage.

The classic 1940s bust shape was definitely 'divide and conquer', as seen in this Mexican bra advert. Spiral or 'whirlpool' stitch bras gave pointed form.

143

A sturdy 'deep' brassiere manufactured by the company Avro, who also made bomber engines for planes such as the Lancaster.

A young apprentice milliner in Prague named Anka remembers Germans coming to ransack and rob her family apartment, after a tip-off from the neighbours that they were Jews. Luckily Anka's mother had an ample bosom: 'she quietly stuffed the family cash into her brassiere when the Germans' backs were turned.'[9]

If bras were in short supply, women were ingenious in fashioning them from any fabric remnants available, using an old bra as a pattern. An advert in *Vogue*, July 1941, recommended the best parts of worn out net curtains for this purpose. The trend for perky breasts (sometimes known as 'teenage torpedoes') led to ads for 'brassieres to make your torso, more so'. Flat-chested girls were offered remedial tips: 'Camouflage can be successfully carried to the lengths of sewing ruched baby ribbon inside your bra.' Where available, cotton wool made good bra padding also.[10]

Fabric restrictions led to shorter hems, which meant stockings – and their snags – were more visible. This posed problems for wartime women living in countries where bare legs were permissible only at the beach or in the privacy of the home. Keeping up standards meant old stockings were darned, professionally or at home.

Silk stockings were rare commodities, to be saved for special occasions. The silk dyes had evocative names, such as mist-beige, rose, midnight, or bronze skin. While unsuitable for most war work, they conjured up an elusive lost world of glamour and indulgence. More usual were strong cotton lisle stockings in shades reminiscent of wet concrete or boiled shrimp. Stockings were to be washed each evening in lukewarm water and dried overnight. Spare pairs were to be kept folded in a cellophane or cloth bag to avoid runs or wrinkles. Shoppers were advised not to begrudge spending an extra sixpence or so for good quality. When they absolutely couldn't be mended any longer, old stockings could be cut into strips and used for crocheting bath mats and table mats: *waste not, want not.*

The need to wear stockings was an added burden for servicewomen in skirts. Even the heavy-duty kit-issue stockings (in ghastly military shades) were soon worn through. One ATS member remembered a shop where, 'if you came on leave and

A wartime darning kit for cotton lisle hosiery. With shops low on stocks and consumers hoarding precious coupons, stocking mending was more important than ever before.

produced your paybook and what not, they would often let you have a pair of khaki silk stockings if they'd got them.'[11]

One of the women interviewed for this book – a young office worker during the war – confessed that in later life she never adopted 'new-fangled' tights, even when old age and infirmity made fiddling with stockings a daily nightmare. In old age she lived in an ancient farmhouse surrounded by derelict, moss hung sheds, like a character from a fairy tale. Her face brightened when she remembered one of the other wartime office girls coming to work in nylons – a gift from a brother in the navy. 'We were *gobsmacked*,' she said.[12] This fine Yorkshire word sums up the response of women to the wonder fabric of nylon. Nylon stockings had been a sensation at the 1939 New York World Fair, where DuPont exhibited nylon goods. They went on sale nationwide in the US in May 1940. On the first day of sales, over three-quarters-of-a-million pairs were sold.[13] As soon as the US officially entered the war, nylons were harder to obtain, unless you had connections with military men, or money to spend on the black market.

After several years of war, some women simply had to give up on the luxury of stockings altogether, wearing slacks with socks or going bare-legged for as long as feasible, until cold weather demanded warm woolly stockings. The illusion of hosiery could be created with commercial skin dye products, or home-sourced alternatives. Parisian women favoured iodine staining; British women experimented with dark sand, used tea leaves and even gravy browning, although one woman confided, 'I think I attracted more flies than men…'. Audrey Pratt, in the Women's Auxiliary Air Force used Oxo for stockings: 'it smelt a bit at first but you got used to it.'[14] The arrival of US servicemen in Britain from 1942 at least meant the possibility of nylons. Silk stockings were a popular gift from service personnel serving in the Far East.

Six years of war took its toll on everyone's underwear. Cold water dyes could refresh a drab colour; tea or coffee were also recommended as tints for tired items. There were also unexpected threats to underwear being laundered. In one incident, sailors in Scotland broke into a naval billet and stole Wren undies from the laundry room, leaving them strewn about lamp posts in town.[15] Miles away in Egypt, ATS officer Winifred Phillips was horrified to find that the local cleaners were responsible for many missing 'smalls'. When confronted, the men took off their djellabas to reveal bras, pants and slips wrapped round their midriffs. 'A most amusing sight,' she commented – presumably with gritted teeth.[16]

In general, anything to do with underwear was a discreet affair, with clothes made, washed and dried in private. Magazines and movies may have touted images of underwear flaunting sex-appeal; most women preferred to keep it under wraps, unless revealed by choice. They didn't always have that choice. Underwear was a symbolic barrier at best, and it's the little clothing details that make accounts of sexual violence truly sobering reading. A woman in a Berlin bomb shelter towards the end of the war whispered that she'd fastened her wedding ring to her pants, joking that if Russian rapists got that far 'the ring won't matter much anyway'. A few floors above, another Berliner endured the latest rape by a marauding soldier. She later recorded in her diary, 'No sound. Only an involuntary grinding of teeth when my underclothes are ripped apart. The last untorn ones I had.'[17]

Nightwear could hold similar stories of privacy invaded. A Swiss girl named Hélène was only 13 when, in 1942, one of the Swiss soldiers billeted with her family raped her in her bedroom. The next morning Hélène crept to the bathroom to wash her nightgown – a stained symbol of her pain and humiliation. The trauma never left her.[18]

Sometimes nightgowns literally have their stories embroidered onto them. Falstad concentration camp in Norway now has in their collection a white nightgown with a blue pattern. It belonged to a former prisoner named Margrethe Venæs. She had been arrested as a hostage when the Gestapo failed to capture her husband Trygve, who was in the Norwegian resistance. Margrethe embroidered a dark blue heart on the front of the nightgown, with the names of her husband and children in neat, white stitches.

Above left: *A pink crepe nightgown with lace insets, swansdown slippers and home-made dressing jacket with marabou trim.*

Above right: *This beautiful silk nightgown with floral embroidered waist and hem was part of a home-made 1945 trousseau set.*

A rayon lock-knit nightgown advert from 1939. During the war years boudoir glamour was a far-off fantasy for most women.

Her prisoner number – 14642 – was sewn on the left, and the date of her imprisonment on the right. The story continued on the back of the nightgown, where Margrethe was able to record her survival and release back to her family in more white stitches: 'Heim 25-4-45'.[19]

Journalist Lee Miller, writing for *Vogue* magazine in April 1945, wrote that Moroccan soldiers found plundered white nightwear invaluable as winter camouflage, wearing them 'with the style of Roman Senators'.[20] Out in the Russian Gulag, peasant women were shocked to note that some Polish prisoners working in Siberian labour camps had special garments for sleeping in, assuming these must represent outrageous riches and filthy bourgeois luxury.[21] Western women had no problems coveting such so-called luxuries, if they had the sewing skills to make them or the money to buy them, and assuming shops still stocked them.

Above left: *Pyjamas were a staple in the wartime wardrobe. They could be adapted from pilfered men's pjs, or made up from cotton flannel, pretty crepe or slinky satins. US 'Kayser' brand pyjamas of 1939 came in attractive 'sweet dream' colours such as Rose Petal, Mystic Blue, Aqua and* Coral.

Above right: *Warmth was a prime consideration for nightwear in bitterly cold winters without adequate fuel. Here, snug designs from* Elle *magazine, January 1941. One high fashion pyjama set was titled Au Coin De Feu – by the fireside.*

Quilted or knitted bed-jackets were ideal for invalids, or for an idle breakfast-in-bed sort of morning.

This gaudy rayon housecoat features the innovation of a full-length zip fastener. Housecoats were strictly for informal wear at home – one step more public than bedroom dressing gowns.

150

Women on duty craved a bit of glamour, even in freezing billets. A WAAF named Tina knotted her pyjama top under her vest declaring it was the only way to make the striped flannel glamorous. Wrinkled pyjamas soon became an outward sign that a WAAF was having sex with someone.[22] Beryl Escott, a WAAF billeted in the North of England, dressed for bed 'as though going on an Arctic expedition'. She described the Nissen hut billets as 'shaped like igloos and just as cold'. Her companions also readied for bed in striped pjs and tin hats (in case of air raids), and with cocoa mugs, hot water bottles and cigarettes.[23]

Since nightwear wasn't considered a priority use of coupons in ration-controlled economies, women had to be ingenious, as ever, in creating their own garments. Dressing gowns could be made from worn candlewick bedspreads or blankets. Slippers, completing the bedtime ensemble, were knitted from oddments and

A wartime pattern for slippers made from fabric scraps.

crocheted from old stockings. Moccasins lined with rabbit fur could be made at home, or there were more adventurous ways to source slipper material: one ATS member confessed 'When I was in the Forces we used to make slippers from jeep cushions, I don't know where they'd come from, nobody enquired.'[24]

Underwear and nightwear may be something which modern women take for granted, but they are soon missed if not available. Even such simple, intimate garments take on a world of meaning to someone with next to nothing, as shown by the story of Leokadia Majewicz, a young Polish refugee being transported to safety on a hospital ship. Desperately ill, she was donated clothes by the on-board doctor. The doctor clearly had good taste as well as an immensely generous spirit. Leokadia was overwhelmed to receive 'two pairs of such beautiful silky satin pyjamas, that I felt like a princess. One pair was of a pastel pink colour, while the other a pale green. I just couldn't believe that someone, a stranger, could be so kind to me. I felt like Cinderella going from rags to riches.'[25]

Chapter 11

UNDER COVER
Spies, codes and computing

'Yes, there will be danger. I've been told what to expect,
I'll do my best to stay alive.'[1]

Diana Rowden, SOE saboteur codename *Paulette*, letter to her mother.

There's no secret to Bletchley Park these days. The one-time code-breaking hub in an inoffensive area of the English Midlands is now a well-advertised heritage site attracting worldwide visitors. The approach road has queues of modern cars and coaches, not a stream of 1940s bicycles at shift-change time. During my research visit, the rather ugly hall at the centre of the site hosted a display of costumes from the 2014 film *Imitation Game*, which focused on the efforts of mathematician Alan Turing and team to break the Enigma code. I later interviewed an elegant lady named Patricia (Tricia) Hales. Enquiring about her wartime work at Bletchley she modestly replied, 'Oh you don't want to hear about that.'[2]

For many decades after the war no one heard about the achievements at Bletchley Park. That was the point – they were top secret. From the 1970s onward people slowly began to open up about their covert duties during the war. Others died with their secrets unspoken.

Countless women worked undercover in the 1940s, at great personal risk. Military planning was pointless without reliable information. Conversely, it was vital to keep manoeuvres, capabilities and innovations secret. Misdirection, intelligence gathering, covert communications, sabotage and weapon development all benefited from women's skills. In some respects, the assumption that women followed purely domestic roles helped them escape scrutiny while working undercover, particularly in the early years of war. Other undercover operatives emphasised their femininity to manipulate potential targets. Large-scale code-breaking and computing projects – in the sense of human computing skills – needed the best brains available, even if this went contrary to accepted notions about female abilities. Two-thirds of the 10,000 staff at Bletchley were women.

'This is confidential work for intelligent women. Good eyesight is essential. You must be able to keep your head in a crisis. Pay 2/6d a day. Ages 17½– 35'

WAAF recruitment leaflet for clerk (special duties)

Casual gossip could reveal potentially useful information to enemy listeners. This 'Don't Say A Word' advert, along with others such as 'Loose Lips Sink Ships,' aimed to curb indiscreet conversations. Those who worked undercover contradicted the stereotype of gossiping women by keeping their secrets well-guarded.

153

Women's secret roles were many and varied. They were important links along established escape routes for those at risk in occupied territory. Homes, farms and businesses provided hiding places for refugees and resistance workers, as well as operating as supply stores and contact points. Those who felt helpless to alter the course of the war could at least do their bit to show their humanity. Hélène Berr, a young Jewish musician in Paris, worked with *L'Entraide Temporaire*, a clandestine organisation, to save Jewish children from deportation. Tragically, Berr was not herself saved, dying in Bergen-Belsen shortly before the end of the war.[3] Georgette Capt was a Swiss hotel concierge and keen *alpinista*. She used her knowledge of secret paths to ski

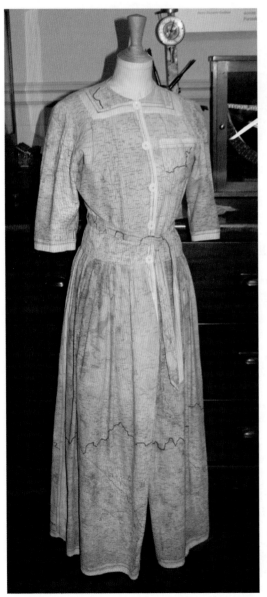

the mountain border between France and Switzerland, escorting fugitives who were not always dressed to suit the conditions. One woman attempted to hike to safety in high heels, and eventually had to be carried by Capt. Arrested by Germans on the border, Capt said even her long braids were searched for evidence. She was young enough to find the risk exhilarating, and said she spat at danger.[4]

There was no question of chivalrous treatment if caught. Prison or execution were the usual punishments for women and men, following harsh interrogation. Belgian Elsie Bell and her daughter, known as Young Elsie, were proud to help run the *Comète* Line for Allied servicemen escaping from occupied to neutral territory. Once arrested they endured lengthy imprisonment. Young Elsie noted that her interrogators removed her corset before beating her so the pain would be greater. Eventually they entered the nightmare of the concentration camp

Allied aircrews landing or crashing behind enemy lines were issued with silk maps to aid their escape to neutral or friendly countries, in the event that they couldn't link with underground networks. Silk could easily be folded and hidden. It also had the advantage of being less noisy than paper. This housecoat has been made entirely of such maps.

system, surviving Ravensbrück thanks to the acquisition of padded Russian jackets. They were wore these jackets after liberation, arriving back in Belgium penniless and homeless and smelling of the crematorium smoke. Journalists looking for a scoop taunted them as 'unfeminine' when they refused to divulge stories or have photographs taken.[5]

Hiding fugitives at home carried the additional risk of putting family – including children – at risk. Women's resistance activities often took place in the absence of men, highlighting the difficulties of managing childcare and domestic tasks while

Stories of the 1930s and '40s featured plucky girls with excellent orienteering and camping skills. The international Girl Guide organisation encouraged resourcefulness. Some acted as couriers. Polish Guide Cecylia Skryzypczak forwarded messages to Britain once a month. They were written in code on tissue paper, stored in an ironing pad filled with sawdust. 'We didn't think about the danger of knowing such valuable things,' she said. 'We just accepted that we might be killed.'[6]

defying the enemy. Norwegian resister Jan Baalsrud was shipwrecked on the coast near Toftefjord in northern Norway. Ill from exposure and hobbled by frostbite he was eventually found by two 14-year-old girls. They took him home and he was cared for by two elderly women while children of the household looked out for Germans. His hostesses found him ski boots, skis, and warm clothes so he could eventually continue his journey across the border to Sweden and safety.[7]

The pressure of avoiding scrutiny as well as managing homes, children and businesses without men must have been extraordinarily stressful for ordinary citizens, yet many were still brave enough to resist. Louise Gould was a housewife on the island of Jersey during the German occupation. She dared to shelter a Russian prisoner who'd escaped from a nearby slave labour camp. Denounced and arrested she eventually died in Ravensbrück. Irene Sendler was a Polish social worker whose network is credited with rescuing 200 Jewish children from the Warsaw ghetto and finding them hiding places, which she never revealed, even under torture.[8] Gertrude Seele was a German nurse executed in 1945 for her anti-Nazi beliefs, and for helping Jews escape persecution.[9] These are just three examples of those who are known – there are thousands more acts of bravery and resistance.

Women were particularly effective at smuggling messages and supplies on resistance networks. On a basic level, they could assist in sourcing food on the black market, if occupying troops requisitioned supplies. During the 1944 'hunger winter' in Holland,

Liesbeth Langford cycled out to farms to barter for food. The punishment for being caught was deportation to a concentration camp. An elderly Dutch lady suggested she disguise herself with different coloured hats and scarves to fool soldiers at checkpoints. Some of Langford's friends were imprisoned by the Germans. She managed to get BBC news updates to them by hiding tiny notes in the seams of pyjamas which she had collected to launder.[10]

A stylish Italian woman waits with a bag. Her name and errand are unknown. Italian resistance couriers found charm and confidence useful when under suspicion. They became adept at carrying food, small arms and dispatches in underclothes, purses and packages. One courier was stopped and asked what she was carrying. 'A bomb,' she replied with a smile. She was allowed to pass.[11]

Female Italian couriers were known as *staffette*. Their work was highly dangerous, but vital to resistance organisations. Laundry – that classic female occupation – was a common disguise for clandestine activities. Ten-year-old Laura Cristina's mother was a laundress in Italy. Laura delivered laundry, communications, weapons and hand grenades to anti-fascist resistance groups. If stopped and questioned she told them she had clothes to wash and iron, and she was allowed to pass. Other children were told by their mothers that they had to play a 'game', by never talking about the subterfuges. Seamstresses also had a useful cover for delivering bundles to various addresses. Italian resistance groups were usually headed by men and organised with women in auxiliary roles. While the men had to acknowledge the female contribution, many were uneasy in the company of emancipated women. It was simpler to assume women would have domestic roles, such as acquiring, washing and mending clothing for combat groups.[12]

Using domestic roles as cover wasn't always successful. A German laundress used her laundrette as a letterbox for resistance messages. Mail arrival was announced via coded message – 'Your washing is ready'. In 1941, the laundress was arrested after a tipoff, along with her laundry phone book, which was actually a list of her underground contacts.[13] Sadly, women were also active as informers. They were perhaps motivated by patriotism, if they supported the dominant regime. All too often informants were motivated by greed or spite. They could be bribed not to go to the police, or they could profit from plunder left by those arrested.

In Poland, the underground state was dominated by men, yet women were active in covert activities from the start and some took leading roles. One of these was Maria Witteck, head of the Polish Women's Military Service of the Home Army HQ. She had a cigarette holder and a hairbrush for hiding conspiratorial post. Courier Katarzyna Sosenko also adapted feminine accessories, including a bullet-shaped perfume phial, powder-box and lipsticks. She later stated, 'good looks and neatness – strongly recommended by the Polish underground movement – could save the women's lives.'[14]

Actress and photographer Pelagia Bednarska was a soldier in the Home Army, based in Krakow. Her photographic studio was a depot for parcels, dispatches, explosives and trainees. Bednarska also stored the letters and photos thrown from cattle trucks by prisoners being transported. She took covert photos of occupying German soldiers. The most extraordinary images she developed in her studio remain unique in Holocaust history, although her part in the process is rarely acknowledged. In 1944, she instructed Teresa Lasocka, also a member of the underground, how to use a camera with an 8mm film. The camera was then smuggled into the Auschwitz camp complex, where prisoners working special duties at the crematoria in Birkenau took secret pictures of the mass execution process, under great duress. When the film was returned only three frames could be salvaged – pictures of women being driven into the gas chamber and a pile of burning corpses.[15]

It was a network of women who supplied explosives for the October 1944 rebellion in Birkenau, when men of the special corpse commandos blew up one of

Rs. 26/8 (£2)—**WHITE**

Army Form W-5192A
(Modified for India)

H. M. FORCES OVERSEAS

DUTY FREE CONCESSION FOR GIFTS SENT TO THE UNITED KINGDOM

The following declarations must be completed and signed by the sender   of the package :—

I declare (1) that the contents of this parcel, are as shown below,

and are sent as a gift,

and (2) that, including the contents of this parcel, I have not sent more than four yards of silk material (including artificial silk) or of silk garments Duty Free parcels from the 1st January 1946 to date.

Goods	Quantity	Value
Dress Material (Silk)	3 yds	£1. 10. 0.
Head Scarf (Sil	Signature of sender... *J. Morgan*	
	Date... 6 July 46.	

This ... st not be affixed to any parcel which weigh ... 5 lb (including packing) or which

(able spirits.

... ½ lb total weight of tobacco, including ...nd cigarettes (200 cigarettes or 50 cigars = ½ lb)

... y tobacco goods marked "H. M. Ships only".

... ore than ½ pint scent.

More than 2 lb on any one foodstuff.

Any communication other than the name and address of the sender.

6. Any imported article.

Warning : If the above restrictions are not observed the full duty will be charged on the whole contents of the package.

Censorship Stamp.

Label issued to... *1456 0499 Sgt. Morgan*

Signature of issuing officer... *[signature]*

SEE INSTRUCTIONS ON REVERSE.

P.T.O.

Censorship helped control information flow. This packet containing dress silk sent from India to England, was checked by the Indian Censorship department, where Indian or European women in khaki uniforms and green berets worked. Their motto was 'We Work in Silence'. They censored telegraph, post, film, images, and even knitting patterns.

the crematoria. Auschwitz inmates labouring at a local metalworks factory were able to buy the explosives using jewels smuggled out of camp plunder warehouses by the women who worked sorting goods. Ala Gertner was one of four smugglers, hiding the gunpowder in underwear or twisted into the knots of headscarves, then returning to barracks in the centre of marching columns to avoid being searched at the camp entrance. She had a fierce spirit of resistance and independence, even daring to wear a ribbon or a hat while enslaved. Gertner and the other conspirators were publicly executed after torture.[16]

As part of official military operations, women intercepted and sent secret messages. Sensitive information was heavily coded. Those working in cyphering handled immense volumes of information, gaining a surreal close connection with distant military engagements even while sequestered underground or in blacked-out barracks. There were sad coincidences of women deciphering the news that their loved ones had died when their ships were sunk or their aircraft shot down. Wireless interception stations could be in remote areas, adding to the sense of dislocation. In India, Veronica Downing exchanged a privileged life of riding and tea-parties for code work with the Enigma machine at the RAF base near her tea plantation. She found it a very male world. In contrast, Sydney Ralli volunteered as a 'cipherette' in Delhi, in a very female world of blowsy haircuts and fashion.[17]

Bletchley Park, now perhaps the most famous code-breaking centre in the world, was both a military and a civilian establishment, so there was a mix of everyday fashions and uniforms. Little details give an impression of life and work there. Wealthy debutants wore their pearls tucked inside jumpers to preserve them; Wrens found their blouse cuffs turned black from fine spray of oil given out by the large bombe machines. One Wren confessed to drying her underwear above the super-hot Colossus machine: the world's first programmable electronic digital computer.[18]

Tricia Hales, interviewed on a quiet spring morning, confessed she joined the Wrens as an 'escape route'. Her mother 'didn't believe in education for girls' so Hales knew almost nothing about maths. Her training for work at Bletchley was

Sylvia Bailey was an intercept transcriber at Bletchley Park – messages were translated from encrypted to decrypted text in German, and then into English. Only in later life did she talk about her work, saying the machines were awkward to work with.

Even simple stitches can tell a story. This wartime Wren insignia and collection of names was embroidered as a keepsake. There are sixty-nine legible signatures in total, the majority female. Research to date has tracked down at least ten of the names to Bletchley and Eastcote. These include Betty Ranken and Joy Ward working on naval and Japanese codes; Ethel Ramsden, Jeanette Hannah, Audrey Clark, Margaret Hall and Jean Ireland, were bombe operators. Ruth Farran helped operate the cutting-edge technology of the Colossus computer.

a revelation: 'All of a sudden algebra turned up and it was like second nature. Extraordinary.' The bombe machines made complete sense to her – and she was tall, so able to reach all banks of drums and plugs with ease. However, the work had a dark side. During our conversations Hales talked of staff breakdowns: 'At least once a week they had someone go off their head because of the intensity. Just screaming, screaming and screaming and then an ambulance came and took them off.' Tricia Hales was no exception. Because she found bombe machines easy she was transferred to a new machine – presumably the Colossus – and found herself in 'dark days' of confusion. This led to a complete nervous breakdown. In later decades she disliked the attention regarding Bletchley, saying, 'War was a waste of lives, and so badly organised.'

After the war, personnel involved in intelligence had to keep quiet about their achievements. Hilary Bedford worked on ciphers and Bletchley bombe machines as a teenaged Wren. She became a fashion photographer with closets full of stylish clothes. In 2009, she finally broke her silence about the war, saying, 'The spirit of the time was incredible. We were really fighting with gusto.'[19]

Above: *Coming from a seafaring family, Mary Sherrard naturally volunteered for service as a Wren. She spent three years as a bombe operator then supervisor – working on German codes at both Bletchley Park and at an outstation at Eastcote. Although she enjoyed wearing her uniform, when she left service as a married woman in September 1945 she was ready to move on.*

Right: *An American cotton print dress similar to those seen on photographs of female staff working in conditions of intense secrecy for NACA – the forerunner of NASA – or at 'Atomic City' in the US, contributing to the Manhattan Project. Computer programmer Betty Snyder said the only way to survive a 1940s' work environment was 'Look like a girl, act like a lady, think like a man, and work like a dog.'[20]*

The pervasive stereotype of a scientist or mathematician depicts a man with spectacles, labcoat, bow tie and either wild 'Einstein' hair or sleek 'geek' hair. Real boffins were fairly usually ordinary in appearance, and sometimes female. Historians are now shining light on the 'hidden figures' in wartime technology, including the hundreds of African American women called up to be 'computers' in the defence industry. Human computers were programmers and data processors. Dorothy Vaughn was one such woman. The industrial laundry at Langley Memorial Aeronautical Laboratory in Hampton Virginia paid better than her teaching job and it was considered 'suitable' work for a woman of colour. However, Vaughn was a gifted mathematician, and escaped the labour of helping process 18,000 bundles of dirty linen weekly by answering an appeal to fill computing positions. She still had six children to care for. In addition to her new day job she sewed all their clothes and wore her shoes till the soles had holes. All the African American women at Langley experienced discrimination despite a presidential executive order ending segregation in the defence industries. Their professional clothes became a kind of armour to ward off negative stereotypes. Employee badges with the winged NACA logo were an important symbol of status and worn with pride. In 1947, it was female computers who analysed the data from pilot Chuck Yeager's Mojave Desert flight, proving a human had broken the sound barrier for the first time in history.[21]

From 1945, female computers – including Kay McNulty Mauchly Antonelli and Betty Snyder – programmed one of the world's first and fastest electronic computers, ENIAC, which was used to calculate precise firing trajectories for artillery. Calculations which would previously have taken forty hours' work could now be done in minutes. Antonelli said they were left to figure out what the machine could do, using only blueprints. Despite their skills the women were not visible in histories of computing until recently, becoming known merely as 'operators'.[22]

'My superiors told me the results of my work saved thousands of British and American lives. I was involved in situations from which respectable women draw back, but wars are not won by respectable methods.'

Amy Elizabeth 'Betty' Thorpe, codename Cynthia, American wartime spy.
Times obituary 21 January 2017.

The ultimate undercover wartime work was spying. Female spies were adept at using their appearance to attract possible informants, and also to evade notice. The work itself was usually more seedy than seductive, but alluring clothes played their part. Iby Knill, a young Jewish woman undercover in Hungary, used her dressmaking talents to turn a piece of brown silk into an evening dress with a deep cleavage. She later recalled, 'In that dress, with my throaty voice and a long cigarette holder I could give

Josephine Baker was an illustrious performer throughout the war and a daring spy for the French military intelligence service, doing important clandestine work across Europe, North Africa, the Middle East and South America. She was one of only a few women to achieve recognition for their work by the French government, being awarded a post-war Medal of the Resistance.

a plausible imitation of Marlene Dietrich singing *Lilli Marlene*.' The persona was an excellent way to make contact for the resistance.[23]

More high-profile spies tended to be charismatic, well-educated society women with excellent contacts. Secret agent Christine Granville smuggled intelligence for the British, hiding torpedo design specifications, as well as detailed plans of German ammunition factories and aerodromes inside her gloves. Granville even obtained footage of Wehrmacht preparations for the top secret 1941 invasion of Russia. She definitely prized freedom, telling a friend, 'You don't need more than two dresses and two pairs of shoes … you have to travel light in this life.'[24]

Active secret operatives working undercover in enemy territory had to be very careful about clothing. It could be a matter of life or death. If something about their appearance was out of place they could be arrested and interrogated, and their networks compromised. If they got it right, women found they could move more freely around occupied territories than men, perhaps because they were overlooked as 'just' women, with domestic, not military roles. Phyllis Latour, a fluent French teacher, joined the SOE from the WAAF. Codename *Genevieve* she posed as a chatty teenage girl whose family had moved to Normandy to escape the Allied bombing. Any military intelligence she gleaned was encoded for transmission using one-time codes. She kept these hidden on a piece of silk used to tie up her hair – the one place German authorities didn't think to search when she was brought in for questioning, so she was released.[25]

> 'In my view, women were very much better than men for the work. Women, as you must know, have a far greater capacity for cool and lonely courage than men.'
>
> Captain Jepson, SOE recruiting officer.[26]

Subtle details of clothing could help a secret agent blend in – or make them stand out. British operatives dropped into occupied France had to ensure their all their clothes looked authentic, which meant removing English labels and even using French knitting styles.

The British Special Operations Executive employed female operatives to be dropped into enemy territory. They were given almost identical training to the men, although not usually permitted to carry weapons or to practise hand-to-hand combat – a distinction which ignored the fact that women faced the same threats as male operatives. Women weren't awarded coveted paratrooper 'wings' like the men, no matter how perfect their parachute drops.

'Freedom is the only thing worth living for.'

Nancy Wake, secret agent, saboteur and fan of Chanel lipstick.

Parachute clothing included overalls and a large, round padded hat. These would be jettisoned on arrival for specially prepared civilian clothes. SOE agent Jacqueline Nearne was given French-style clothes with French labels for her undercover work, made up by specialist SOE tailors: two suits, two blouses, two pairs of pyjamas and two pairs of shoes. The pyjamas were such poor quality they were almost useless after the first wash – very authentic for wartime France. On one occasion Nearne was washing underwear in a basin in her room. Answering a knock at the door she found a plain-clothes policeman was making enquiries. Embarrassed to be caught holding wet undergarments she stammered her apologies. The policeman was disarmed and a raid was averted. Surviving the war, Nearne received an MBE for her service in the face of extremely active Gestapo operations. She was one of many undercover heroes.

A plaque at Dachau concentration camp near Munich commemorates the murder of four SOE officers who served the resistance in France. WAAF Noor Inayat Khan was one of these women. She was taken to her death wearing navy-blue slacks, a light grey woollen jumper and plimsolls – looking like an ordinary French girl. Codenamed Madeleine, Khan worked as the sole SOE Paris wireless operator for a time. She was betrayed to the Gestapo. After a failed escape attempt she told her interrogator, 'I have served my country. That is my recompense.'[27]

Chapter 12

ON THE DANCE FLOOR
Leisure activities

'There are about 90,000 officers, trying to have fun; the battles in the
desert here are treated like a game'[1]

Christine Granville, a spy in Cairo

Getting ready for a ball, a party, a disco, a date – these have been features of women's lives for centuries. The anticipation, anxious decision-making over what to wear, critical review of the final ensemble – dress triumphs, dress disasters – the possibility of romance... The transformative power of clothes cannot be underestimated, turning daily life into something special. During the war, leisure activities such as dancing and sport were crucial to keeping up morale and helping young people in particular let off steam during highly emotionally-charged years. In fact, fun was so important to national and military health, governments devoted considerable resources to promoting mass entertainment, such as the Nazi *Kraft durch Freude* (Strength through Joy) recreational organisation, designed to stimulate morale among workers.

The desperate need for distraction could be hedonistic, and a live-for-the-moment attitude pushed away morals as well as the horrors of war. Mary Morris, a nurse attending an Allied New Year party in Brussels in 1944, noticed Belgian girls in evening gowns and turban-style headscarves and wondered if the same girls had attended the glittering dinner dances of the German Wehrmacht during occupation. She later saw one girl being chased through the streets of Brussels by a crowd of women who cut off her hair as retribution for such collaboration.[2] There were harsh judgements on those who took their fun too far, or with the wrong crowd.

For some war workers, leisure meant a lunchtime music recital, laughing at a radio show, or a quiet moment with a book; others indulged in the escapism of cinema and theatre, a trip to the beach or a spot of sport. Clothes for leisure had their place in war.

Cairo, only two hours away from harsh desert battles was a place of frantic gaiety for Allied civilians and service personnel. Freya Stark, travelling with government propaganda work in 1941, showed off one of the last Molyneux designs bought in Paris before the designer fled Nazi occupation. She said cinemas and restaurants were crowded, 'and people with arms in slings or bandaged heads were going out to dinner parties.'[3] American army auxiliaries in Cairo were forbidden to appear out of uniform

Chapel Allerton High School girls, glammed up for a dance in an array of shop-bought and home-made evening styles.

even in the evening, so they hid dresses under khaki coats and caps until they reached their destination, such was the desire to dress up for a night out. Germans advancing from El Alamein broadcast the message, 'Get out your party frocks, we're on our way!' Local Egyptian dressmakers dropped English clients to start stitching for a German Victory Ball.[4]

War understandably had a major impact on leisure activities and leisurewear. Earnest promotions for civilians to have 'Holidays at Home' were essentially putting a brave face on the fact that working hours were long, borders were closed, holiday destinations had become battle zones, fuel was precious and families too scattered for

Above left: *Home-made velvet and floral crepe evening dress embellished with marcasite dress clips. Long sleeves were a bonus during fuel shortages, and also welcomed by older women.*

Above right: *Those who had full-length gowns made them last as long as possible, adding variety through different accessories. This early 1940s dress features an innovative rayon fabric with heat-sealed cut-out designs, like a colourised wearable doyley.*

holidays together anyway. Those craving society came up against the usual problems of how to make fewer clothes go further, and how to look fabulous without seeming unpatriotically over-indulgent. Fashion magazines regularly addressed this issue. The wartime solution was day-to-night ensembles. Plain outfits were glamorised with chic bolero jackets or a change of bodice. Lace shawls added warmth without looking frumpy. Long wool frocks were in fashion in England. Black wool sweaters were stylish for evening wear, with added embroidery, lamé details or statement pearls. Silk stockings might be saved for special occasions, although wartime transport – walking, the subway or Jeep rides – were not friendly to delicate evening wear. Fabric length was an issue. Long gowns had been de rigueur for formal evening wear, yet they were hardly compatible with austerity. British dressmaking patterns slowly dropped designs for long hems. Women began to eye up floral curtains or bedspreads for the fabric.

In America, mobilisation from 1942 onwards meant young women had an endlessly renewing source of military men as paying escorts to dinner dances and gala dances. US Army dietician Caroline Morrison Garrett smiled to hide the pain of feet that ached from dancing too much, conceding 'Dancing slippers were no match for army boots'. Her weapon of war was a small travel iron, used to freshen up the layers of net and rhinestones on her formal gown. During an evening event at the Chinese Embassy she admired the Chinese ambassador's wife Mrs Wei, looking distinctive in a white floral cheongsam and jade earrings.[5]

It is on record that an attractive member of the WVS accepted as part of her duties an invitation to go to a dance in a Polish Officers' Mess. Her first partner, after the first dance, clicked his heels, bowed low, kissed her hand and said, 'I thank you. You dance divine, you glamorous bitch.'[6]

Dancing had a major profile in the social calendar. Professional and competitive dancers set high standards for steps and costumes. Ballroom dancers were advised not to have too full a skirt, even if this could be wangled – immense ballet-style skirts waved behind your dance partner's knees, 'giving him the appearance of an over-anxious mermaid,' wrote Irene Raines, British dance expert.[7] Fans of old-time dancing got a shock when American servicemen came to Britain eager to share heady dances such as the jitterbug, swing, jive and boogie. These were perfect for flat shoes and short skirts – and a decent pair of knickers for if the dance got wild.

Most Saturday night dances were as home-made as the dresses of the dancers. Teenagers often had to cycle to the venue, and music might just be from a gramophone. Girls swapped clothes with friends, to get variety for each new dance, and refreshments (inevitably spilled onto frocks) were simple – one Yorkshire village dance offered sausage rolls and KitKat chocolate bars. Fancy dress balls gave the greatest scope to creative ingenuity, with costumes crafted from oddments and crepe paper. Granted, generous doses of imagination were needed to appreciate some concoctions, but there was a war on – every small achievement was significant. Doris Lihou, from the British Channel Isles, was interned as an enemy alien in a French camp. She celebrated her twelfth birthday by tap dancing at a concert, wearing a Hawaiian-style costume. Her 'grass' skirt was mattress straw, decorated with pictures of fish cut from the labels of tinned salmon, courtesy of Red Cross parcels.[8]

The greatest influence on evening styles was cinema. Picture Palaces offered shelter, escapism, and opportunities for semi-private courting. Film tickets were cheap and programmes changed frequently. Shows ran through the day. Hollywood actresses offered star appeal, selling an ideal of wealth, ease, glamour and romance. Housewives escaped from home and into a world of the imagination. Big names commanded big fees, and their images were used to promote beauty products and

Peggy Colbourne met her sailor husband while working at the milk bar attached to the Gaiety Cinema in Southampton. Milk bar staff were allowed in to watch the ends of the films, sometimes taking their fish and chip suppers in with them.

fashion in women's magazines. Top Hollywood designers such as Edith Head and 'Adrian' had their own headaches trying to create spectacular fashions during a war economy. Far from paring down every ensemble, they found that the more extravagant the frocks, the more popular the film.

Cinema showed ordinary people what they craved. Designer Walter Plunkett's fantasy 1860s-style gowns from the 1939 film *Gone With the Wind* are a classic example – hooped exuberance and excess embellishments. The scene where heroine Scarlett O'Hara, has her maid Mammy convert thick green curtains into a bold outfit would have resonated

LUCILLE BALL and HENRY FONDA
the co-stars of Damon Runyon's "The Big Street"—a sentimental story peopled by Damon Runyon's inimitable characters. (Cast on page 80.)

Right: Lucille Ball is pure loveliness in cascades of net for the 1943 film The Big Street *with Henry Fonda.*

Below: Film poster for Lakharani, *starring Monica Desai and Durga Khote, 1945. The Indian film industry was a vibrant and creative force in the 1940s.*

Actress and comedian Hattie McDaniel was the first African American entertainer to win an Academy Award. Persistent racial stereotyping gave Black women limited roles as slaves and domestics. Hattie fought for wider roles, but defended her Oscar-winning portrayal of Mammy in Gone with the Wind *– 'I'd rather make 700 dollars a week playing a maid than 7 dollars being one.'[11]*

with women used to being resourceful in wartime. It was also symbolic of fashion's power to give confidence against the odds.[9] The film was a huge hit worldwide, and remade in Shanghai with a Chinese cast as *A Beauty at a Turbulent Time* – part of the Japanese Imperial Army's ideology of the Greater East Asian Film Sphere.[10]

Few wartime films could credit women for work behind the camera as directors or technical crew. Leni Riefenstahl was an exception to the rule, bringing her talents to German cinema to glorify the Third Reich. Nazi Propaganda Minister Josef Goebbels had tight control over entertainment during the war, distorting storylines to promote Aryan ideals, in which all black actors would play African savages, and all heroes were strong Caucasians. Concentration camp survivor Doris Reiprich and her sister Erika Ngambi ul Kuo came to Berlin for the movies and met a small community of Africans working there.[12]

'One evening, in the middle of a performance, my panties fell to the ground; they were French knickers with a button to hold them up. My father had always said, do not stop playing for anything! So I finished playing, picked up my panties, bowed and walked off the stage to catcalls!'

Joan Folkard, Royal College of Music, entertaining troops with jolly martial tunes.[13]

Music fed the soul during war. Songs such as *Lili Marleen*, first sung by Lale Anderson and popularised by Marlene Dietrich, connected people separated by war. Music nourished a spirit of resistance. In besieged Leningrad, musicians died of starvation while rehearsing Shostakovich's new symphony in 1942, but Russians craved culture – music, ballet and theatre.[14] Music was vital for dancing, and a soundtrack for all

Above left: *Singer Elisabeth Welch had a big wartime following, giving sophisticated, stylish interpretations of popular songs. She sang for troops across the UK and abroad. Although she could glam up for shows she also performed in everyday clothes, including trousers. John Gielgud wrote of one show where she wore a black dress against a white satin curtain: 'You can hear a pin drop while she is singing, but when she has finished the thunder of applause can be heard in the street.'*[15]

Above right: *ENSA dancer Mildred Turner in her official uniform. Mildred was a former Windmill dancer – not one of the nudes, she always stressed. She entertained men evacuated from Dunkirk, and was also weeks at sea on various Atlantic convoy troop ships, which she said was quite enjoyable, as the three girls in the company were the only females among a couple of thousand men. During a bomb raid at the Finsbury Park Empire she had to shelter under the stage and hope for the best.*

wartime experiences, whether a pulsing night out with Glenn Miller's big band sound, or quiet heartbreak hearing Vera Lynn's *We'll Meet Again* serenade.

Radio tunes played in kitchens, across factory floors and in military outposts. For those wanting the live experience there were multitudes of wartime artistes, from celebrity entertainers, to Music Hall variety shows and amateur theatricals. The worldwide range of talent is staggering, as is the diversity. In Harlem, Gladys Bentley performed with a chorus of drag queens at the Ubangi club, wearing men's clothing, and singing racy lyrics to popular tunes. She matched top hat, silver-topped cane and glistening lipstick.[16] In Paris, the singer Mistinguette defied advancing years to show off her famous legs, although her low-grade costumes had none of their pre-war flamboyance. Legendary Josephine Baker's Folies Bergère show incorporated scenes of her dressed as Mary Queen of Scots, singing Schubert's *Ave Maria* in Latin.[17]

Baker's wartime performance schedule was prodigious, and yet she took care to appear smart at all times. Noel Coward spotted her outside Shepheard's Hotel in Cairo, September 1943, 'looking the last word in chic and bright as a button'.[18]

Entertainment was a highly effective way for women to support those in military service. For British Armed Forces, it was ENSA which became synonymous with wartime entertainment – the Entertainments National Service Association. Established in 1939, ENSA groups crossed continents, travelling and performing in terrible conditions, all on a shoestring budget. There may have been sporadic complaints about quality, but given wartime conditions ENSA staff have to be admired for their fortitude. For many troops serving abroad, ENSA entertainers offered memories of home. Clothing was a key component of performances. Women were encouraged to look attractive, but not too alluring.

'Whenever I wear the uniform I get the 'hi-babe' looks, approach and conversation with the soldiers. I never meet with anything but extremely friendly and easy manners when I'm in my ordinary clothes.'

Joyce Grenfell[19]

The official ENSA uniform was universally detested by those who wore it. It was known as Basil dress, after Dean Basil, the dictatorial founder of ENSA. ENSA veteran Joyce Grenfell called it 'as unbecoming a little outfit as ever you could see: stiff, hideous in colour.' Its only virtue was that it saved on civilian garments, which suffered the perils of travel-packing, climate damage and over-vigorous scrubbing at local laundries. Grenfell lamented the hours spent mending her gala clothes until they were almost rewoven with darning. Her journeys in North Africa and the Middle East were helped by fur-lined boots and an inflatable cushion. In India she was warned to check her shoes for snakes.[20]

Singer Vera Lynn – nicknamed the Forces Sweetheart – also clocked impressive mileage for ENSA. For her, India meant long sleeves because the mosquitoes were so bad. Perspiration was her greatest challenge on stage. All make-up slid off, except for trusty red lipstick. Her favourite pink dress grew darker and darker with sweat as the show went on. When her luggage went astray in Burma, Vera gallantly sang in a pair of trousers borrowed from an army major. She was a nimble seamstress and used her time between theatre sets to run up new clothes.[21]

It is through ENSA travelogues that we catch sight of local women, albeit through a somewhat colonial filter. Joyce Grenfell observed Maltese good-time girls in uplift brassieres, Egyptian royalty in organza and diamonds and Egyptian housewives in black abbas and veils. Married women in Bethlehem wore a white cotton headdress over raised foundations, which Grenfell described as 'Crusader' style and 'most becoming'. In India, she envied women wearing 'ravishing' saris at a Bombay Yacht

As part of an ENSA dance troupe Mildred Turner travelled in North Africa, Italy, India, Iceland and the Middle East. She described the gunfire from frontline battles as 'a trifle noisy' during shows. Here she poses with a wrecked tank in the Algerian desert.

Club lunch – rich delphinium purples, flame reds, spring yellows and incredible greens. The Darjeeling women she saw had nose rings and shawls.[22]

In the theatre, professionals and amateurs alike struggled to concoct decent costumes out of very little. English actresses often had to provide their own outfits for plays with a contemporary setting, putting further strain on their purses and coupons.

Home entertainment usually involved simple pleasures such as board games, puzzles, or a sing-song round the piano. The Women's Institute recognised the value of taking a break from war work and war worries. Their meetings included a social half-hour on the programme where members could enjoy a brief bit of laughter and relaxation. A wartime handbook gave ideas for games to play, including some gems involving clothes. There was the *Oldest Hat Parade*, where the history of hats brought from home was given. One winner was an early nineteenth-century hat which the WI owner said had been 'quite a nice hat till my husband used it to cover his head when he was re-creosoting the fowls' pen!' There was a fancy-dress character-guessing game, a dressing race and – so reminiscent of the war years – a frantic game called *Queuing*, in which players rushed around 'shopping' for items on a quest list.[23]

The idea of specific leisurewear is relatively new. 'Sportswear' in the early twentieth century often referred to jersey knits and comfortable, informal styles – suitable for

Moments of relaxation during wartime might be rare, but at least no special outfits were required for an evening at home with books, a paper and the wireless.

watching sports rather than participating. Previously people relaxed in their regular everyday clothes. Companies such as Janzen latched onto the trend for informality, where fashion played second fiddle to utility. Their wartime clothes, including trouser suits and battle-dress-style jackets, were designed for 'comfort, freedom-for-action, gaiety'. Creases were sewn in to save ironing.

Most sports – walking, cycling, tennis or baseball – could be enjoyed without specialist gear. People simply adapted the clothes they already had. There were basic sturdy boots for hiking or plimsolls for ball games – if there was enough leather for the boots and enough rubber for the plimsolls. Team sports required a 'strip', or if that wasn't feasible, teams played with coloured vests or sashes. Aside from charity matches, women's team sports were usually limited to school tournaments. Women weren't

176

Planned For Your Leisure

For Victory Garden Chores

. . . For Active Sports

2478 Butterick. Saucy sailorette in a two-piece nautical suit . . . blouse and trim slacks. Size 16, 4½ yds. 35 in.; 1 yd. 35 in. tie; 5 yds. narrow braid. 10 to 20; 28 to 38. Price, 35 Cents.

2477 Butterick. One-piece Princess bathing suit for the slim or not so slim figure. Size 16, 1½ yds. 35 in. ⅞ yd. contrast ruffles. Sizes 12 to 20; 30 to 44. Price, 35 Cents.

2483-D Butterick. When you're in a country or suburban locale, you'll want a sun frock. This jumper has a smart fitted midriff and dirndl skirt. Size 16, 3 yds. 35 in. 12 to 20; 30 to 40. 35 Cents.

1943 Butterick Fashion News ideas 'Planned for Your Leisure – For Victory Garden Chores For Active Sports' The outfits give a sense of freedom, lightness and informality. They look more fun than practical for gardening and sport.

Deutsche Moden-Zeitung

vereinigt mit Beyers Modenblatt
Frau-Volk-Welt

Ausgabe
mit 4 Schnittbg.
15 Rpf.

A 1941 German tennis outfit, offering a refreshing antidote to ongoing warfare. Tennis was a pastime for the privileged during war. Skirts were considered more respectable than shorts. In 1949, American Gertrude 'Gussie' Moran dared to play at Wimbledon wearing lace-edged pants visible under her dress.

usually encouraged to form professional leagues while male players joined the military, although the American initiative for a female professional baseball league thrived during the war years, giving athletes the opportunity to showcase their skills before admiring audiences. Baseball was an American gift to Japan after the war, with Japanese schoolgirls training and competing in popular leagues.

Of all sports, swimming was the one which required specific clothing, although Joyce Grenfell stooped to bathing in men's underwear with a scarf round her breasts when she lost her own swimsuit in Haifa. Commercial swimming costumes combined wool with Lastex elastic to help keep the shape. Home-made versions could be stitched with shirring elastic which caused bubbly air pockets in the water until the elastic inevitably perished and the costume went limp.

The ultimate home-made swimsuits were knitted. No matter how tight the tension, these always sagged when wet, becoming frontless as well as backless, and often drooping to the knees. Knitted swimsuits were also notorious for collecting sand. Swimming accessories might include rubber caps, velveteen beach slacks and terry towelling robes.

Two-piece suits pre-dated the bikini. On a good figure they had a certain amount of glamour (although the navel was always covered). They had the advantage of needing roughly 10 per cent less fabric than a full costume, which was handy during thrifty years. The original bikini, with exposed navel and buttocks, evolved from these two piece suits. It was something of a publicity stunt by French designer Louis Réard. The slim model wearing it for the photo shoot attracted more attention than the actual garment, which was far too risqué for most women in the 1940s.

178

Above: *Canadian skiers show off 1940s knitwear, and trousers tucked into boots. Few women had specialist ski-wear. The emphasis was on layering for warmth. Ski-wear was worn in unheated homes and offices during wartime fuel shortages.*

Right: *Healthy, happy and unselfconscious – English friends model a selection of swimwear styles. Home-made, shop-bought, one-piece or two-piece, the main thing was to enjoy the beach in whatever you could get to wear.*

Cycling for shapely legs – 'Although lovely legs are enhanced a hundred-fold by modern hosiery, its very sheerness reveals every fault, so lady, watch your legs!'[24]

However women spent their leisure time, the clothes they wore gathered memories and ghostly perfume scents. One nurse in India packed her civvies in tissue paper for the return to England. Each of her three evening frocks represented significant eras of her service abroad, from the demure broderie-anglaise dress worn for a gentle sweetheart, to the red sari-fabric gown worn when dancing with a man she could never marry, and finally a duck-egg blue crepe frock, worn for the night of a 1945 Victory Ball, where she was first spotted by her future husband.[25]

Women sparkling in cocktail bars or stepping out in home-made party gowns had their moments of fun but they were also the women who were ferrying planes, driving ambulances or working with TNT in a munitions factory. Sometimes the lace and the glamour hid heavy hearts that needed the uplift of music and the elegance of fashion to carry on.

A sunny cotton playsuit, for those with time and inclination to spare for sunbathing.

Chapter 13

IN THE LOOKING GLASS
Cosmetics and grooming

'Very busy but very lovely. It's your duty these days to be beautiful,
because beauty inspires happiness and cheerfulness both
in yourself and others.'

Wartime ad for *Icilma* beauty products

One August afternoon in 2013, I joined a group of hikers to scramble along a dilapidated section of China's Great Wall. On the approach route our guide touched my arm and gestured to an ancient woman in black resting at the side of the road. He knew I was interested in women's history, so he was discreetly pointing out that her feet were bound. The custom of breaking young foot bones and rotting the flesh to achieve a small, deformed foot was mainly out of favour for Chinese reformers of the 1940s. In rural areas the custom persisted, and the process was irreversible. The woman I saw, hobbled by her own 'Lotus' feet, was a remnant of earlier ideals of beauty.

Sketch of a Parisian hat by Paulette, 1943. Hats, hairstyles and make-up were key components of women's identity in the 1940s.

The pursuit of beauty in wartime was not usually so extreme, nor was it limited to glamorous actresses or even to women in civvies. Poster pin-up girls, army officers and household drudges all knew the power of a good beauty pick-me-up such as a fresh application of lipstick. The fact that personal grooming and vanity seemed the antithesis of warfare was the element which made them so powerful. Hairstyles, cosmetics and accessories were all means of defying the coarse

181

Traditional Japanese cosmetics favoured a matt white face and dainty red lips. Popular media criticised glamorous 'Western-style' make-up and hair as vulgar and unpatriotic.

brutality of war, however arduous it was to source products and find the time for self-care.

Appearances mattered, arguably more for women than for men, since the female wartime roles were often considered a mere interim phase before attracting and pleasing a mate. Ultimately, societies usually saw marriage as the main goal for women, placing great premium on female attractiveness, as well as virtue. For many women this created an uneasy conflict between looking desirable and not being tainted by suspicion of immodesty – unless the women in question were in the business of using their looks immodestly of course.

In the mid-twentieth century, as now, different cultures had different standards for what it meant to be 'feminine'. There are common threads. In many Western societies, slender figures were prized because of the association with youth, although to be gaunt was not desirable, as it implied malnourishment or illness – both prevalent during war. 'Trim', 'neat' and 'ladylike' were popular descriptives for acceptable Caucasian physiques. One British beauty expert critiqued extreme thinness as likely to promote nervousness and irritability, while stoutness led to shortness of breath '…and you get an inferiority complex because you can't find clothes to suit you, and don't feel as smart as other women.'[1] Magazines were full of advertisements for products to help banish the 'rubber tyres' of middle-age spread. Bile beans promised the consumer would 'Keep radiant, slim and attractive all through the year!'

Some cultures were uncomfortable with the association of artifice – beauty products – with immorality, particularly if they were keen to promote strong domestic and functional roles for women. In these cultures, feminine ideal was for 'wholesome' good looks, perhaps with help from subtle powderings of rice flour or commercial face powder. Inevitably hypocrisy crept in. Thus, official Third Reich policy may have been to deplore the seductive techniques of French coquettes, but French perfumeries were plundered as soon as the Germans had invaded Paris. Film-maker Leni Riefenstahl told a journalist: 'The Fuehrer detests make-up. You can never tell when he's going to show up, so I've quit using the stuff altogether.'[2] While it may have gone against the stated public image of German women to be artificial or alluring, German men and women were happy to enjoy the results of quality time in front of the looking glass: Hitler gifted his mistress Eva Braun with a beautiful silver lipstick case.[3]

Judging by the products being marketed, skin colour and condition were major features of the beauty regime. Lotions in India and the Far East promised lighter skin tones for 'the pale loveliness that men admire'[4], while Western adverts promoted ultra-violet treatments to create 'that healthy tan that men and women admire'.[5] An English department store sang the praises of sunbathing with Nivea skin oil: 'ideal for acquiring a lovely tan without looking like a boiled beetroot.'[6] This hardly took into account the limited opportunities women had for sunbathing during wartime. A more serious problem was the lack of sunlight for shift workers, who suffered ill health from depleted vitamin D levels.

In 1941, the French fashion magazine *Elle* gave readers a rare insight into the wide range of beauty ideals around the world, along with relevant beauty products. Inuit women – termed Eskimos in the article – used seal oil to moisturise; Norwegian and Japanese women favoured hot bathing and massage, while the American specialities were described as 'putting

'If the embarrassment of dark skin hinders your social and business progress …' begins an Indian advert for skin whitener in Bombay. Culture pressures to look lighter created a demand for potentially harmful skin-bleaching products.

on her face what could equally go in her stomach – milk, tomatoes, grapefruit, banana skins' – most of which would not have been wasted on the face when the stomach needed filling. Arab women were said to use rose water for the skin, as well as intricate henna tattoos.[7]

'Your war work starts with beauty care. To remain attractive – stimulating – inspiring is as important as your new job. Although office or other work now claims most of your day, your first duty is still to be and to look charming'

1945 advert for Pond's Creams.

TANGEE
LIPSTICK
for Beauty on Duty

All the nice girls love — TANGEE! Orange in the stick, this unique, incomparable lipstick changes on the lips to the *exact* colour needed to make them look their loveliest. Blush rose, coral, carmine—whichever shade is called for, TANGEE gives it according to your type. By enhancing *natural* loveliness, TANGEE has banished that garish 'painted' look for ever — made 'beauty on duty' open to all.

Tangee was a top lipstick brand of the 1940s. They cleverly marketed to women in the services in order to boost sales. A key selling point was 'enhancing natural loveliness'.

Cosmetic adverts often showed pretty young women embraced by manly chaps in uniform. If older women were portrayed it was to suggest they dealt with constipation problems, or quickly bought beauty products to make themselves look younger and less fatigued.

A typical 1940s' look required foundation cream, or powder at the least, with light blusher, blue eye shadow, black eyeliner and mascara, and red lips. Popular lip shades such as 'Don Juan' and 'Victory Red' hinted at orange, although pink shades – including the suggestive 'trousseau pink' – were available. Painted nails hardly tallied with manual labour, but they were popular in the US in particular. In North Africa, Westerners were impressed at the strong eye make-up of local women, who left off rouge and lipstick to concentrate on kohl and mascara. What was normal for one culture seemed exotic to another.[8]

'Owing to circumstances over which we have no control, slight alterations in packs will have to be made but the high quality of Max Factor cosmetics will remain unchanged. Save your lipstick containers. Packed so as to conserve vital metal for the war effort, Max Factor Lipstick Refills are ready to fit the container we hope you have saved.'

Max Factor advert, 1942

Coveting cosmetics was all very well; acquiring them was a different matter altogether. It was a notable joy to find odd stocks of beauty products, particularly for servicewomen abroad, bereft of their accustomed treats. A Queen Alexandra nurse shopping in Brahmaputra, Assam, was astonished to find Elizabeth Arden powder and lipsticks in a local bazaar. She quickly bought

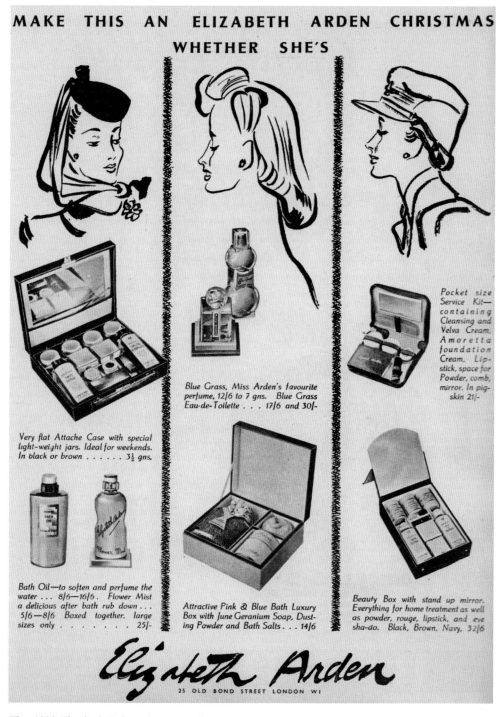

This 1939 Elizabeth Arden advert appeals to servicewomen, sirens and the girl next door but cosmetic companies would soon struggle to source raw materials and to distribute goods in a wartime economy.

Bourjois Evening in Paris *was a best-selling perfume of the 1940s, along with* California Poppy, Miss Dior, L'Air du Temps, Black Satin *and* Yardley Lavender. *Wartime customers were advised to treasure their scents and use them sparingly. Cheap Eau de Cologne was a pick-me-up when feeling hot and jaded.*[10]

the lot for nurses and VADs, commenting, 'There were few delights out in the wilds to equal the opening of a new box of fragrant-smelling face powder when one has been reduced to scraping the last scraps from the edges of a compact.'[9]

Enterprising individuals learned how to eke out their lipsticks, by using sparingly, and by dabbing up every last spot from the tube. Local chemists with an entrepreneurial streak concocted coloured lip salves and filled (unused) suppository cases with them, for sale. In Calcutta thousands of rupees were raised for the East India Fund charity by a two female chemists inventing their own cosmetics. Their ingredients included beauty classics such as cucumber, oatmeal, lavender and jasmine. Boiling and emulsifying the cosmetics was hot work in a stifling climate.[11]

As cosmetic products gradually came on the market once more they were snapped up by eager consumers. Mary Morris, nursing in Louvain, France, had a trip into town in late 1944, after liberation. In her diary she recorded buying lipsticks and Chanel No. 5 perfume, an experience she described as 'blissful!'[12]

Servicewomen in Allied countries were not exempt from the desire to wear make-up, nor the expectation to. Vinolia cosmetic soap adverts played to the concept of beauty on duty: 'Because many women are now in uniform, it doesn't mean that they should abandon their femininity and charm. On the contrary, men expect them to be just as attractive as ever.' Servicewomen were encouraged to hide blemishes under face powder; to boost morale (and attract admirers) with lipstick, and to remove body hair with Veet. Then, as now, Veet optimistically claimed to be pleasantly perfumed and not messy to use.

'Will she have a chance to wear it?' asks the cover of Picture Post *in 1945, contrasting an ATS woman's 'masculine' uniform with an utterly frivolous 'feminine' hat.*

Eunice Fairless was a talented ATS hairdresser, employing her skills in Europe after D-Day.

'Went to Bayeux to have my hair shampooed and set. Was enjoying the luxury of having my hair dried and in rollers when the electricity was cut off.'

Nurse Mary Morris, 1945.[13]

Hollywood actress Margaret Lockwood endorses Drene shampoo.

Hair was washed and set far less frequently in the 1940s than now. With a few exceptions – noticeably Hollywood actresses such as Veronica Lake and Jane Russell – long hair was worn rolled up and pinned, using Kirby grips. Permanent waves were popular, as were home-set waves made from crocodile clips and Dinky curlers. Despite the rigours of war work most women preferred not to crop their hair – anything shorter than a bob was considered rather masculine. Hair salons struggled to source products for perms and colouring. They did not struggle for customers. Having one's hair dressed was a treat that helped make daily drudgery bearable. Busy women kept their styles simple – a 'Victory' roll could be effected by turning the hair up over a pad of old stocking, then gripped into place. Those with deft fingers rolled curls to be pinned high on the head.

Shampoo, like soap, was a prized commodity in wartime. One advantage of the fashion for hats was that they hid greasy, dirty hair. Headscarves and turbans were the easiest and most practical head coverings, along with woolly caps and berets. They kept the head warm and the hair out of the way when working. They were also inexpensive, stitched or knitted from leftover scraps and yarns. By 1945, even *Vogue* magazine resorted to giving make-do-and-mend tips on how to turn oddments of fabric into stocking caps or draped turbans.

Fashionable hats could be as flamboyant and frivolous as the wearer wished. Elsa Schiaparelli dared to wear a hat exported to the US from occupied Paris, via Buenos Aires. It was promptly reported that she was buying from

*An American red felt hat with cheeky flowers –
great with Victory rolls and matching lipstick.*

*An American hat of striped rayon, worn at an
appealing slant over the brow.*

*Felt hats were most common, often with neat veils
and feather or fur embellishments. Trilby styles
were also popular.*

Nazis. She defended the outrageous, hideous hats in wartime Paris, declaring they showed the French capital as 'convulsed and trampled but still possessed of a sense of humour.'[14] *Vogue* editor Bettina Ballard was in Paris after liberation, in time to see the insolent fashion for vast headwear, said to have been worn despite shortages and in defiance of the German occupation. She described seeing a very elegant woman in a towering pink felt hat nestled with birds and clouded with a haze of tulle – 'something even beyond Cecil Beaton's dreams'.[15]

Left: *Straw hat with velvet ribbon from Ukraine. In April 1942, Lancashire housewife Nella Last recorded the exquisite pleasure of successful hat shopping, writing in her Mass Observation diary that she ignored the so-called Hollywood styles suggested by the hat shop assistant, saying she hadn't got a 'Hollywood face'. Mrs Last settled on a 'dream hat' of wine-coloured straw only 16 shillings and 6d.*[16]

Below: *'However much, or however little money a woman may spend on clothes, she will attain quiet distinction and individuality in her dressing only if she pays attention to details.'*
    Wisdom from a wartime Sew and Save *booklet. A bright home-made belt such as this jazzed up an old or worn outfit.*

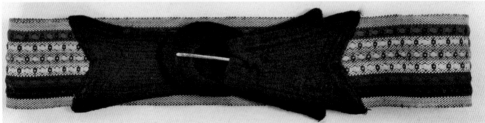

Chapter 14

UP THE AISLE
Weddings

'What will I look like tomorrow? Perhaps I won't wear my white dress.
I'll wear navy blue. I'm not in the mood to dress up, but I want to look
nice. I hope in years to come, Walter will remember.'[1]

Trudi Kanter on the eve of her wedding, 1938

I have many wedding dresses in my vintage collection, from Victorian crinoline gowns to 1980s' meringues. Some have names and pictures associated. Many keep their stories secret.

I find the gowns of the 1940s most poignant. The printed acetate for a bride in Kenya who was thousands of miles apart from her fiancé who still made it home for the wedding. The luxurious silk of a gown embroidered with silver thread, worn by a bride who carried calla lilies in 1942. The plain, light silk for a bride named Jean who met a handsome naval officer on a train while she was promised to another man. She broke off that engagement to marry the sailor. He survived two ship sinkings, but died of a brain haemorrhage at the end of the war.

I have a wedding dress dyed blue, with pink ribbon swags added, and one of white lace given a dramatic black bow. These are the gowns of thrifty brides who knew they had to make the most of their clothes. Rather than leave them languishing in tissue paper after the wedding they cut off sleeves and trains to transform the frock into an evening outfit, and turned the remnants into christening gowns. 'Make your wedding frock with an eye to the future,' advised Leach/Way fashion catalogue in spring 1946. 'Belle pour un beau jour,' declared *Elle* magazine in January 1941 – beautiful for one fine day.

Regardless of the fortunes of war, a wedding was to be a moment of loveliness. *Elle* recommended satin, crepe, drapes, gathers, orange blossom, roses, camellias or a corsage of tulle. How many wartime brides-to-be read this advice and wondered – *how*?

Where there's a will, there's a way. War divided couples and families, but it also threw people together in heightened circumstances. Passions were easily ignited in a live-for-today world where the future seemed so uncertain, or frighteningly short. Romance was a wonderful way to escape from the everyday grit of war; a wedding was the only way to escape the stigma of unwed motherhood.

Plan a Pink Wedding

Here again is the pretty pink bride on the cover, with her two bridesmaids who are wearing duplicates of her dress. Slipper satin, with huge skirts and quaint swathed bodices, they were adapted from First Empire styles, could be worn after the wedding for evening wear. The little satin bonnets are trimmed with ostrich feathers. Turn the page for ideas on the pink wedding itself, the bride's going away outfit.

MARGARET KAY.

Magazines, novels and films reinforced the idea that every girl's dream was to be a bride. In 1939, Woman magazine indulged in the overblown sweetness of pink bridal fashions. Romance stories always ended in marriage. What happened afterwards was left to the Agony Aunt columns.

Marriage in many cultures was an expensive affair, involving feasts, new clothes, gifts and even dowries. It often meant the linking of dynasties or businesses rather than the legalisation of a love affair. War certainly shook up conservative foundations in many societies. There is an enduring theme running through the cultures of countries at war – that weddings were as important as ever.

Cairo during the war was considered open season for husband hunting. One American motor transport girl pulled a crumpled white satin wedding gown from the bottom of her kit bag when she arrived in town, saying she'd bag a husband soon enough. Men too had need of marriage as an antidote to the violence and unpredictability of the world around them. It wasn't all a question of ensnaring a new husband: young women also had more freedom to explore their own passions – if they could escape chaperones, get back to billets by curfew, and keep their reputations intact. As one commentator wryly put it, 'buttons had a way of coming undone in Cairo'.[2]

Historically, young women would prepare for future married life by planning a trousseau. This might include new clothes, nightwear, bedding, household linens, baby layettes and even a shroud. War hastened many plans, particularly if the fiancé was in the military with limited pockets of leave, and had just sent a telegram saying 'FORTY-EIGHT HOURS TO CHANGE YOUR MIND'. Thrifty brides-to-be did their best to stretch resources to cover a few wisps of lingerie, a dress to be married in and a going-away outfit.

Margaret Wishart née Robinson changed out of her Land Army breeches for a white wedding, but she still had a Land Army guard of honour. Her husband was a former PoW from Stalag VIII, and in poor shape at the end of the war. 'But what a marvellous chap my Jack was,' Margaret wrote to me years later.

Claire Atkins née McNie married in New Zealand, June 1940. She was a talented seamstress, although dust from fabric gave her asthma. She started with nothing, worked hard on the family farm, and was keen for her daughters to be educated. The pleating and tucks on her wedding wool two-piece show excellent dressmaking skills.

Iby Knill's trousseau was gathered against the odds. She was a survivor of Auschwitz and lucky to have any family left to join her wedding to a British officer. Because it was winter, she chose a wool costume – a suit – with a white blouse and white turban. She created the blouse herself from German parachute silk. Her mother packed a trousseau for her to take to England. It included outfits for four seasons, hand-made shoes and boots with matching bags, gloves and hats; twelve nighties, six negligees and twelve sets of silk knickers and petticoats. This was an extraordinary achievement. Inside the whole box of delights was a selection of fabrics – a godsend in fabric-rationed England. Remnants of the trousseau and the fabrics were later worked into a quilt for her son. He called it a 'story-telling' quilt.[3]

Not every trousseau would be wanted. Rena Kornreich, Polish-born but living in Slovakia, had to pack hers away when Germans began deporting all Jews to ghettos and work camps. She folded up her wedding nightgown, her new shoes and new tailored dress: 'everything I own has been packed, and with my dreams, put away.' She survived the Holocaust; her fiancé did not.[4] In Russia, Valentina Pavlovna Maximchuk's friend Vera coveted a new chiffon dress with ruffles. Valentina offered it as a wedding present for Vera's upcoming nuptials. Then the war intervened. Valentina went off to serve as an anti-aircraft gunner and the dress was accidentally burned in a dormitory fire.[5]

For the actual big day some brides had to scramble everything together in a hurry. This was the case for one unnamed pregnant WAAF who needed to get a ring for respectability's sake. The other WAAFs pooled coupons and money to buy her a blue dress with a matching coat and sandals. After the wedding, the new bride sold the coat and got drunk on the proceeds in a field, thereby wrecking the dress. The pregnancy turned out to have been a false alarm. No information survives about the success of the marriage.[6]

American brides of 1943 were invited to buy War Bonds as well as trousseau items. (Vogue, January 1943)

Joan Hackney née Bell was lucky even to get to her own wedding. Working as a teleprinter in a top secret RAF receiving station she had advance knowledge of the D-Day landings, when all leave would be cancelled. She left the station not knowing if her fiancé had received the message to bring the wedding date forward, ahead of D-Day. Fortunately all was well. She tied the knot in a dusky pink dress that could be worn afterwards.

More dramatically, in April 1945 Eva Braun finally obtained her wish to marry long-time partner Adolf Hitler. The high-fashion salon of Annemarie Heise received a last-minute order to make the dress, even as Russians bombarded Berlin. A courier fetched the dress through the burning city to Hitler's bunker. Braun wore it with Ferragamo black suede shoes.[7] And on a lighter note, the WVS were able to rustle around for a wedding dress when two bombed-out octogenarians decided to get married.[8]

Particularly at the start of the war, brides thought it made sense to save their money – and their coupons – by not buying a special white wedding dress. Alternatives might be a smart white suit, such as that worn by singer Vera Lynn when she married her sweetheart Harry in August 1941. A white pillbox hat and white lace-up shoes accessorised nicely and a white gardenia completed the outfit.[9]

For those brides determined to have the full indulgence of a formal white wedding dress, help was at hand. Romance novelist Barbara Cartland promoted a wedding-dress-hire scheme. Eleanor Roosevelt – First Lady of the United States – oversaw something similar for British and European women who married American servicemen. These were famously known as G.I. brides. Lord Nuffield, founder of Morris Motor Co. arranged for 200 dresses to be made in America for the use of anyone in the British Armed Forces who was unable to obtain coupons for a dress. They were stored in a London warehouse and could be borrowed with twenty-four hours' notice.[10] An enterprising nurse decided she wanted a film-star dress so she wrote to Gainsborough Studios in London begging for the loan of an Elizabethan gown. A week later she

Mary and George Bennett's wedding photos from July 1941 were colourised afterwards, with lovely pastel tints. Popular fabrics for British wartime weddings were powder-blue crepe and dusky pink crepe.

Above left: *An Air Force couple – WAAF Doreen Lane married in 1943, wearing her uniform, with a corsage and a couple of horseshoes for luck.*

Above right: *Newly-weds from Philadelphia, USA - Agnes Louise Wells née Halbe and Tom Eckle Wells. The bride is wearing a two-piece suit and fabulous white hat instead of a formal gown. Her fiancé wasn't Catholic, as she was, so they couldn't be married in church.*

Above: *Christine Cole's Aunt Nancy (centre) was well known as a 'live wire'. She played lacrosse for England, and loved tennis and hockey. She was also a robust member of the League of Health and Beauty. She took time away from her wartime role as officers' chauffeur, to be married in September 1940.*

Left: *A beautiful lace wedding dress and veil worn by Ann Abbott née Parkinson in 1942.*

had her reply – she could borrow the white Elizabethan gown worn in a recent Flora Robson film, with a matching full length veil.[11]

Lorna Carr née Summerton had her 1948 wedding dress made locally. She obtained the white crepe from an aunt in Windsor who bought it on the black market. Her sister Jean was a bridesmaid in red wool georgette. Showing me a newspaper clipping about the day, Mrs Carr still felt annoyance that the only flowers available to carry were red carnations. 'I *hate* red carnations!' she laughed.[12] There was always the chance of borrowing someone else's dress. In 1945, Lilian Briggs borrowed a wedding dress from her sister, who'd just been jilted by a G.I.[13] Brides on the islands of the Torres Strait browsed fashion catalogues for fashionable dresses and wedding regalia, sending to Brisbane for their purchases.[14]

With silks and satins in short supply it's no wonder many brides resorted to using parachutes for their dress and trousseau. Winifred Smith was a WAAF Parachute Packer. Her best friend was set to marry a French Canadian, and wasn't eligible to borrow an Air Ministry dress as she would be wed abroad. The packers collected ivory silk panels from a 'chute returned from France and began to sew. Just before the final fitting, the illicit dressmaking was discovered when the Duty Officer walked into the Repair Section where the gown was on display. Luckily she was amused to learn why the women had been working so late and full of compliments for the dress.[15]

One of General Montgomery's Eighth Army 'Desert Rats' met his future wife living in an Italian ex-pat community in Alexandria. She was a genteel lady; he was down-to-earth Irish working class. Her wedding dress was of parachute silk with a scalloped hem and long train, decorated with thousands of tiny glass seed beads, each with a silver thread running through.[16]

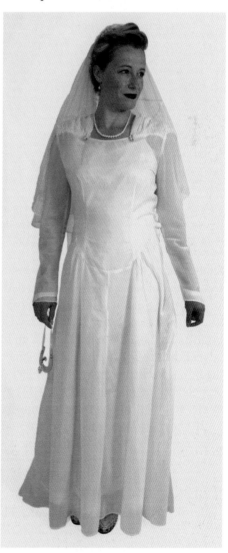

A nylon wedding dress from 1945, sewn from parachute fabric. It is rather transparent, so a white slip is essential. The silver horseshoe was a traditional 'good luck' accessory.

'I got married in the war years, what a scream, the dress was new and cost £5, which was a lot then, the bridesmaid (my sister), her dress was made by our next door neighbour who was a seamstress, it was made out of a parachute dyed a pretty blue.'

War bride Marjorie Norton.[17]

Even when the dress had been safely sewn or sourced there was the threat that it wouldn't survive intact to the wedding. Winifred Keeling's lace dress was shop-bought – 5 guineas from Binns department store in Sunderland. On 7 April 1942, the night before the wedding, there was an air raid. Sitting in the air raid shelter a neighbour said, 'What about your dress? If the house is bombed you'll have no dress for your wedding tomorrow!' They both dashed back to the house to collect the dress and veil, and waited out the air raid with the dress

A 1940s Indian bridal doll, stitched as part of a charity scheme designed – ironically – to generate a modest income for Indian widows.

stretched over the knees of everyone on one side of the shelter, and the veil across the knees of those sitting opposite. Seven decades later the dress was still safe. It went on display in the local church.[18]

Wartime weddings around the world could be solemn, formal affairs, or parties lasting several days involving a whole community. A wedding defied war. By its very nature it looked to a future of companionship and connection, not dislocation and destruction. Of course, not all marriages lived up to the promise of the wedding. Often a young woman was merely being handed from one household to another. In her 1943 novel *War Tide,* Lin Taiyi describes a wedding in Hangchow, just as China faces invasion from the Japanese. The bride's $1,000 trousseau is delivered in the rain: eight trunkfuls of soft red feather quilts, fine dresses and jewels. She barely knows her husband – away in the air force – or her new family. Her married life consists of sewing uniforms for soldiers.

Travelling in the Middle East, propaganda officer Freya Stark encountered several weddings. She described a 1940 Jewish matrimonial in Yemen where the very young bride had her hands stained blue with indigo, her torso loaded with gold necklaces and silver beads as big as eggs. In Palestine, Stark was invited to an Islamic wedding where the bride was hennaed for the holiday and wearing red trousers with a flowing dress of magenta satinette. Stark recalled, 'They seized my hand and I was soon dancing in the circle, stamping and waving a handkerchief and saying *hah* to the beat of the music.'[19]

If the marriage was a joyful union then the whole village could celebrate. Preparations in Palestine might be a female-only affair. The bridal outfit would be brought from town carried on the heads of walking women. The cloth wrapping the clothes would form the bride's veil and then become her girdle. Singing, trilling and hand clapping accompanied the inspection of the bride's new garments, all lavished with silk, cotton, silver or gold cord. The gifts bound makers and recipients. Trousseau items were as practical and symbolic as those of Western brides. By the 1940s, urban Palestinians enjoyed white European-style dresses.[20]

Descriptions of the new bride's going-away outfit was often featured in press reports of the wedding. It symbolised her new start, and it often formed the basis of her wardrobe as a married woman. Suits – known as costumes – were a popular,

This post-war Japanese wedding group shows a fusion of traditional bridal silk kimono, obi and wig for the bride, and Western-style suits for the guests.

practical choice for the going-away outfit. During the war years, British and European honeymoons were often brief. They could be weekends in a seaside boarding house, strolling past barbed-wire coiling on the beaches and wrangling over meat coupons with the landlady. More elaborate trips would have to wait until peacetime. There was also the question of what to wear on the wedding night. Iby Knill, whose trousseau we explored earlier in this chapter, had a silk nightdress and seductive negligee trimmed with marabou feathers. After a luxurious bubble bath she appeared in the bridal suite. Her new husband Bert had passed out drunk. She opened a book and drank the champagne waiting in the ice bucket.[21]

One of the most extraordinary wedding night stories I came across involved Greek nightgowns. Despina, a village woman from the mountains, gave testimony that a new bride still had to give proof of virginity by wearing a gown that went from her chin to her ankles, then showing it the next morning to her mother-in-law. Blood stains on the gown were supposed to prove the breaking of the hymen. One bride with an unstained gown was thrown out of the house, her clothes were tossed after her, and she was sent back to her home village.[22]

1945 wedding of Elsie Patient and Geoffrey McGarry. On their Golden Wedding anniversary Elsie slipped into her dress once more, and, like Cinderella's slipper – it fit! Afterwards it went back in the 1940s utility wardrobe where it had been stored for so many years.

Elsie Patient married Geoffrey McGarry on 10 June 1945. She was an immensely vivacious and creative woman despite learning to adapt to disabilities as a child. Geoff adored her. His diary entries about the wedding are charming, detailed and loving: 'At last the most important day of our life had dawned and it was raining. Nothing dampens the wonderful excitement of the day. We smiled and I stared with silent admiration at her frock, the beautifully cut vee neck. The two doves in her hair with orange blossom was a wonderful idea … . It was lovely to dance with Elsie in her white frock flowing round her … . At last I was alone with Elsie and we kissed our first kiss of married life. It was a very enjoyable journey … .' Their first night of married life took place in their new home. Geoff had decorated the bedroom with flowers and set out her new nightie of white satin trimmed with red, white and blue to match her camiknickers. The moment was slightly marred by the lights fusing, with Elsie and Geoff chasing round to fix things in their dressing gowns. Geoff concluded his journal entry: 'I went to bed with my darling Elsie for the first time and glorious sleep swept over us both. It was an end to our wedding day which had been successful in every way. Nothing could have been better it was just perfect as we wanted it.'[23]

If they were lucky, the wedding was the start of a couple's long married life together. Those who survived the war had to hope initial romance and shared goals would help

Maureen McNeil-Smith married in 1944 wearing a white taffeta dress – 12 yards of fabric brought from Canada by her RAF fiancé Alan. Her going-away outfit was a brown dress and jacket and 'Mrs Miniver' hat. The honeymoon was spent in Edinburgh and it rained five days out of the seven. The trains were all having problems and it took them eleven hours to get back home - travelling overnight – and arriving very tired and hungry.[24]

them overcome the inevitable difficulties of reconnecting after wartime separation. Former WAAF nurse, Eileen Little, faced the long sea voyage from England to Canada to reunite with her husband who lived in a remote farming community on the west coast. She began married life by packing away the ball gowns, evening shoes and fur wraps she'd so optimistically brought with her. Furs and woollens were now her daily essentials, in a house with no bathroom and no running water.[25]

In February 1945, a bridal couple were spotted setting off together on the Paris Metro. The groom wore a rented suit with a white button hole. The bride was ready for winter weather in a white raincoat, white rubber boots, white sweater and skirt, and white turban. The couple were holding hands. A group of American soldiers across the train tracks shouted good wishes to them. The rest of their story is unknown.[26]

Chapter 15

ROCKING THE CRADLE
Maternity and childcare

'I dried the swaddling clothes on my body. I would put them in my
bosom, warm them up and swaddle the baby. Everything
around us was burning.'[1]

Maria, a Russian partisan who gave birth to a baby girl while hiding in
a swamp in 1943.

Crossing by ferry to the island of Zanzibar one bright January morning I watched passengers with their luggage. I carried only my tourist kitbag. Local travellers were loaded with big laundry bags, fridges, mattresses – and babies. It struck me how remarkable mothers are, to do everything that needs to be done with a baby on a hip, or in a pram, or swaddled to the back; with toddlers exploring their limits; with older children growing and questing. Parenting is a demanding job at the best of times, made so much worse by war. While absent fathers might have missed their children and worried about their welfare during the 1940s, the mother was left to draw on all resources to protect, clothe and nourish her young ones, often in the face of terrible adversity.

A Japanese mother proudly cuddles her child – names unknown. 'Having babies is fun,' declared Katsuko Tojo, mother to seven children and wife of Japan's prime minister. In Japan child rearing was seen as a public matter and a patriotic duty. Laws assisted impoverished single mothers; the state sponsored match-making agencies to encourage procreation in marriage.

Memoirs of the Second World War show wonderful moments of joy and play between parents and children, as well as countless instances of enduring love and sacrifice. Scenes of mothers parting from children being evacuated still have the power to move the modern viewer to tears, as do images of children clinging to their loved ones in the shadows of the bombs, or at the end of a rifle barrel.

In propaganda of the 1930s and '40s, images of strong, weaponised men were regularly set in contrast to vulnerable, nurturing women. This was partly to encourage mobilisation – giving men something for fight for when military leaders wanted to attack or defend. It was also to reinforce social structures built up around the biological role of motherhood. Women's primary duties were to be mothers, carers and consumers, with domesticity and community as their hub. For example, Mussolini's fascist state glorified pictures of fresh young rural mothers in peasant costumes, untainted by the feminism and artifice supposedly spoiling town girls in Italy. There was no pageant of older, exhausted mothers in baggy black dresses and aprons. The Italian National Olympic Committee even controlled female sport participation, fearing women would be distracted from their fundamental mission – maternity.[2]

Both idealised images and the daily realities of motherhood reveal a great deal about a nation's attitude to women, to wider gender roles and to race. Universally, mothers were held up as an ideal of womanhood, yet invisible in most histories. They were essentially unrewarded at a civic level and unremunerated except with what the father chose to give. Mothers were often considered guardians of the household, yet required to work outside the home if the war economy demanded it and given little legal protection in the domestic sphere they supposedly presided over. Birth control was frowned upon if a nation needed higher birth rates – ironically, in the 1940s and '50s, to replace those killed by war – but terrible state measures could also be imposed to stop the reproduction of people considered racially or mentally 'unfit'.

The modern mother is to be 'slim, active and never over-tired' according to this Beechams pills advert. It would take more than pep pills to counteract the strain of parenting in wartime.

In Hitler's Germany those deemed 'worthy' of reproduction were supported by a comprehensive system of social and medical support, as celebrated by these Reich stamps commemorating ten years of state support for mothers and children.

Nazi Germany is a complex and often chilling example of attempted state control of birth patterns. The infamous T4 euthanasia program carried out forced sterilisation of patients with mental and physical disabilities, and eventually condoned their murder. State-promoted anti-Semitism evolved into legally sanctioned segregation, deportation and mass murder, with any groups categorised as 'sub-human' to be targeted, including

Roma and Sinti gypsy families, Slavic eastern Europeans and Jews. Iron sculptures of shoes on the banks of the Danube river in Budapest are mute testament to the 20,000 people believed to have been murdered there. The children's shoe sculptures are now found filled with flowers and sweets, to commemorate the brutal loss.

Conversely, the Third Reich's gendered division of roles gave 'acceptable' mothers highly focused support through the *Frauenschaft* Women's Bureau and numerous other welfare organisations. Gertrud Scholtz-Klink, leader of the *Frauenschaft*, was proud that motherhood courses had already benefited over 1.6 million women by 1938. Thousands of women were mobilised to staff clinics, promote maternal welfare and support families. Some of the welfare was racially orientated – such as tolerating single mothers as long as the father was Aryan – and some was a genuine belief that dividing society into male and female spheres was for the best.[3] Mothers dreaded the labour service and excursions of the girls' youth group *Bund Deutscher Mädel,* Madel, since an estimate 50 per cent of the girls came home pregnant.[4] Birth control was prohibited. In the Third Reich the essential female role was breeding and nurturing.

In her powerful essay, *Three Guineas,* Virginia Woolf touched on one of the fundamental issues of war – it glorifies male combat and leadership, and puts parenting in jeopardy. Comparing the gaudy uniforms of Great War military and civil leaders, Woolf wryly noted: 'A woman who advertised her motherhood by a tuft of horsehair on the left shoulder would scarcely, you will agree, be a venerable object.' Hitler's Germany was one of the few countries in the world that paid more than lip service to the idea of honouring motherhood, awarding the *Mutterkreuz* - or Mother's Cross – from 1938. There was a bronze medal for mothers of four children; silver for six and gold for eight or more children. Only Aryans were eligible of course. An estimated

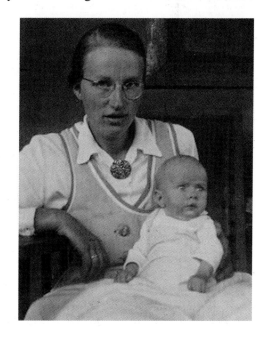

Gertrud Mampe, pictured here with her first child Kurt in 1939, was a qualified teacher of agriculture in Germany, also working for two years at an uncle's farm in Namibia. She moved to Colombia with her husband Rudolf in the 1930s. When his export business was halted in the 1940s, Gertrud rallied by growing and selling vegetables to support the growing family. She even managed to spare money to send home to relatives struggling in Germany. Evenings were spent knitting for the war effort, inspired by her strong belief in the family ideals of the Third Reich. Gertrud's mother was a committed leader of the Nazi Women's Bureau in Germany, who handed herself in to be interned war by the Russians, dying in captivity. Two of Gertrud's children died young.

Attractive

Maternity Frocks

Salons: *Third Floor*

Moss Crepe

21/ML/19. *A charming Dress in heavy quality Moss Crepe which tailors so beautifully. It has a becoming new neckline and excellent adjustment. In Navy, Firmament Blue, and Wine.*

£8.7.8

(7 Coupons).

Spot Rayon

21/ML/29. *A trim little Frock, youthfully styled in good quality spot Rayon, with a clever adjustment to preserve perfect balance. Rose, Red, Powder Blue, Navy, all with white spots.*

£3.1.5

(7 Coupons).

Housecoat

21/ML/39. *Practical in Wool of useful weight for present wear, cut on graceful slimming lines. Ideal to wear at home, and it will pack easily too. In Carnation Red, Pastel Blue, Summer Green, and Gold. In Medium Women's size only.*

£4.17.7

(8 Coupons).

DRESSING GOWNS
Salons: THIRD FLOOR

Please state normal hip measurement in each case.
A personal visit is advised to see the variety of styles specially designed for the mother-to-be.

Derry &Toms
Kensington

Telegrams: Derrys, Kensington, London

This advert for maternity wear from Derry and Tom's department store is typical of the era. Illustrations always show young, white, slim mothers-to-be with slender waistlines. The housecoat is 'cut on graceful slimming lines'. The spotted dress has 'clever adjustment to preserve perfect balance' – the pockets are higher.

4 million German mothers earned the medal. They were to receive the same privileges as war wounded.[5] Alongside this cultish worship of motherhood, there was also a pragmatic acceptance that women were needed for industrial labour and in education, particularly once men were mobilised en masse.

This same need for women to be carers at home yet labourers in the economy is seen in most of the countries affected by war. Cultures demonised spinsterhood and promoted a happy ideal of motherhood. Babies were seen as an investment for a brighter future. Young single women were expected to be attractive enough to raise morale but not to lower morals. The now-or-never mentality that characterised a lot of wartime couplings inevitably flagged up a sexual double standard – women were promiscuous if they got pregnant; men were simply being men. Condoms were issued to military men for use with sex-workers and girlfriends, but they were essentially to protect the men from venereal diseases. The women were left with the baby – and the judgement.[6]

A certain coyness characterises advertising for pregnancy wear. Maternity wear is first sold commercially in Britain during the Great War, usually in relatively upmarket magazines. By the 1940s, there's still a reluctance to talk frankly about maternity, or to depict it. Images of storks and cradles are pleasant euphemisms. Maternity clothes were definitely designed to conceal. Commercial maternity dresses were usually limited to designs with tie-waists that can be let out, or voluminous shirt styles. Women resorted to smock tops, often home-made, although in Britain Marks and Spencer's produced cotton smocks in zinging colours and patterns.

Wartime pattern catalogues from the Leach/Way company advised expectant mothers: 'Don't make do with old clothes, stretching them here, letting them in a bit there, feeling and looking depressingly turned out; instead, make new – then make over the garments into smaller sizes after you have regained your figure.' There were no extra coupons for pregnant women in Britain.

'Attractive youthful styles concealing your secret. Easily adjusted without alterations. Adaptable for after wear.'

Advert for Maxlim maternity gowns, *Vogue*, February 1949.

Mary Firth, a WAAF nurse during the war, was pregnant in 1948. We chatted together over coffee and cake one afternoon and she confessed she'd made a maternity dress out of her father's kilt, telling me 'you didn't flaunt pregnancy in those days.' Her father merely commented at the time, 'A lot's gone on under that kilt but not *that*.' Mrs Lorna Carr's face lit up during our conversation about maternity wear in the war years. She had a well-loved Jaeger tweed coat for pregnancy – dark green with orange checks. The sides eventually split after the third child.

> 'The dress was lovely; small black and white checks with a small jacket. The jacket hid the stomach a little. And it was trimmed in black velvet. A magical dress. And right for the purpose.'
>
> Marianne Karlsruhen describes an outfit chosen to hide her pregnancy in 1944. She was German, unmarried and in love with a half-Jewish man, Peter. Marianne and Peter were joyfully reunited just after their daughter was born at the end of the war. (Owings, *Frauen*)

Pregnancy could be a lonely time. Nora Brown conceived her daughter Judith on honeymoon in August 1939. War was declared shortly afterwards and Nora's husband was sent from England to Canada then New York on government business. Nora wasn't allowed to join him until the baby was born. She give birth in a Home for Mothers and Babies with no visitors. Her husband sent frequent insistent cables for her to leave England (he was privy to knowledge of Hitler's impending invasion). Nora sailed from Liverpool with her newborn and a trunk containing wedding presents.[7]

Other women were undeterred from joining their partners on military expeditions. Ethiopian women famously gave birth on the march as unofficial army auxiliaries, nursing their babies en route.[8] There are accounts of Ethiopian women fighting while pregnant. These are matched by stories from the Soviet Union. Stalin reversed female-friendly policies concerning birth control and safe abortions mid-war – the need to encourage new births was necessary for post-war reconstruction. Women still needed to do their patriotic duty if pregnant. Two examples give an idea of the challenges facing Red Army mothers a cryptographer suffered the anguish of an illegal abortion because she couldn't give birth on the job. A radio operator gave birth while hiding, with comrades, from German hunting dogs. When the hungry baby became dangerously noisy she was forced to drown it to protect them all.[9]

Dorothy Kelly, a midwife in Britain, would cycle to deliver babies in the blackout, with a tin helmet on her head and a gas mask over her shoulder.[10] Babies ready to be born did not wait for the All Clear of bomb raids, or for when a nice layette was prepared. Newborns who arrived in traumatic conditions needed to be cleaned, fed and clothed. It is a great testament to human love to read of people rallying round after a birth in extreme circumstances. In Malta, a young mother hid under a hospital bed as bombs made window glass shatter all around them. She tore strips of white towelling for nappies.[11] Prisoners in Ravensbrück concentration camp wrapped a baby in paper and rags, marvelling at the miracle of its survival as pregnant women were usually murdered on arrival at the camps…or taken for hideous experimentation.[12] Doctors at the women's hospital in Warsaw tended babies hit with shrapnel during a bombardment.[13]

An Eritrean welfare clinic pamphlet with instructions in Tigrinya language on how to bath a baby. New mothers needed helping learning the basics of childcare. Training was offered to girls from the bush wanting to learn maternity work. The midwives would then walk to attend births across a wide area with only the equipment they could carry by hand.[14]

After the wonder of a successful birth came the endless cycle of washing and drying nappies, when cloth could be in short supply, soap was rationed and hot water limited. American wartime advice on washing diapers gives an idea of labour involved. Scrape first, rinse in cold water and soak in a pail; use a plunger to work suds through the cloth; place in the washing machine – this was manually operated – with thick hot

European mothers in India readily devolved day-to-day childcare to Indian women. The sari-clad Ayah here is Mona, taking care of baby Elizabeth Walker, born 1945, and her siblings. The Walker family also employed a Tibetan nanny while living in North Bihar.

211

suds; rinse, sterilise in lukewarm water with acetic acid. Rinse. Boil thoroughly twice a week. Dry in the sun and fold.[15] In bunkers of bombed-out cities there was little water for drinking and almost no washing facilities.

'War or peace, most mothers like to knit their babies' clothes themselves. They are very quickly done, and the making of them provides a restful occupation.' (Chase, *Sew and Save*)

Ingenuity was required to clothe growing children. Eileen Webster was an English housewife who sewed for the family at home, unpicking old dresses exchanged for butter or margarine coupons.[16] Iris Origo, managing a farm in Italy, spun their sheep's wool and made it into babies' jackets for the local hospital. She also made clothes and nappies out of old sheets and curtain linings.[17] Women around the world turned old frocks into romper suits, and cut trousers down into boys' shorts. The ever-efficient WVS went to extraordinary lengths to help clothe thousands of evacuees and refugees at short notice. The Central Hospital Supply Service in Britain supplied an army of volunteers to make children's clothing, issuing over 2 million buttons, a quarter-of-a-million knitting patterns and nearly a 100 thousand needles.

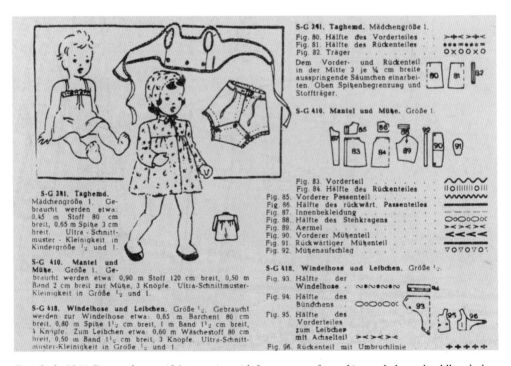

Detail of a 1944 German housewife's magazine with free patterns for making up baby and toddler clothes.

STRETCH, BEND, AND TOUCH YOUR TOES

As free as air to bend as you like — that's you in your 'Liberty' Foundation. The 'Liberty' Bodice for the "under-sixteen", or the 'Liberty' Corselette for the grown up, is so soft and well-cut that you forget you have it on.

'LIBERTY' SLIP-ON BODICE

Rubber buttons for suspenders. Infants to 16 years, 1/0¾ to 2/6½ Also in All Wool.

'LIBERTY' SLIP-ON CORSELETTE

Tea-Rose and White. Small, Medium and Large Sizes. Also in Celanese Locknit. Art Silk, 3/6.

'Liberty'

FOUNDATIONS

from Childhood to Womanhood

Should you have any difficulty in obtaining 'Liberty' Garments, or if you would like an illustrated catalogue, write to 'Liberty' Foundations, 14, Libertyland, Market Harborough, for the name of the nearest stockist. EIRE enquiries to 33, Clanbrassil Street, Dundalk.

British girls often wore the fleecy corset-equivalent known as the Liberty bodice. It had buttons to hold up stockings, carefully placed seams to give structure and rubber buttons that were very fiddly for young fingers.

Left: *Young girls were usually dressed in frocks and bows regardless of temperament or activity. Elsie Walton, pictured here, much preferred Meccano sets to mothering toys and was happiest playing outside.*

Opposite: *Promoting the evergreen myth that menstruating women adore vigorous activity in white clothes, this advert for Tampax tampons is also educational – disarming popular wariness of internal sanitary products. Obtaining any kind of sanitary protection was exceedingly difficult. They were not luxury items. Brands such as Mene, Kotas and Modess offered washable towels, as well as Terry towelling pads. These were fastened to a maternity belt with loops or clips. If no commercial products were available women were economical and practical, fashioning sanitary napkins from cotton wool balls, knitted string, torn sheets, curtain cords or burlap sack thread.*

Knitting needles were in constant motion, producing clothes and blankets to keep children warm. Hildegard Schwartzdahl, growing up in Paderborn, Germany, remembers wearing knitted underwear, also red and blue knee socks called *gamaschenhosen*. These were like tights, held up at the waist by elastic. At school one day, Hildegard's teacher made her stand on the desk, declaring 'It was a sensible mother who dressed this child.'[18]

War, separation, hardships and shortages compounded post-birth baby blues. Sometimes a treat was needed. British mother Joyce Storey felt the desolation of bringing up a baby alone in lodgings while her husband served with the RAF. Her landlady forbade her from washing nappies on Sunday – 'the Lord's Day'. A friend offered to make her a new dress from a roll of moss green jersey fabric acquired on the black market. It was cut with a slight flare and a Peter Pan collar. 'Having that dress meant so much to me,' Joyce wrote in her memoir, 'a kind of reward now the long months of pregnancy were over, and I wanted to feel attractive again.'[19]

In some ways, war forced governments to appreciate the hardships of motherhood. If they needed women with children to work full-time to support war industries then they had to provide childcare facilities. Without children there'd be no future nation to fight for. British working mothers were likened to the defenders of Stalingrad, fulfilling their obligations against massive odds.[20] I suspect many of them would have been proud to be told this – or perhaps they would have preferred a cup of tea and quiet sit down.

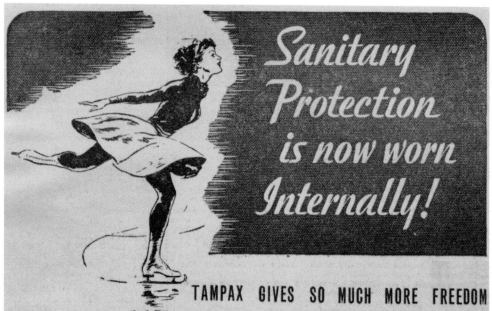

TAMPAX GIVES SO MUCH MORE FREEDOM

Be rid of all the discomfort, embarrassment and handicaps of those trying, critical days! Tampax sanitary protection worn internally enables you to feel as comfortable and carefree as on any other day of the month.

A doctor's own invention—adapted from the tampon used in medical and hospital practice—Tampax is recommended by doctors as a far more hygienic, comfortable and sensible method of sanitary protection. Women everywhere are welcoming it as the greatest boon and blessing in the history of feminine hygiene!

Try Tampax once—and you'll never return to the bulky old-fashioned methods of the past again! A packet containing a month's supply of Tampax costs 1/6, and slips easily into your handbag. Full instructions are enclosed. Tampax may confidently be used by all normal women. Some young girls may not find it possible to use Tampax, and should do so only after consultation with their doctor.

WARNING *This doctor's invention has been patented and registered under the trade mark TAMPAX to protect the public against inferior imitations. TAMPAX alone has the patented central stitching process which ensures complete removal.*

NO BELTS
★
NO PINS
★
NO PADS

TAMPAX *Sanitary Protection*

REGD. TRADE MARK *Prices: 1/6, 1/- and 6d.*

WORN INTERNALLY

TAMPAX **is sold by Boots,** TIMOTHY WHITES & TAYLORS, *and all other good-class Chemists.* HARRODS, SELFRIDGES, LEWIS'S LTD., *all good departmental stores and drapers, and* WOOLWORTH STORES, MARKS & SPENCER LTD., BRITISH HOME STORES, LTD., LITTLEWOODS LTD. **TAMPAX Ltd., 10 Bolton St., London, W1**

Chapter 16

RUNNING FOR COVER
Air raids and recovery

'It is very odd to be torn from one's deepest sleep as through the open window comes the dreadful hollow howling of the siren, a ghastly sound promising death. One jumps out of bed, pulls on garments with trembling fingers, stuffs a few precious things into a small suitcase, takes a blanket and pillow and dashes for the lift.'[1]

Mathilde Wolff-Mönckeberg, German housewife

Whitaker's Almanac of 1940 announced the Uranium Atom Split, following the work of Professor Otto Hahn, Dr Lise Meitner and Professor Enrico Fermi. The piece concluded, 'One of the most striking facts of the experiment was the relatively small amount of energy needed to liberate the enormous amount of energy obtained.'

Mid-twentieth century Japanese cotton kimono fabric showing paper lanterns. In the aftermath of bomb raids, fire from incendiaries, lanterns and hearths spread quickly in the wooden buildings of densely packed Japanese streets.

Standing under a cloudless sky in Hiroshima, one morning in 1994, I looked up at the big blue and tried to imagine the same scene on 6 August 1945, as the US bomber *Enola Gay* crossed the sky to deliver its atomic payload. The 'enormous amount of energy' from the single bomb dropped was enough to obliterate solid buildings and vaporise human beings, leaving their shadows burned onto concrete. Thermal rays set clothes aflame over a mile from the epicentre. On one victim these rays burned through the dark-coloured parts of her kimono, searing the fabric pattern onto her skin. Rikio Yamane, a PE instructor described the aftermath: 'Soon I found myself watching, like some hellish marathon, a procession of ghastly, inhuman figures fleeing from the city. Their burned skin had peeled and was dangling in shreds. Shirts had been ripped to tatters and appeared more like night garments.'[2]

This chapter explores life under the bombs for civilians around the world during the war, looking at how to prepare for an air raid, how to endure life in a shelter; how women were a crucial part of emergency response teams and how women attempted to rebuild their lives in the rubble.

Naval bombardments and aerial bomb raids by Zeppelin and aeroplane had been a shocking feature of the Great War. In the 1930s, the world media gave ample warning of how modern warfare was waged, reporting on devastating bomb attacks in Spain, Ethiopia and China. Martha Gellhorn, war correspondent during the Spanish Civil War, described the aftermath of a bomb raid, seeing fly-blown corpses in the road, 'and then, a sewing machine, blown out onto the street.... The whole place was infinitely dead.'[3] The blasted sewing machine is a stark reminder that the female sphere of 'home' was not safe. Bombs and bullets are no respecters of boundaries. April 1937 saw the deliberate targeting of the Spanish town of Guernica, with staggering death toll and destruction. Ethiopians learned to fear the noise of aircraft engines as invading Italian forces bombed indiscriminately. Shanghai and other Chinese towns trembled under the Japanese onslaught. The year 1939 found many countries still believing that the bombs couldn't possibly shatter their peace. Others, heeding the warnings, began to prepare. By 1940, when bomber planes reached the British mainland,

A 1942 British dressmaking pattern for children's hats also includes a gas mask handbag pattern, which could be made to match your outfit, in leather, velvet or even satin.

217

civilians had already been issued with gas masks, against the possibility of chemical warfare. 'Terrible things they were,' recalled one woman born in the aftermath of the First World War. 'A Tasmanian Devil couldn't have looked any worse.'[4]

Shops quickly stocked thick 'blackout' fabric to comply with regulations against showing light from windows at night. When German bombers reached London, local women were asked to help out making blackout curtains for a particular street. Lengths of material were duly measured. By the time the curtains had been made the houses had already been bombed. In Hamburg, soon to be targeted by British bombers, one housewife wrote to her daughter: 'To begin with we stuck black paper over all the windows and doors and it felt as if we were sitting in a large coffin.'[5] European cities saw civilians wearing white gloves for the blackout, or walking with white shirt tails hanging out. Metal and fabric flower brooches painted with luminous paint were a new fashion accessory.

In the Pacific islands, Polynesian women were warned not to wear brightly coloured lavalavas – the traditional wrap skirt – in case they were spotted by enemy planes. Shopkeepers shared rolls of dark-coloured cloth – 'pale-brownish material,' recalled one islander. 'Something like canvas, really strong but it was hot.' The warning was not an over-reaction. A fisherwoman on Mabuiag Island quickly stripped off the red silk dress she was wearing when a plane passed over the lagoon three times.[6]

In threatened areas, whole communities worked to build air raid shelters. A few examples set the scene. On the Japanese mainland, women and children worked at this task. Sulochana Simhadri, a schoolgirl in Vizagapatam, on the Indian east coast, remembers digging trenches in her house, 'deep in the garden and covered with planks and palm leaves.'[7] Moscow residents, unexpectedly threatened by the Germans' lightning advance in 1941, were advised to jump in a ditch or lie down if they heard the 2-3 second warning of a bomb. Under Hitler in the 1930s, the Germans themselves had ample time to prepare for war. Air raid shelters were obligatory in all Berlin buildings from February 1936. Air raid and blackout tests were common. When the war reached the German heartland, civilians were already prepped with supplies of rags and water cans, to use as a moistened filter against the smoke of spreading fires.

Civilians quickly learned how to set their clothes out when they went to bed so they'd be ready for getting dressed in a hurry. Sometimes, in a panic, it was just a question of grabbing the clothes and dashing to the shelter. What to wear in an air raid is hardly a frivolous question, given the need to be half-decent and protected from the elements. The wail of the siren brought a terrible disconnect between the expected peace of civilian life and the indiscriminate damage of war. It's not surprising that many people clung to their sense of identity through familiar clothes. Writer Eileen Chang described this phenomenon in her 1944 short story *From the Ashes*. When a dormitory of students is bombed in Shanghai, one girl – Suleika – lugged a heavy leather trunk of her most lavish clothes to safety. Even while working in the defence force as a Red Cross nurse, Suleika wore a fancy silk gown, embroidered with Chinese characters for longevity. 'What a waste,' comments the story narrator, 'but for her it was all worth it. This smart outfit endowed her with an unprecedented confidence.'[8]

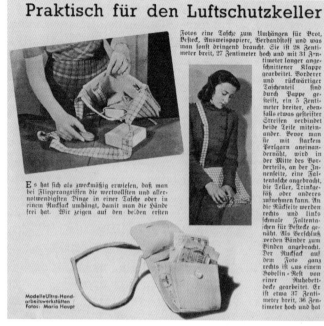

Praktisch für den Luftschutzkeller

Fotos eine Tasche zum Umhängen für Brot, Besteck, Ausweispapiere, Verbandstoff und was man sonst dringend braucht. Sie ist 28 Zentimeter breit, 27 Zentimeter hoch und mit 31 Zentimeter langer angeschnittener Klappe gearbeitet. Vorderer und rückwärtiger Taschenteil sind durch Pappe gesteift, ein 5 Zentimeter breiter, ebenfalls etwas gesteifter Streifen verbindet beide Teile miteinander. Bevor man sie mit starkem Perlgarn aneinandernäht, wird in der Mitte des Vorderteils, an der Innenseite, eine Faltentasche angebracht, die Teller, Trinkgefäß oder anderes aufnehmen kann. An die Rückseite werden rechts und links schmale Faltentaschen für Bestecke genäht. Als Verschluß werden Bänder zum Binden angebracht. Der Rucksack auf dem Foto ist ganz rechts aus einem Gobelin-Rest von einer Ruhebettdecke gearbeitet. Er ist etwa 37 Zentimeter breit, 36 Zentimeter hoch und hat

einen 14 Zentimeter breiten Boden und ebenso breite Seitenteile. Die der Rückwand angeschnittene Klappe reicht bis zum unteren Rand und wird durch Stoffriemen und Schnallen geschlossen. Sehr praktisch ist die der Vorderseite aufgesteppte, etwa 20 Zentimeter hohe, 25 Zentimeter breite Faltentasche, die in der Mitte durch Steppnaht geteilt und durch eine Klappe geschlossen ist. Etwa 11 Zentimeter breite, 20 Zentimeter hohe Faltentaschen sind auch den Seitenteilen aufgesteppt. Links unten zeigen wir noch einen Brustbeutel zur Aufnahme von wichtigen Papieren, Geld und Fotos. Die ganze Länge des auseinandergenommenen Beutels beträgt, mit angeschnittener Klappe, 10,5 Zentimeter, zusammengelegt ist er 16,5 Zentimeter hoch. Die Breite ist 12 Zentimeter. Die vordere Hälfte hat eine aufgesteppte, in senkrechter Richtung mehrmals durchgesteppte 10,5 Zentimeter hohe Faltentasche. An der Rückseite dieser Tasche ist von innen ein gesteifter, 13 Zentimeter hoher, an den oberen Ecken abgerundeter Taschenteil aufgesteppt. Zur Aufnahme eines Ausweises oder Bildes steppt man der Rückwand einen mit Stoff bezogenen 1,5 Zentimeter breiten Rahmen an drei Seiten auf, die obere Seite bleibt zum Einschieben offen. Knopf und Knopfloch dienen als Schluß. An den oberen Ecken sind flache Ösen befestigt, durch die Schnur zu ziehen ist.

Es hat sich als zweckmäßig erwiesen, daß man bei Fliegerangriffen die wertvollsten und allernotwendigsten Dinge in einer Tasche oder in einem Rucksack umhängt, damit man die Hände frei hat. Wir zeigen auf den beiden ersten

Modelle Ultra-Handarbeitswerkstätten
Fotos: Maria Haupt

Not a fashion accessory, a bag for survival. The January 1944 issue of Das Blatt der Hausfrau *(The Housewife's Journal) shows how to make a practical bag or rucksack for the air raid shelter. It features internal pockets for bread, papers and emergency necessaries.*

Most people were pragmatic when choosing air raid clothes. Japanese mothers made their children special padded cotton air raid hoods called *bokuzuki*. The Japanese government exhorted civilians to 'Carry something white at night'. Patterns for air raid suits suggested a touch of red for femininity: red underwear was also considered lucky for Japanese women.

Dorothy Blewitt, only 5 years old when the bombing of England began, remembers 'mothers going to jumble sales to look for clothes that could be made over. They especially looked for old coats which could be turned and made into siren suits for the children for when we had to go into the air raid shelters.'[9]

Siren suits are perhaps the most famous British garment of the war, and a dramatic contrast to the everyday female fashion of frocks and skirts. The 1946

A 1942 siren suit pattern with matching gas mask holder, showing trousers gathered at the ankle, a practical zip fastening and a roomy pocket.

novel *Miss Ranskill Comes Home* describes a spinster heroine surviving shipwreck on a desert island, only to be rescued and returned to England in the middle of the Blitz. She encounters a siren suit for the first time, worn by her hostess, Mrs Bostock: 'She pushed her hands into the pocket of a blue-serge garment that reminded Miss Ranskill of the one-piece pyjama suits worn by small children. "I'm sure I don't know what I should ever have done without this one, though my husband did pretend to be shocked when I bought it. "You'll be going into rompers next," he said."'[10]

Jantzen manufacturers claimed their siren suit was 'simplicity itself to doff or don' using zip fastening throughout: 'The ideal suit for any emergency.' Speedy dressing was obviously crucial. However, Marjorie Pugh, a teenager in Birmingham during the war, admitted that when the air raid siren went off she rushed to shelter so quickly she forgot to put her new siren suit on. An elderly aunt in Norwich was rather less speedy during a raid on the town. Passing a truck which had spilled tins of condensed milk onto the road, this redoubtable lady stopped to gather up the treasure, stuffing it in her baggy knickers.[11]

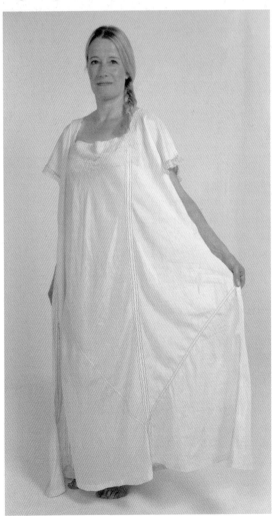

High-end French designers soon capitalised on the need for air raid fashion, known as *Tout ce qu'il Faut pour Descendre a l'Abri* (Everything you need for going down to the shelters). Couture collections in Paris featured padded waistcoats, fleecy hoods and wool jersey siren suits. Bettina Ballard, *Vogue* editor, noted that her maid set out slacks, sweater, tennis shoes and a flashlight along with night clothes: 'This was her idea of the proper garb for a *Vogue* editor to wear in an air raid

This nightgown is made entirely from parachute silk, the original seams incorporated into the design, with a touch of lace at the chest. One victim of a bombing raid on Malta wore a similar silk nightgown, given to her by a legendary daredevil pilot, who later joked she should have trusted to her 'parachute' and escaped from her wrecked flat by jumping from the window.[13]

An improvised family shelter on the island of Malta, heavily bombarded and under siege.

shelter.' Ballard thought Molyneux and Piguet made very chic air raid costumes, and considered Piguet's jersey suit the forerunner for Churchill's 'one-piece teddy suit'.[12]

Conditions in air raid shelters were challenging, particularly for those caring for elderly relatives or young children and babies. Sing-a-longs and 'Spirit of the Blitz' could only go so far to alleviate the discomfort of nightly vigils in damp, overcrowded, verminous and unsanitary shelters. Savitri Choudary, married to a doctor in Kent, recalled sleeping in an Anderson shelter in the garden with her husband and children 'like primitive cavemen and women, hoping and praying that they wouldn't drop their load on us.'[14]

Boredom was a big problem, Wren Roxane Houston said her fellow naval friends 'brought out yards of knitting which grew in length and inaccuracy the fiercer the raids became.'[15] Not only was knitting soothing for frazzled nerves, it could also produce the warm clothes so desperately needed while sheltering in winter. Weldon's knitting series capitalised on this, offering patterns for *Quick-Change Siren Woollies*, included a hooded jacket, a child's shelter suit, Norwegian mittens and a baby's shelter bag.

Bombs were great social levellers, with rich and poor sheltering together wherever they could find safety. Catacombs, sewers and even palace dungeons were used as bunkers. A refugee in a Rome shelter described slum families mingling with an ancient princess wearing three rows of pearls and carrying the family jewels.[16] Taking

221

the jewels was no mere snobbish vanity. Valuables had to be kept safe from the bombs and from looting. It's fascinating to see just what people consider too precious to be left behind. A young boy remembered his mother during the Coventry bomb raid taking her knitting bag, insurance policies and the pet budgie.[17] In Cologne, one giant suitcase in a bomb cellar fell open to reveal only a black straw hat and a jar of marmalade.[18] A Berlin woman was very particular about saving her mink – and her vacuum cleaner.[19]

Personal safety is another issue rarely mentioned in history books. Sexual predators took advantage of dark nights and confusion, leading some women to disguise themselves in worn and dirty clothes to avoid attention. A German girl in Berlin was even more creative, dressing in trousers and horn-rimmed glasses to pass as male.[20]

As for the looting, it wasn't only professional criminals who targeted unwatched shops and homes. Desperate civilians weren't above helping themselves, once all state

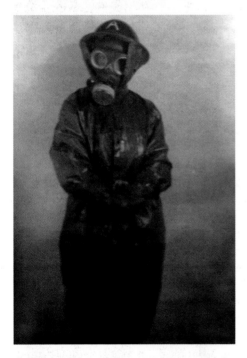

Kathleen Atkins in full Air Raid Precaution kit, including tin helmet and belted, rubberised oversuit. British ARP volunteers – called 'citizen warriors' by writer J.B. Priestley - became known as the Civil Defence after September 1941, at which time there were over 2 million people in action.

The British Civil Defence uniform was a smart dark blue wool with neat badges and lanyards. Many women won decorations for gallantry under fire.

services had disintegrated, although many thefts were presumably minor, such as the Manchester pensioner who was given a one-month sentence for stealing a curtain and a lady's vest from a damaged house.[21]

Women played vital roles for support and emergency services during air raids, ranging from school girls and Girl Guides who helped fire-watch and do basic first aid, to volunteer defence groups and trained firefighters. In Japan Neighbourhood Association groups and the Women's Defence Association – dressed in sashes to show their status – were the backbone of wartime social infrastructure. In Germany, youth groups were tireless in support of bombed areas. In England, keen Air Raid Precaution volunteer Enid Ellis of Birmingham often cycled to her shift in an air raid with shrapnel bouncing off her bike or her 'battle bowler,' as she called her tin helmet. Eileen May Rice, from the heavily bombed city of Hull, was one of 400 local women working in Civil Defence. During a doodlebug explosion, her scarf was blown away. Every Remembrance Day after the war she used to say 'I wonder what happened to my scarf?' Little details such as these fix traumatic memories in the mind.[22]

It took relentless bomb raids to persuade the British government that professional female fire

Londoner Alice Morgan had to knock a good ten years off her age to be accepted into the AFS in 1940. She poses for a portrait in the smart double-breasted coat, tin helmet at the ready.

Some firewomen wore skirts, but after 1943 battledress was common.

officers were acceptable. The Women's Auxiliary Fire Service provided drivers, watchroom workers, clerks, cooks and dispatch riders. Dire shortages of the navy gabardine uniform soon meant the few items issued could not be replaced when worn; they had to be patched like quilts. Some local authorities provided siren suits and duffle coats. From May 1941, the auxiliaries became fully-fledged members of the National Fire Service, wearing their uniforms with pride. At its peak the NFS benefited from 80,000 women.[23]

A fireman at East India Docks set off to attend a blaze at Rum Wharf in September 1941 and encounters a woman of the Auxiliary Fire Service:'Standing nonchalantly by it was a young WAFS, outwardly not taking a blind bit of notice of the stuff that was falling pretty thick all round. Seeing her I strolled past as if I was used to walking out in the middle of falling bombs every Saturday afternoon. We gave each other a sickly smile and I passed on.'

(HMSO, *Frontline*)

Firewoman Marjorie Davies was killed with twelve colleagues when a Balham fire station canteen suffered a direct hit in November 1940. She was given a guard of honour at her funeral.

When the all clear sounded, survivors emerged to assess the devastation. At this point, emergency services were already searching through debris for the living and the dead. Sadly, many human remains could only be identified by their clothes. Small items became the focus of grief for loved ones – the socks and satchels from an infant school in Lewisham that received a direct hit; shoes and torn trousers after a bomb on Cinderella Night Club on Putney High Street, London. Sometimes it was only the clothes that remained, blasted from bodies. Among the debris of a station near Hiroshima after the atomic bomb were shoes, wooden clogs, sandals, sunshades and air raid hoods, 'like the dressing-room during school theatricals,' wrote Matsuo Ibuse in his harrowing novel *Black Rain*. For those under the bombs, the Home Front was as lethal as the front line.

These CC41 pyjamas belonged to Winifred O'Donnell of the Auxiliary Fire Service. Wartime work offered Winifred relief from a stifling family environment. The fire crew slept above the engines, sliding down a pole to the ground floor. In later years Winifred loved to demonstrate her ability to give a fireman's lift. 'Teddykins' is an original 1940s teddy bear crafted out of old cotton lisle stockings, made for a girl called Jenny by her aunt.

'An image from the street: a man pushing a wheelbarrow with a dead woman on top, stiff as a board. Loose grey strands of hair fluttering, a blue kitchen apron. Her withered legs in grey stockings sticking out at the end of the wheelbarrow. Hardly anyone gave her a second glance. Just like when they used to ignore the rubbish being hauled away.' (Anon, *A Woman in Berlin*.)

225

The Italian town of Cassino suffered horrendous, relentless bombing due to the strategic position of a nearby hilltop monastery. When the dust settled, survivors had to rebuild their lives, faced with food shortages, destitution and disease. Refugees from bombed areas lined the roads of Italy, owning only what they wore and what they could carry.

After first aid and shock treatments (usually involving a cup of tea for British survivors), the next priority was to re-clothe victims. This was no mean feat in economies already suffering clothing shortages. Every country rallied to take care of refugees. Among the Western allies, this work was famously undertaken by the Women's Voluntary Service (WVS), essentially an organisation of unpaid housewives who, amongst other duties, acted as shock absorbers after raids.

It was agreed that a WVS uniform would give a sense of identity and communal pride. However, women were encouraged to add their own touches of individuality in the tilt of their hat. This was no military organisation – it went far beyond that in its tireless efforts to help where needed. Rest centres in bombed areas had an iron ration of spare clothes and screens for fitting. If shrapnel were still a threat, WVS members staffed the centres with tin pans and colanders on their heads for protection. Regional clothing depots sent out tens of thousands of garments to affected areas and refuge billets. Generous donations of funds and clothing came pouring in from American, Canadian and New Zealand branches. The WVS then wrestled with the

The Women's Voluntary Service were known as 'Women in Green' because of their uniforms. Other practical colours had already been adopted by the services, so green-grey was chosen. Top couturier Digby Morton created the first uniform designs. However, this WVS dress was dyed and adapted from a civilian dress by its wearer.

226

steel bands that fastened the great bales of donations prepared. They assessed each case and gave out clothes accordingly. It wasn't merely a case of covering flesh or warding off the cold. Being clothed restored some sense of dignity and self-identity to traumatised and homeless survivors. Some had only the clothes they stood up in.[24]

'An elderly Yorkshire woman was having a bath when the house collapsed. Six hours afterwards, when the rescue squads were getting near her, she called out: "Ee, you'll get a surprise, lads. I've nowt on."'
(Graves, *Women in Green*.)

In Germany, the state raised funds and gathered clothing via *Winterhilfe* (winter help) donations. Contributions were as good as obligatory under the watchful eye of Third Reich officials, usually from the Women's Bureau. Hundreds of thousands of garments were requisitioned for civilians after the devastating Bomber Command raids on cities and towns. This was far short of what was required. However, the authorities had other, more sinister, sources to draw on. Goods plundered from Jewish people deported to concentration camps and extermination centres were sorted on site then returned to Germany along the same train lines which had seen the cattle-truck transportations of the rightful owners, most of whom were murdered. It is desperately sad to think of citizens in Essen, Hamburg and Cologne being grateful for new shoes and a new coat, not knowing the origin of their bounty; even sadder to think that some took the goods with full awareness of the provenance. There were muted fears that the bomb raids on German towns were some kind of punishment for mistreatment of Jews.[25]

Not every family was helped by the German War Reparations office. Hildegard Schwartzdahl, a young woman from Paderborn, luckily escaped the total destruction of her home in March 1945. The only help offered came from foreign PoWs who'd been forced to work in the family businesses. Because these foreign workers had been well treated by the Schwartzdahls (against regulations) they now brought the homeless family clothing and food. In her donated outfit – knitted dress, red knee-socks, a brown coat and white jumper – Hildegard had met a friend she'd known since they were in prams. The friend, a seamstress from the local department store, looked her up and down and said, 'Couldn't you dress any better?' Decades later Hildegard was still angry at the thoughtlessness of this comment. 'For forty years I never spoke to her,' she said defiantly, as we took coffee and cake together in a floral sitting room decorated for Christmas.[26]

By the latter years of the war, conditions in Japan were so severe for civilians that some relinquished their clothes just to buy food. Heirloom kimonos were regularly bartered to rural families and farmers to avoid starvation. This was the case for many survivors of the A-bomb. Friends and relatives helped with clothing donations where they could.

This American dressing gown was stitched from 1940s' Japanese kimono fabric, woven with the atomic symbol – an ironic and poignant connection between the two countries linked by atomic bombs.

After the bombs, women had to be resilient for the sake of their families if nothing else Journalist John Hershey wrote a Pulitzer-winning report on the Hiroshima bombing for *The New Yorker* magazine. He collected eyewitness testimonies, including the account of tailor's widow Hatsuyo Nakamura who, having pulled her children from the burning wreckage of her home, next salvaged her sewing machine as it was the symbol of her livelihood. She knew it was essential to work and earn as quickly as possible. At the same time as a Catholic priest in Hiroshima watched a young woman with a needle and thread mending her torn kimono, thousands of miles away a hungry young woman in Berlin was picking summer nettles from the gardens of ruined buildings, elegantly plucking them using the fishnet gloves she'd saved from her air raid gear. Life goes on, with needles and thread and oddments of clothing – all have stories to tell.

Chapter 17

ON CALL
Medical staff

'Once our role was to play the ministering angel, scraping up lint for
bandages. A cool hand on a man's hot brow. At a healthy distance from
the shooting. Now there's no difference between a regular hospital and a
field hospital. The front is everywhere.'[1]

A Berlin journalist, 1945

There was a time when nursing was not considered a respectable profession for women.
The drunken slattern nurse was a familiar caricature in Victorian literature, only
tempered by images from the other end of the spectrum – holy ministering angels who
healed by generic goodness. As ever, reality was
less dramatic and more quietly impressive: for
centuries women were primary caregivers in the
household, aided by oral histories of herb lore,
then printed home medical guides. The duties
of the sickroom were tiring, repetitive and often
repugnant. They did not tally with an stereotype
of delicate femininity that would swoon at the
sight of blood, much less phlegm, pus and faeces.

Scientific medical knowledge was jealously
guarded by a male elite. It was in their interest
to perpetuate the myth that women were not
suitable for the medical profession, despite the
resilient pioneers who proved otherwise. From
the 1850s, Florence Nightingale demonstrated
the potential for female managerial skills in
military hospitals; Mary Seacole also excelled at
hospital care in the Crimea conflict, successfully
applying her own medical remedies and care
regimes. At the start of the twentieth century,
nursing was consciously established as a 'female'
role, thanks in part to Nightingale's robust

Ada Arrowsmith, English Red Cross nurse,
in her uniform and cape, 1942.

229

example and the training school she established for professional nurses. Doctors and surgeons were less visible and far less acceptable – they contradicted claims of female intellectual ineptitude. These old-fashioned attitudes informed recruitment of medical staff during both world wars.

'They were the invisible heroines. They did wonderful, important work without carrying weapons and without making a big fuss. They were the ones who, silently, would be on the front lines during the street battles in Athens, secretly taking the wounded to the hospitals and retrieving the dead for burials.'[2]

Greek relief workers.

Excluded from combat, nursing seemed an excellent way for women to show their allegiance to a cause and to have an active, compassionate contribution during war. Those who volunteered their services during the Spanish Civil War quickly found that the role of ethereal ministering angel was obsolete. The work was tough and bloody. War correspondent Martha Gellhorn was exasperated by unprepared amateurs – 'untrained peroxide blondes with long, brightly coloured nails.' The regular nurses were inevitably nuns, who supported Catholic General Franco.[3] British Medical Unit volunteers quickly acclimatised to extreme temperatures and endurance nursing. Winifred Bates had to wear her blue flannel dressing gown as a shawl until she could acquire a sheepskin jacket. In the winter of 1937-8 she wrote, 'I have slept in all my clothes and my camp eiderdown *and* shivered all night.' Joan Purser, a theatre nurse, found herself washing hospital sheets in a river, but she loved the freedom: 'Spain was the best part of my life. I had no personal possessions, none of this clobber.'[4] British, American, Australian and New Zealand medical staff used the skills and experiences of the Spanish war during the following six years of world war.

'No time for rest – a furtive dab of powder puff, a meal of bread and black coffee, and again all ready for work.'

Nurse Lilian Urmston – veteran of Spain, Dunkirk, Eritrea and Italy, preparing a hospital in a tunnel during a bomb raid. (Fyrth, *Women's Voices of the Spanish Civil War*)

Uniforms were considered essential to promote high standards of hygiene and to instil a professional attitude in nursing staff. White clothing was both a remnant of nursing's origins in Christian religious orders, and it was practical – sturdy white cottons and linens could be boil-washed to kill germs; white showed up dirt quickly. Keeping uniforms clean and neat was a trial in a war zone, particularly the more elaborate starched, white headdresses.

Voluntary Aid Detachment staff had to provide uniforms at their own expense – dresses, aprons, capes, walking out uniforms – with only a small grant towards tropical uniforms. In America, volunteer nursing aides were issued a uniform, an event which fashionista Bettina Ballard considered 'the most depressing day of our training'. She compared her blue-grey summer

Stella Eves trained as a Red Cross nurse aged 18, driving an ambulance during air raids in Southampton. She kept her distinctive apron as a memento of service.

uniform to a loose Chanel style but promptly sent all outfits to a local tailor for alteration, then teamed them with pretty designer blouses for a little touch of vogue – 'not entirely in the group spirit but at least thoroughly feminine'. Ballard had romantic notions about nursing which did not include packing sensible items such as flannel pyjamas or warm underwear for service abroad. Instead she took pink shantung silk pyjamas and a dotted Swiss negligée, along with moisturising creams and hair dye. Her one practical item was a cashmere rug, which was a godsend during North African winter nights. Nursing in Italy brought the bonus of having a Rome dressmaker make up parachute silk into civilian frocks. Mustered out of the Red Cross in July 1945 Ballard commented, 'I took off my uniform with no regret.'[5]

Most Red Cross recruits were not as fashion-orientated as Bettina Ballard. They accepted the new wartime uniform of navy blue gingham dress with turn-down collar and an organdie cap that did not need starching or ironing. The square-bibbed apron clipped into place, to avoid shoulder straps sliding off. In Italy, the Red Cross ensemble was considered the only respectable female uniform. It came complete with blue veils on white headbands. The modesty pleased Mussolini when women marched before him at a Rome rally in 1939.[6] The St John Ambulance Service also provided outstanding auxiliary service worldwide, in very challenging scenarios. In India, for example, they helped those suffering during the famine, they nursed patients during severe epidemics of cholera and malaria, and evacuees from Burma. Some work was in hospitals, some on hospital trains – much was out in the field. The SJA nurse was a familiar sight cycling in Indian towns – 'easy to pick out in her white dress and veil. In winter she wears a short swinging pale-grey cape.'[7]

Colonial attitudes influenced nursing roles, yet the demands of war also broke down social barriers – for the duration of the war at least. In India, rich and poor trained in hygiene, first aid and home nursing. Volunteer medical staff were among the first white women to nurse sepoys, which went contrary to the usual racial segregation. Nurses from different castes and cultures worked alongside each other in the East. One 1945 parade in the grounds of Government House at Singapore saw Chinese, Malayans, Indians and Europeans ranked together. While some were in full uniform, others had only a badge or a button. These were survivors of the Japanese invasion, when to be in any kind of uniform triggered severe treatment from occupying soldiers.[8]

In India, the ANS – Auxiliary Nursing Service – was inaugurated in 1941. It included British, Anglo-Indian and Indian women. They wore a khaki drill overall and khaki cap. Indian nurses could wear a plain khaki sari under the overall. Class and money still created distinctions among nurses. Joan Boss, nursing at an army hospital in Secunderabad, found she was barred from attending the local club unless in uniform, 'which frequently cost nearly a month's salary,' she complained.[9]

While a red cross was an international symbol of aid, war was not always a respecter of medical uniforms, nor the people wearing them. In occupied Warsaw, there were over 4,000 female doctors and nurses staffing first aid posts and providing hundreds of medical patrols during the 1944 Uprising against German forces. When the Germans invaded the Old Town hospital, all staff, including Girl Guide nursing volunteers, were put in rows against the wall and shot. One eyewitness survived to tell of the girls

and women singing the Polish national anthem until the last possible moment. Other Guides worked as nurses in children's homes, as well as running first aid stations in schools, providing medical supplies to the resistance, and organising auxiliary hospitals. It was no game – these Guides could not wear uniforms or earn badges. Those who were captured alive were transported to concentration camps for execution.[10]

Professional medical women were needed on the home front too. Civilians suffered the usual ailments and injuries; babies were born or grew sickly; old age needed special care. Some nurses had been in service before the outbreak of war, trained by old-school veterans of the First World War. Neatness, cleanliness and order were emphasised. There were often strict uniform distinctions between probationers and experienced nurses. Dresses might be coloured differently for each year of progress. Rules about appearance helped reinforce discipline

Young German nurses with short sleeves and white aprons. Nursing took on an acutely nationalistic character during the Nazi era, although recruits were still motivated by the desire to help and heal.

and rank, breaking rebellious tendencies towards individuality and dissension. Matron was the ultimate authority, described by one Irish nurse as 'a terrifying figure as she sits behind her large desk in full regalia – severe navy dress with a stiff starched collar, starched cap with frilly edges and a large bow tied under the medley of chins.'[11]

Military nurses were very much in demand, to be sent where they were needed. When 17-year-old Eileen Little arrived at the RAF recruiting office to be a driver she was told it was nursing or nothing. Modest in later years, Little would only say 'I did some nursing' but she witnessed the terrible injuries of RAF patients, particularly on the 'gangrene ward' with amputees.[12]

Queen Alexandra's Imperial Military Nursing Service (QAIMNS) outfits were particularly splendid, with scarlet and grey outdoor uniforms, or white tropical dresses with scarlet and white epaulettes. These dresses had a dozen round pearl buttons, which had to be taken out of each dress and slotted into a new one for the laundry – and dresses would be changed once a week.

Mary Firth nursed evacuees from Dunkirk, Jamaican WAAFS and PoWs from Japanese camps. She recalled, 'The first patient I had who died, I cried.' To cheer up the patients, wheelchair races were held in long hospital corridors. She said, 'Aircrews were all bursting with energy and dying to get back to the job.'[13]

Hot, damp climates took their toll on white rayon or lisle stockings. New QAIMNS arrivals in India keenly darned stockings during their first monsoon season. After that they learned to request permission to wear white ankle socks. In extreme heat the top two uniform buttons could be undone. Eventually nurses were issued bush shirts and trousers as a protection against mosquitoes. The trousers caused some merriment, since they were male sizes and took some adjusting to fit the female form.[14]

Racial segregation persisted in the US Army Nursing Corps, despite the logistical difficulty of insisting that patient care had to be provided along racial lines. Three African American medical units served overseas, in England, Burma and the South Pacific, including 512 nurses. It was rare to see publicity images of African American women in any wartime roles, even as nurses.[15]

Stereotypes about women's role as doctors also took a battering during the war. It was not enough to break the limitations imposed on women, but at least to crack them. In *Matilda Waltzes with the Tommies*, Dr Mary Kent Hughes describes how her services were refused by Australian authorities because she was female, so she joined the Royal Army Medical Corps in England in 1940, serving there and in the

This 1944 German stamp emphasises the perceived gender roles of medical staff – the male doctor has the stethoscope; the pleasant female nurse looks on as a subordinate.

Middle East, 'trussed up in a uniform that made me feel like a small bottle of beer in a large crate of straw.'[16] Chinese women, in contrast, were accepted as army doctors, as well as providing a full range of roles in the Women's Aid Corps.

Naval nurses, among others, played a key role nursing traumatised inmates of Japanese PoW camps in the Far East. Hospital ships criss-crossed the Atlantic rescuing and repatriating Allied prisoners. The work was very distressing, but the women found the convalescent men responded well to female company, having been starved of it for so many years.

Equally harrowing were the experiences of women who nursed survivors of European concentration camps. News filtered out in letters from medical staff to friends and family, describing Nazi camp conditions and the horrific experiences of survivors, as well as the high mortality rates. Allied medical personnel worked alongside German doctors and nurses, which created some tensions.[17]

In addition to static sites and hospital trains, Allied naval and air forces offered an air ambulance service. The nursing sisters were known as 'Flying Nightingales'. Parachutes were locked away while tending patients in the Dakota planes – nurses were ordered to stay with the wounded. Marjorie Clark enrolled in the WAAF in August 1941. Since leaving school at 15 she had worked as a tailoress in an English clothing company, repairing uniforms. Her air ambulance service took her between France, Belgium and Holland, wearing a flying suit. Flying sisters were invaluable in the Pacific theatre of war, where some naval sisters flew in army jungle gear – bush shirts, khaki trousers and a fur-lined jacket for the flight.

Tragically, medical staff could all too easily become patients. Thea Wolf, Head Nurse at the Jewish Hospital in Alexandria, devoted much of her time to helping Jewish fugitives fleeing European persecution, aided by Arab Egyptians. Ever compassionate, she was dismayed to discover the patients on a commandeered civilian train were actually Canadian nurses who'd been injured when their ship was torpedoed. She promptly set to work nursing the nurses.[19]

Being on duty during a bomb raid was a particularly fraught time. London nurses learned to harness very young patients so they didn't wander while taking shelter

Above left: *Minnie Lindsell joined the Queen Alexandra's Royal Naval Nursing Service in 1938 and was called up in 1943 as a theatre sister. 'When you're young it's all quite exciting. No use saying otherwise. It was a great challenge,' she said of her years in service. Joining a medical air evacuation unit she worked with Australian 'flying sisters' ferrying patients from Pacific Islands. She remembers the beautiful sunrise over coral reefs. Having worn trousers to fly she vowed she'd never wear them again after the war.[18]*

Above right: *Epaulettes of the Queen Alexandra's Royal Naval Nursing Service (R). Minnie Lindsell's reminder of war work, friendships and hospital life.*

Red Cross design for a burn mask. Civilians had to learn how to act as first responders during bomb raids or maritime incidents.

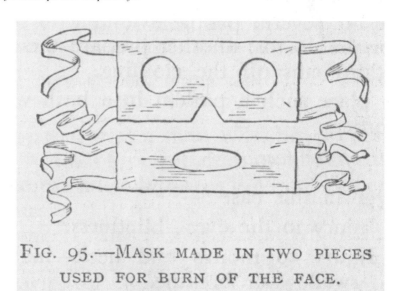

FIG. 95.—MASK MADE IN TWO PIECES USED FOR BURN OF THE FACE.

under the cots and beds. Mary Firth, on duty during the London Blitz, wore navy blue woollen trousers for her night shifts, in order to be ready for action. As soon as blown-out hospital windows were boarded up, they were blasted open again. Firth recalled an Irish nurse running away from bomb damage calling 'Oh Jesus, Mary and Joseph', with her cap scandalously awry. Firth stayed with patients who could not be moved. One elderly lady told her, 'If they come tonight nurse, save yourself. You're only 18, I'm 80. I've had my life. I'm ready to meet my maker.' On the night of a bombing the patient was not at all ready to meet her maker, shouting, 'Get me out of here!'[20]

Nurses were part of the forces landing in Normandy after the 1944 invasion. Flying Nursing Orderlies made landfall on D-Day+7. They were more afraid of cockroaches than the enemy as they set up tent camps, despite prolific landmines and not-so-far-off gunfire. One Queen Alexandra nurse was disgusted by the uniform issued for her crossing to the continent – hilarious elasticated-waistband trousers, and hideous khaki knickers. Mud was thick after heavy rain, and wellingtons were in short supply, leaving the nurses looking more like farmers than medical staff. Further along in the Allied advance across Europe, hospitals in Belgium began to notice a shortage of blankets for patients. These were later spotted in town – Belgian girls had turned the blankets into stylish blue coats.[21]

The ultimate hard core service was offered by frontline medics. In the Soviet Union more than 40 per cent of all frontline medical personnel were women. Initially 400,000 women were trained as doctors, nurses, orderlies and stretcher-bearers.[22] Most had no clue what war meant. Vera Iosifovna Khoreva, an army surgeon, packed very little as she left for the front, supposing it would all be over soon – just a skirt, two pairs of socks and one pair of shoes. She even packed perfume, reasoning, 'It was hard to renounce all at once life as it had been up to then.' She soon found herself operating around the clock. Among the waiting wounded, every third man was dead. Somehow the women endured. Appearance helped. Cossack medic Olga Vasilyevna recalled, 'I always tried to look neat, trim. I was very afraid that if I was killed I'd lie there looking unattractive.'[23]

> 'I watch films about the war: a nurse on the front line, she's always neat, clean, not in thick pants, but in a skirt, a pretty forage cap on top of her head. Well, it's not true! How could we have pulled a wounded man out if we were like that?'
>
> Sofya Konstantinova Dubnyakova – Russian medical assistant. (Alexievich, *The Unwomanly Face of War*)

There was a high death rate among the Russian medics and orderlies, second only to the infantry. Medical assistants in tank units died quickly, pulling burning men from burning tanks under fire. Medics were traumatised by treating battle injuries, hearing the crunching noise of hand-to-hand combat, and having their uniforms permanently crusted with blood and lice. Surgery nurses slept where they stood, with feet so swollen they wouldn't fit in their tarpaulin boots. If captured, women could expect to be executed. Hospital trains were targets for enemy planes. The sensory overload was horrific.

The impact of war continued long after hostilities had ceased. PTSD was undiagnosed and often unacknowledged among women. When those who'd served for the duration left off their uniforms and got into civilian clothes again there might have been a sense of relief. There would also be the memories of what had been suffered by patients and staff. Others kept their uniforms and continued in service. Work was their healer.

● TRAINING WITH PAY ● FREE UNIFORMS ● NEW SALARY SCALE
● HOLIDAYS WITH PAY ● WIDE RANGE OF SPECIALIST SUBJECTS
● PENSION SCHEMES

Nursing is a key profession in our National well-being. Nurses are needed to give us fitness for battle, and when the time comes, for peace. Fill in the coupon for details of the war job that can be your career.

TO: THE MINISTRY OF LABOUR AND NATIONAL SERVICE (Dept. N.R.), 24 KINGSWAY, LONDON, W.C.2.

Please send illustrated literature on Nursing as a war-time job and as a career. Also details of TRAINING PAY, &c.

Name...

Address...
 (Including Town)

(USE BLOCK LETTERS) County.. HN6

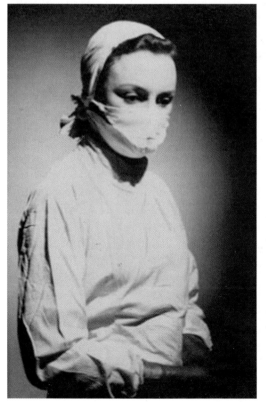

Above: *British recruitment advert from 1943. Some women found fulfilment continuing to nurse after the war. They'd certainly earned respect and appreciation for service under pressure and under fire.*

Left: *Margery Hall was a wartime theatre nurse. She never served abroad, but her war touched far off countries when she married John Watts, an RAF officer involved in dropping food supplies to PoWs in Malaya. He was 24 and they'd only been married for six weeks when his plane went missing. The wreckage wasn't discovered until 2009. John's wedding ring and a bracelet engraved with Margery's name were recovered from the remains.*

Chapter 18

BEHIND BARS
Internment, prisons and concentration camps

'One matron, six years ago renowned in Paris for her elegance, had become a bent, dazed, shabby old woman. When her smartly attired brother, who met her, said, like an automaton, "Where is your luggage?" she silently handed him what looked like a dirty black sweater fastened with safety pins.'[1]

A survivor of Ravensbrück concentration camp returns to France

A fraction of the shoes found stored in the Auschwitz camp complex after Russian liberation, January 1945.

It's the shoes that get you. The tangible evidence of industrial scale murder. The tens of thousands of pairs of shoes that represent millions of feet walking to their fate. Shoes on display at the Auschwitz State Museum in Oswiecim, Poland, are not a pleasant panorama of vintage style. They are the slowly degrading remnants of life and death behind bars. Prisoners' names were often erased with their lives. Clothing – essentially ephemera – survived.

Prison existence forced wartime women to shed their familiar comforts and clothes and endure fundamental levels of loss, pain and hardship. In concentration camps, internment camps, gulag camps or plain prison cells, appearance was about more than vanity. It was about holding onto dignity, normality and identity, for as long as humanly possible.

Internment could come with very little warning. In North America, the shock waves of the Japanese attacks on the US naval base at Pearl Harbor in December 1941 rippled across the nation. Then came an order in February 1942 for everyone of Japanese ancestry on the

238

west coast to be interned as enemy aliens, including American citizens. They were dispersed to impromptu camps with very little notice. 'Pack up your suitcase now,' commanded one mother to her family in California. They could take only one case each. It begs the questions – what would you pack and what would you have to leave behind? Even after the internment order was revoked in 1944, families were still in shock from the humiliation and the terrible financial losses of abandoning farms and businesses. Women picked up the pieces as best they could. For many, the only work they could find was sewing or doing laundry. In 1944, Jennie – a second generation Japanese-American girl – left a camp to work at the Bemus bag factory in Minneapolis, sewing potato sacks. She came home with her blouse ripped from the coarse fabric. Even as citizens picked up the pieces of former lives, there was silence and shame about their time in internment.[2]

Those captured abroad were even further cut off from their usual support networks. They quickly learned to form new communities in order to survive. Southern Sumatra hosted the prison camp of Palembang, for Europeans captured after the surrender of Singapore to Japanese forces in February 1942 (ironically just as Japanese Americans were being interned in America). Among the prisoners were Australian army nurses, including Jessie Simons, who spoke with gratitude of local Malayan women, former servants of Dutch families on Sumatra. The Malayans were able to help new prisoners with food, as well as clothes – presumed to be looted from abandoned Dutch houses. Being too well-dressed was a liability – the nurses discarded all known beauty tricks to look as unattractive as possible. They wanted to avoid being coerced into sexual slavery.[3] Margaret Dryburgh was an English missionary from Sunderland in the north of England, also interned at Palembang. She helped found the camp orchestra as well as organising other community groups to keep morale strong. In gratitude she was given a colourful apron, stitched by internee Mary Brown. It was pieced from precious scraps of cotton clothing in a 'crazy' quilt pattern, and embellished with feather stitch. Dryburgh died in captivity in April 1945. Her apron can be seen on display at the Imperial War Museum North. The Imperial War Museum collection also holds a simple kimono made from a hospital sheet and embroidered with the signatures of internees at Stanley Camp in Hong Kong. It belonged to nursing sister Margaret Lee.

Perhaps the most famous examples of crafting behind-the-wire are the Changi quilts, stitched by prisoners in the infamous Changi gaol in Singapore. Inmate Ethel Mulvany came up with the genius idea of using quilts to send coded messages to loved ones in the separate men's barracks. Squares were cut from rice sacks. They were embroidered with individual names then sewn into quilts. Each quilt had sixty-six squares, some with wistful imagery, some with patriotic pictures. British nurse Elizabeth Burnham embroidered 'Hope springs eternal in the human breast' on her square. Needle and thread kept that hope alive. Two quilts survive and are in Australian collections. One mysteriously surfaced at the Red Cross museum in London in the 1960s.[4]

Further north-east in Shanghai, Europeans learned to make a new life behind the wire. After food, clothing and textiles were most precious, from needles and shoelaces to mosquito nets and underwear. Peggy Abkhazi, interned in Lunghua camp, recorded daily life in a diary. She watched free Chinese women walking past the camp, wearing faded blue cotton clothes with white cotton head wraps. She dried her worn clothes on the dormitory stove. She took up knitting and darning with a vengeance, and spent each winter wearing everything she owned to keep warm. By March 1945, some internees could sign IOUs for 'Dire Need' clothes from the British government, via the Swiss Consulate.[5]

At Frontstalag 142 internment camp in France, a batch of linen mattress covers were discovered in a storeroom. Creative prisoners decided to make spring clothes, producing skirts, slacks and blouses. New outfits gave the women a renewed sense of optimism after a hard winter. Occasional gifts from home made it through, lovingly packed by families who had little spare themselves. Rosemary Say, an Englishwoman trapped and arrested in occupied France, fortified herself against winter temperatures by wearing Lucile Manguin designer ski-wear, which she'd luckily packed in her luggage.[6]

Keeping warm was very much on the minds of civilians interned in cold climates, with only sporadic Red Cross parcels as treats. This ski wear is Italian, from 1942.

In Europe, the greatest numbers of internees were to be found in ghettos, and they were Jewish. Under Nazi racial policies, Jewish families were uprooted from their own homes and crowded into walled-off areas of selected towns, invariably in the poorer districts. Here people attempted to re-establish some sense of routine, eking out precious belongings – all with daily indignities, frequent violence, and the ominous threat of deportation hanging over them.

Deportation swept up anyone who was considered an enemy of the ruling state. Nazis mainly categorised their enemies by race. The Soviet Union filled the Siberian Gulag system with political prisoners or anyone

240

Jewish seamstresses at work in Warsaw. Ghetto labour meant the possibility of food and a temporary escape from being rounded up for deportation. Many thousands of factories were operated in European ghettos. Conditions were harsh; hours were long. Textile workers produced uniforms for the German army as well as civilian clothes for sale beyond the ghetto walls.

even remotely suspected of a crime against communism. Whole families were deported from Poland after the Russian invasion, to be used as slave labour. There were countless camps and an endless supply of prisoners. Eugenia Semyonovna Ginzburg's political opinions fell foul of the Communist authorities. She arrived in Siberia after a hard spell in prison cells where she'd been dressed in convict clothes of stiff material with brown stripes. It was a demoralising transformation: 'No woman of 30 likes to be transformed into a scarecrow,' she recalled, 'even if no one is going to see her.' Conditions were far worse in the gulag camp. Within the barbed wire were women with faded, patched, ragged dresses and thin, sunburnt faces. Overseers had quilted coats, felt boots and warm mittens. One of the few ways to earn pieces of clothing was to trade sex.[7]

Political prisoners in various regimes sometimes had contact, albeit limited, with the outside world. Families were asked to send in wool, sewing materials and old clothes, which inmates unpicked and turned into sweaters and bags for themselves. Some of the activity was to ease anxiety as well as boredom. Prison labour might even be welcomed to pass the long hours. Female prisoners were given jobs such as sewing buttons on cards, darning socks for male prisoners, or knitting garments for the guards. Sometimes these tasks became crafts of resistance: Greek women imprisoned just after the war for their resistance affiliations taught each other lace-making, knitting and embroidery, eventually selling the items they made. Winifred Green, a waitress from the Royal Hotel on Guernsey was imprisoned for six months for refusing to say *Heil Hitler* as she served German occupiers their rice puddings. She calmly spent her time in prison embroidering *Heil Churchill* on a square of cloth ripped from a bedsheet.[9]

The Third Reich went beyond incarceration and ghettoization. They imprisoned millions of people in concentration camps for slave labour, and for so-called processing ie, mass murder on industrial scale in extermination centres. As the war progressed, rumours began to spread of previously unremarkable places with names such as Treblinka, Terezin, Ravensbrück, Sobibor and Auschwitz. Deportees to camps were told to take one suitcase only. Even this was taken from them on arrival at their

Embroidery pattern from Everywoman *magazine, 1947. Among the many Polish Christians deported to the Gulag was Leokadia Majewicz. Her mother was a talented embroiderer who traded her skills for food, having had the foresight to pack needles and thread when forced from home. During a long journey out of Siberia as refugees, Leokadia became separated from her mother. By extraordinary coincidence they were reunited on a beach in Persia, when Leokadia recognised the rose pattern cross-stitch embroidered on a woman's white blouse – it was her mother wearing it.*[8]

destination. Forcing new arrivals to strip was a deliberate tactic in the process of dehumanisation. It also left people bewildered and embarrassed, so they could more easily be herded on to the next stage. Survivor testimonies talk of being degraded beyond belief. It was especially offensive to women, who had always been told that nudity was shameful; decency meant being covered up. Czech actress Zdenka Fantlova later testified that the group of tightly packed naked and shaven women waiting in the changing rooms at Auschwitz-Birkenau was 'like a collection of bald tailors' dummies waiting for their wigs and clothes before being arranged in a window display.'[10]

After the stripping and shaving came showers. The lucky ones had water coming from the shower heads, not poison gas. For the living there was a scramble for new clothing, sometimes blue/grey striped uniforms; sometimes, especially as the camps became grossly overcrowded, civilian clothes distributed at random from a pile. Distribution was carried out with no regard for size, style or practicality. Prisoners could be sent out into sub-zero temperatures wearing only a negligee or silk evening gown or shirt. Underwear was only permitted for more privileged political prisoners, not for Jews. No pads, rags or paper were available to use as sanitary protection, yet blood on a dress meant death.[11]

Prisoners weren't the only women in the concentration camp universe. Guards, often young women and even teenagers, underwent intensive training to deaden potential compassion towards those they were to treat as 'subhuman' and vermin. Distinctions between the guards' clothes and the inmates' degraded appearances

Unnamed SS staff from Auschwitz enjoying a day out. Out of context and out of uniform they could be any group of carefree colleagues.

were deliberate. They created a gulf of 'us' and 'them'. Potential recruits found the SS auxiliary uniforms an incentive to join up. They wore mouse-grey jackets, culotte-skirts and leather boots. A wool cape and cap completed the outfit. Accessories included whips, truncheons and savage dogs. Surviving photographs of camp guards on leave show them smiling and comfortable. Although from 1940 female guards were permitted to wear eagle patches on their left sleeves and caps, they did not have SS rank insignia – a subtle reminder that they were employees in a man's world, not full members.[12] For impressionable young women, sites of mass-murder were seen as places of opportunity – a steady job with good pay and the chance to be powerful and brutal. There were other perks: unlimited new clothes.

'With Nazism I was somebody. Afterwards I was nothing.'

A former Auschwitz-Birkenau SS guard, elderly and full of nostalgia in 1971, shows off her SS uniform, kept impeccable. She suggests to her horrified daughter, 'Why don't you try it on? I'd like to see it on you?'[13]

Inmates sorting clothes outside of the many huts of plunder at Auschwitz. The job had benefits: prisoners often smuggled food and extra clothing out of the warehouses. They had tolerable uniforms, in contrast to less privileged inmates. They were also vulnerable to sudden 'liquidation' in the nearby gas chambers.

Journalist Martha Gellhorn reached the liberated camp of Dachau, near Munich, in early May 1945. At the crematorium she noted that the clothing of those murdered was neatly stacked in piles; naked bodies were dumped like rubbish.[14] The terrible reality was that clothes had more value than human beings. The task of sorting plunder required many thousands of slave labourers and vast warehouses. Guards had their

Detail from a 1941 German pattern magazine. In the summer of 1944, blue polka-dot dresses were in fashion across Europe. Auschwitz plunder warehouses were full of such frocks. SS guards decided to issue them to prisoners working in the admin block. 'What luxury!' remembered admin worker/inmate Erika Kounio, wondering which unfortunate woman had once owned the dress. Kitty Hart-Moxon and other prisoners sorting plunder were also kitted out in navy blue dresses with white polka dots. The dresses were all painted with a red cross to show they were prisoners.[15]

pick from the mountains of clothes spilling out of once carefully packed suitcases. The warehouses of plunder were known as 'Canada' in concentration camp slang – a land of plenty. Notorious SS sadists such as Irma Grese and Isle Koch helped themselves to confiscated fashions, perfumes and jewellery.

Inmate Irene Reichenberg found her sister Frieda's jacket while sorting plunder in the Auschwitz warehouses. She later testified, 'And there I found it, just imagine. In such a heap.' Frieda and her baby had been sent straight to the gas chamber.[16] Jolana Roth, a Czech Jew in Auschwitz, found her brother's shirt among the piles – she'd sewn it for him. Prisoners were told to remove all name labels, and all traces of the yellow star that Jews had been required to stitch to their clothes. Roth defied this order, leaving torn fragments of the star 'so the people outside would know where these clothes came from'.[17] The 'people outside' Roth refers to were ordinary German citizens who received concentration camp plunder in the form of charitable aid. It was distributed to those made homeless or destitute in the war.

In Auschwitz, fabrics and couture fashions were diverted from the warehouses to a select sewing workshop known as the Upper Tailoring Studio. It was staffed by prisoners and its purpose was to create quality outfits for SS Guards and Nazi officers' wives. The women who worked there were mainly Jewish seamstresses, with some French political prisoners. They formed a tight bond of friendship and support. It was a fragile privilege, but conditions were luxurious compared to women enduring hard labour outdoors. The dressmakers had meaningful work and the opportunity to keep clean – so that their 'clients' didn't catch illnesses. The fact that such a workshop existed to gratify the vanity of the SS highlights the grotesque tragedy of a regime which could indulge in high fashion alongside mass murder.

Even in the most extreme circumstances, the human will to love and make connections can survive. There are many instances of concentration camp prisoners sharing what

scraps of food they could glean, and even crafting tiny gifts for each other. These were acts of defiance every bit as significant as more dramatic acts of violent resistance – they showed that inmates were still human. Zusi Giner, imprisoned as a slave labourer in a factory on the Poland-Czechoslovakia border, came back from work one day to find a white dress on her bed, with a row of buttons down the front. It had been stitched in secret by her

Marta Fuchs was the inmate overseer of the elite dressmaking workshop in Auschwitz. She was first commissioned to sew by Hedwig Hoess, the camp commandant's wife. In the workshop Fuchs looked after the twenty-three prisoners creating garments for the SS and their children. This is a portrait taken just after the war. She was lucky to survive. Other seamstresses were shot while attempting to escape.[18]

friends as a birthday present.[19] Erika Kounio's 1944 birthday gifts in Auschwitz included a white head kerchief and an onion with a red bow tied round it – absolute treasures.[20] Charlotte Delbo was a French political prisoner in Auschwitz. Her friends rustled up a bow and a woven rope belt for her as gifts.[21] Shortly before her death in Ravensbrück in 1943, friends of fashion journalist Milena Jesenská made her birthday handkerchiefs embroidered with her prisoner number and tiny hearts.[22] There are innumerable stories of such gestures in wartime prison camps around the world.

'I was given a pair of stockings by Nina Gviniashvili, an actress of the Rustaveli Theatre at Tiflis. "Take them, take them! I've got two pairs, and you've practically nothing," she exclaimed as she looked at my one pair, darned with fishbone and threads of many colours.'

Eugenia Semyonovna Ginzburg, en route from a Russian prison to the Siberian Gulag.[23]

It was new clothing that helped former prisoners regain a sense of self and dignity after liberation. While SS guards rapidly shed their uniforms hoping to escape revenge attacks from inmates, or arrest by Allied troops, those who'd endured the torments of the concentration camp shed their rags – where possible – and rediscovered civilisation through normal clothes. Some broke into the plunder warehouses and SS stores, even adapting SS curtains and gingham bedcovers from SS barracks.[24] Some, bold enough to explore the towns near the camps in Germany, broke into houses to loot from German civilians – acts of vengeance and retribution. Allied personnel attempting to aid former inmates recognised the importance of having decent clothing in addition to medicine and nutrition. One of the Red Cross teams at Bergen-Belsen, headed by a Miss Daniell, set up a clothing centre for the 20,000 former inmates, supplied with clothing requisitioned from local German civilians. It jokingly became known as 'Harrods'. Thousands were transformed there, entering as dazed figures in striped pyjamas or blankets and leaving in entirely new outfits.[25]

For Jewish teenager Eva Schloss née Geiringer the feeling of real re-humanisation came when she obtained a bra. This humble yet invaluable item was often denied women in the prison systems of all regimes. She received hers from a Russian soldier after the liberation of Auschwitz. The soldier had his dream job – measuring inmates for their bra and calling out to a colleague 'small!' or 'middling!' There would be rummaging in a pile of brassieres and a lot of laughter as the bras were fitted. 'We felt civilised again,' she told me, her eyes bright at the memory. Over the bra she wore an olive-green blouse with a hammer-and-sickle, donated by a Russian infantrywoman. This top can now be seen on display at the Amsterdam Museum of the Resistance. Eva's mother married Otto Frank after the war, making Eva a posthumous step-sister of diarist Anne Frank, who died at Belsen not long before the camp was liberated.[26]

This anonymous woman wears a neat striped wool two-piece suit. After the war, many former concentration camp inmates couldn't bear to wear stripes in any form, as it reminded them of their prison uniforms.

In the Far East, survivors of Japanese prisoner of war camps also needed coaxing back to health and confidence. A rehabilitation centre near Manila provided a beauty parlour and outfitting department, with a range of fashionable new dresses.[27] In Australia, recovering internees were overwhelmed by the generosity of local people and the Australian Red Cross. Distribution of Red Cross parcels was always an occasion for celebration among convalescents and former prisoners. It could mean the first hairbrush in years, or face-flannels, or white handkerchiefs – even slippers and socks when they'd been used to newspapers and rags. The WVS were tireless handing out clothing supplies in Burma, Malaya, Saigon, Bangkok, Singapore, Java, Sumatra, Hong Kong and Japan. Those who'd lost uniforms were given flashes and badges to restore a sense of pride and belonging. To civilians and service personnel who'd survived long years of horror the new clothes from WVS stocks were a tremendous comfort – a symbol of a world where kindness was normal.

Chapter 19

PICKING UP THE PIECES
Post-war life

'So when at last I greeted my first American, my hair was bedraggled,
my skirt was wet and uneven, and I was caked with
mud from top to toe'[1]

Ginette Spanier, cycling to Paris for the liberation.

Last summer I travelled with a friend on the famous *Hurtigruten* coastal ferry up the coast of Norway. Along the way I visited museums featuring stories about the *Milorg* resistance in Norway. I read of daring escapes and savage reprisals; of betrayal and supreme generosity. Then the ship docked in Kirkenes, a bleak-looking town high above the Arctic Circle and near the Russian border. Kirkenes was almost wiped from the face of the earth in 1944. As the Nazi occupation weakened, retreating German soldiers were under orders to leave nothing in northern Norway that would support liberating Russian forces. In a matter of hours local people lost their homes, livelihoods and possessions. Those who weren't evacuated hid in freezing caves and dugouts. Many had nothing but the clothes on their backs. Unusually, the modern town of Kirkenes not only commemorates the military aspects of war, it also honours the resilient civilians who survived the scorched earth policy, with a statue of a mother and two children – a rare image among the worldwide sculptures of men of war. The Mother's Monument was unveiled in 1994, on the fiftieth anniversary of the town's liberation. Survivors still speak of their female relatives, knitting with broken wool threads, and making clothes from German flour sacks. The mother of the statue is barefoot, wearing only a light dress and shawl. She looks defiant.[2]

How do you pick up the pieces of life when war has changed so much? What did it mean to hear the word 'peace' in 1945?

For the Allies there was victory. On 8 May 1945 – Victory in Europe Day – spontaneous parties erupted. Flags were out, buildings were floodlit, bonfires crackled and fireworks shot up into the night sky. Outdoor parties enlivened the bomb-damaged streets of Britain. Proper party clothes weren't required – people celebrated in floral aprons, turbans and uniforms. In London, people wore paper crowns or red white and blue rosettes.

For Trudi Kanter, a Viennese milliner seeking refuge as a Jew in England, victory meant relief: 'Escaping our persecutors was like climbing a mountain, arriving at the top with bleeding hands. Now it is over.'[3] For Elsie Walton, a rebellious young Yorkshire girl, victory meant sneaking out to dance the hokey-cokey in the street. She was spotted by her aunt and sent home to bed, but simply but she secretly ran further down the road to dance some more: 'It was something that I shall never forget.'[4]

Victory might mean liberation. Pearl Smith celebrated the end of the German occupation of Guernsey by dancing until dawn. Her feet were rubbed raw in her wooden-soled shoes.[5] Victory could also signify the end of a long hard job. Mary Sherrard, bombe-operator at Bletchley Park, said VE Day was wonderful: the German de-coding machines could be dismantled, although the Japanese cipher staff were still hard at work until August. By the time Sherrard handed in her Wren uniform she was ready to move on.[6]

Russian Army scout Albinia Alexandrovna Gantimurova had three wishes at the end of the war – 'to ride on a bus instead of crawling on my stomach; second – to buy and eat a whole loaf of white bread; and third – to sleep in white sheets and have them make crinkly noise.' Everyday acts that were taken for granted in peace assumed whole new levels of luxury if that peace had been hard-won.[7]

June 1945 saw the British Britannia and Eve *magazine celebrating weddings, homes and fashions. No hint of war. The bride in white looks forward to a romantic idyll out of uniform.*

250

US army dietician Carol Morrison Garrett rode in an Armistice Day parade, in November 1945. She was seated with a frail veteran of the American Civil War. For her, the salutes took on special significance: she was the first woman of her family to serve in the military.[8]

Victory wasn't straightforward, particularly when the final enemy was defeated by terrifying new bombs on Hiroshima and Nagasaki. American writer Mollie Panter-Downes overheard a shabby London matron discussing her fears for the new atomic age. 'Funny thing,' the woman said, 'even though I've taken every stitch off me back every night since VE Day, I can't seem to feel easy.'[9] Maureen Sutton, a WAAF in York, came home from a May Thanksgiving service and took out her knitting as rain pelted down. Life had to go on, and it wouldn't all be joyful.[10]

Victorious or defeated, grief was universal. The dead had to be buried and to be mourned – if they could be found. Black was the colour of mourning in many countries. In Russia, white was worn next to death. Even homeless and destitute, Soviet mourners found a scrap of white – a handkerchief, a shirt, a white embroidered towel. Grave markers spiked roadsides, fields and flattened towns.

Victory for the Allies meant defeat for the Axis powers. Civilians hunted for white material to signify surrender. Towels, napkins and handkerchiefs were all adapted as flags of surrender. German housewives took out their needles and sewing machines to stitch flags of the victors. They hedged their bets by crafting flags of all the major Allies likely to be occupying the country. American and British designs were fiddly. The Nazi flag was easily adapted into a Russian one. White sheets served for the French tricolour; blue was trickier. Tablecloths and children's clothes were cut up for blue; blouses for the yellow Russian hammer and sickle.[11] Appearance-wise there were few pretty frocks or visible uniforms on German streets: local women learned

Greek women offer very public lamentation at a 1945 funeral. Death is so common they mourn in everyday clothes, with black headscarves.

'How to Transform Your Furs' – Petit Echo de la Mode *November 1945. Keeping warm was a major consideration, even for those craving new elegance in their post-war life. Dressmaking magazines offered patterns for snug nightwear and remodelled furs. French fashion publications showed restrained silhouettes and long hemlines in winter, as coal was unobtainable for domestic use.*

to leave their hair filthy and their clothes baggy as the Russians advanced. Epidemic sexual violence emphasised women's powerlessness.

Issues of culpability must have seemed irrelevant to those civilians suddenly on the receiving end of invasion, occupation and humiliation. Allied witnesses found it hard to pity German families displaced by changing boundaries, or looted by those who'd suffered under Nazi oppression. Retribution was sought in formal, legal proceedings, such as the Nuremberg and Hamburg trials in Germany. Now the victors got to scrutinise those they'd fought against, including SS women on trial for murder and torture in concentration camps. Reporters were surprised at how human the accused looked, either in lumpy suits or stylish and attractive.[12] Grey areas of wartime interaction were very quickly erased in favour of simple justice. Clothes were part of the retribution: dresses and underwear were swiftly torn off women in more personal acts of vengeance, specifically against those accused of having sex with the enemy. Images of these 'collaborators' are harrowing to see, particularly when the woman carries a baby. During victory celebrations on the island of Jersey, a local man came across a teenage girl stripped naked by a mob and left terrified. She was an easy target for reprisals, as the enemy occupiers had been escorted away as guarded PoWs.[13]

Peace wasn't tidy. There were huge implications for geographical boundaries. Political regimes collapsed and were replaced – not always by less repressive structures. Whole continents were convulsed by the possibilities of change. Some fought new oppressors; some sought freedom from old tyrannies.

Amongst all this seismic upheaval, people attempted to restore some routines of daily life. In Prague, where communism would soon nationalise the fashion industry and squeeze out the flair of pre-war entrepreneurs, Lilli Kopecky – Auschwitz survivor – found a menial job so she could save and buy a dress. This meant staying hungry for a month. With a decent dress she could interview for better work. Heda Margolius Kovaly, also an Auschwitz survivor, had a warmer welcome in Prague. Desperate for shelter and support she looked up old friends. She met her mother's dressmaker, who promptly burst into tears. The dressmaker went straight to her workroom and made a new dress out of remnants there and then, weeping the whole time.[14]

Even in victorious nations there was an awareness that once the euphoria of peace wore off there would be tougher restrictions to endure. Food and clothing were more tightly rationed in Britain after the war, and housewives bore the brunt of extra economising when belts were already tight and clothes already threadbare.

'Our Post-War Girl is bored. She's sick of advertisements asking her to wait with a smile for something she has needed urgently for five years. But what can we do? For it seems we mustn't make our new Youthlines yet awhile. We must keep our red-hot ideas in cold storage'

Advert for WB 'Youthline' girdles and brassieres. *Woman's Journal,* March 1946

Elle magazine November 1946. Perhaps stores didn't have their pre-war stocks and quality, but post-war women still enjoyed window-shopping and the possibility of new purchases.

Peace meant time to take stock and to re-stock. Martha Gellhorn, war correspondent, was in Paris after its liberation in 1944. Having travelled in so many battle-scarred countries she was impressed by the Parisian ability to create style out of almost nothing. One Paris concierge delighted in wearing high-heeled evening sandals as she dragged rubbish bins across the cobbles and hung out the washing. She'd bought the shoes from *Vogue* editor Bettina Ballard, with cash raised on the food black market. In 1945, Ballard was more in need of money than the couture clothes she'd put into storage in 1940.[15]

'Now women once again have time and opportunity to dedicate themselves to special occasions, to be a beautiful and attractive being, to leave her daily worries behind and throw herself into an intense social life, which of course, requires magnificent outfits which showcase her beauty and character.'

Today's Fashion article in *Negro y Blanco Labores* December 1946, Mexico.

Military surplus gear would soon find its way into civilian wardrobes. Ex-service greatcoats were offered 'coupon free' in England. Ladies' overalls in denim or khaki drill were suddenly available to civilians, as war-workers were made redundant. Ex-ARP stock rubber mackintoshes were pricey but useful. Even khaki battle dress blouses were on sale 'part-worn but in good condition, splendid work wear coupon free 7/6'[16] Ex-service blankets were very much in demand, particularly when the British government announced a cut in wools available to women, in order to favour menswear – necessary for male demob suits. Foreign workers were encouraged to come and fill major gaps in the British labour market for clothing production, while shoppers grumbled that most of the clothing produced was destined for sale overseas in order to bring in export revenue. Criminals solved the problem of shortages by making high-speed raids on West End clothing shops in London, making off with thousands of pounds of garments for black market trade.

'British Celanese Limited – textiles, plastics, chemicals – All will add luxury to everyday life… and all will be released in ample supply just as soon as conditions permit.' *Vogue* advert February 1949.

'Mist-beige, sand beige, rose beige, midnight, bronze skin – art silk, rayon, lisle, silk and rayon.'

Stockings readily available once more in the Oxendales spring 1949 catalogue. French knickers were also on sale, in ivory, azure, apple-green, peach and lagoon blue.

American Fabrics *trade magazine 1947 was full of inspirational synthetics. Nylon was the new wonder fabric – easy to wash and dry, no ironing required. It was the perfect modern material for a future-facing industry.*

Fashions themselves were bravely elegant in the face of continued adversity. Collections launched immediately post-war affected the appearance of abundance through clever draping, dolman sleeves and cheeky peplums. In New York, designers with talent and stamina continued to please the 'middle market' of fashion – creating stylish yet practical clothes for a broad range of women. London designers worked under strong government restrictions on yardage and embellishment. There were to be no pleats, tucks, excessive buttons; no embroidery, quilting or beading. Hems, lengths and collar widths were predetermined. Bianca Mosca, Elizabeth Champcommunal, Captain Molyneux, Charles Creed, Peter Russell and Hardy Amies were among the so-called Big Eight of London style, perfecting cut and pared-back elegance. British fashion was also hobbled by an established mistrust of fashion as if it were something frivolous – a peripheral feminine pastime. This was despite the revenue generated by fashion exports. Across the Channel in France it was a different story. Rich investors saw great potential in the trade. Marcel Boussac, head of the French cotton manufacturing industry, decided to bankroll a protégé from the house of Lucien Lelong. His name was Christian Dior.

Excitement over the launch of Dior's first collection, 12 February 1947, was tempered by the bitter cold of fuel-scarce Paris. France had been re-asserting its place as the heart of world couture via the *Théâtre de la Mode*, a travelling pageant of dolls dressed in exquisite fashions from leading French couture houses. Could Dior deliver on expectations? His collection was shown in a beautiful grey and gold salon. The tension was electric as mannequins swayed past provocatively, in the most audaciously wide skirts. Gone was the boxy wartime silhouette. Instead Dior offered a new 'natural' female form, of padded hips, corseted waists, boosted bust and sloping shoulders. Fashion editors and buyers were on the edge of their seats. After the show, orders poured in. Whatever the world thought, Dior would outsell every other Paris label that season.[17]

What is now accepted to be one of the most significant fashion events of the

A sketch from Album du Figaro *1947 shows the new lines of Christian Dior's revolutionary collection. The shape and length had all been seen before. Dior put them together with particular genius. The fashion world was ready.*

257

Above left: *Dressed to impress in the US. From 1947, fashionable skirt lengths reached mid-calf. Some adored the new glamour; others deplored the excess fabric and the hiding of shapely legs.*

Above right: *A young Blackpool woman shows off her* New Look *outfit. The jacket cut is less extreme than French cinching. The soft, long pleats must have felt divine after the sparse yardage of Utility skirts.*

twentieth century caused great controversy at the time, which, in turn generated more publicity for Dior's work, although he was by no means the only designer experimenting with longer, fuller skirts or tighter waists. In November 1947, *Marie France* magazine gave the results of a referendum regarding the new style. Over 46,000 readers were against it; only 7,000 voted for it. Essentially, it was hard to find money for daily necessities, let alone splashing out on retro styles last popular during the Great War. 'I don't need to sweep my house with the hem of my skirt,' said one respondent. Other fashion critics agreed the leg-covering skirts and petticoats were too backward-looking. Grandmothers who hadn't left off their long, wide skirts suddenly found themselves in fashion again. Hardy Amies called Dior's signature pieces 'unbridled nostalgia', preferring the bravura of Balenciaga's bold cuts.[18]

Emotions ran high. 'Why any woman wants to return to ugliness for the sake of change is more than I can comprehend!' complained Hollywood designer Gilbert Adrian.[19] 'Ludicrous!' said British MP Mabel Ridealgh: 'Too reminiscent of a caged bird's attitude.'[20] *Picture Post* magazine ran an article deploring Dior's manipulation of a woman's natural shape, as well as the restrictions of the skirts: 'Our mothers freed us from these in their struggle for emancipation; in our own active workaday lives there can be no possible place for them.'[21] By 1948, much of the furore had died down. Female opinion had most definitely swung in favour of the 'New Look' as it came to be known. One woman said, 'It is more flattering, more feminine, and above all more exciting to wear. We like it, our boyfriends like it – well, what more have we to say?'[22] Any attempt to regulate hemlines and skirt widths were doomed to failure in the face of women's dressmaking ingenuity. If they couldn't afford to buy the fabric, or if shops simply didn't have fabric stocks, they dyed old blackout curtains, made patchwork variations, or sewed strips into dirndl skirts.

The New Look came to represent optimism and abundance during a time of hardship and scarcity. Mavis Ballinger was 17 when she got her first New Look style suit from Harella. It was a rite-of-passage; a fashion coming of age. Birmingham worker Enid Ellis – not much older than Mavis but a lot shorter – hated the New Look because it swamped her. 'I looked like a little girl in her mother's clothes!' she said.[23]

'When I put on a dress for the first time, I flooded myself with tears. I didn't recognise myself in the mirror. We had spent four years in trousers.'

Russian radio operator Valentina Pavlova Chudaeva faces post-war life. She turned her army greatcoat into a civilian jacket and sold her rubber army boots for food. (Alexievich, *The Unwomanly Face of War*)

Dior's New Look now defines the post-war era, fashion-wise. Yet for women being demobbed from the services, *any* kind of civilian clothing was transformative. The switch from uniform to civvies symbolised a release from structure, homogeneity and belonging. It was an unplanned existence, and often directionless. Returning military kit might mean saying farewell to a vivid, meaningful time of life. Nevil Shute addressed this depressing aspect of post-war life in his novel *Requiem for a Wren*. The fictional Wren in question, Jean Prentice, is sadly unable to come to terms with wartime bereavements and the equal grief of being cast out of the navy as surplus to requirements. 'She was better in overalls and bell-bottoms than in a backless evening frock,' commented a friend.

Naval nurse Minnie Lindsell was eager to start new adventures around the world once her service with the QARNNS had ended. She retrained as a midwife. Even so, she was devastated when a thoughtless relative disposed of her wartime uniform. Audrey Pratt left the WAAF in 1946 and found it difficult to settle down again. She disliked what she saw as the pettiness of civilian life. It made her realise how lucky she'd been to have had wider experiences through the war.[24] Eager to woo new customers, John Lewis of London invited WAAFs to a special fashion display, where they could try on fabulous clothes which were simply unaffordable, but they wanted to dream anyway.

Demobilisation often meant adapting to the roles of wife and mother. Here, my grandmother Margaret – with her first son John – has swapped her naval uniform for comfortable skirt, blouse and cardigan.

New clothes and new fashions – was it really the dawn of a new age? Each country and culture had its own challenges to face. Personal tragedies were buried deep as lives were rebuilt. For all the achievements of women in wartime, most post-war governments were keen to engineer society along gendered lines, giving demobbed men the pick of jobs and continuing pay inequalities. Women who'd received technical training and wartime pay packets, who'd been in positions of trust and responsibilities, now had to navigate a post-war world which didn't value them.

Small acts of social amnesia helped overlook wartime roles that didn't fit the new domestic ethos. Female resistance leaders of Norway were denied a part in a 1945 parade before the king.[25] In New Zealand, there were jokes that men would have to mend their own clothes and do their own cooking. They remained jokes: New Zealand women wore aprons instead of uniforms again. Rosie the Riveter of US poster fame was metaphorically sacked: mass mobilisation of American women was swiftly followed by emphatic mass demobilisation, even though one poll of American working women stated 75 per cent wished to continue in paid work.[26] Black Americans, fresh from a war against racism and oppression, found their battles against violence and discrimination continued, very little of it reported in newspapers. Seamstress Rosa Parks, working as a tailor in a local shop, recalled, 'At times I felt overwhelmed by all the violence and hatred, but there was nothing to do but keep going.'[27] In Africa, India, Asia and America it was clear that war had intensified political consciousness, giving a stark awareness of imperialism in all its forms.

The narratives of war that followed focused mainly on male heroics and villainies. Women's lives and experiences were slowly excluded from mainstream narratives of war, and from many military pageants.

This did not mean women were either inactive or silent. Greek women formed the first Panhellenic Women's Conference in May 1946, emboldened by their wartime fights. They spoke about the continuing devaluing of their work, of deprivation, violence and a fierce desire to participate in the evolution of post-war Greece as citizens not chattels.[28] In 1949, the All-China Democratic Women's Federation was formed, teaching women to be economically and socially independent in the new communist era. Palestinian women gathered with equal determination to have their voices heard, saying explicitly that they were not exotic creatures of veils and harems, they were rational, informed people. The struggle to redefine Arab women's roles was overwhelmed by dramatic changes to national boundaries when the new state of Israel was created. Many Palestinian families joined the swell of refugees seeking safety, even as Jewish survivors of the European horrors came to Israel to start new lives.[29]

Aspiration against the odds is a feature of many post-war stories. In 1948, the former German troop carrier, the *Empire Windrush,* sailed from Kingston Jamaica with a stowaway – a seamstress. She was Evelyn Wauchope and she was coming to England to start a new life, optimistically believing

Frankfurt fashions from a 1949 German Royal Moden *pattern book. New silhouettes for a new era. There are sports clothes, elegant dresses, warm coats and dainty blouses.*

Britain would welcome black West Indians. She was only discovered when the ship was seven days out at sea. A whip-round among passengers – including wealthy Nancy Cunard – generated enough money to pay Wauchope's fare with a little left over.[30] Lucilda Harris was another West Indian on the *Windrush.* She was sailing to join her husband, a tailor. If the English climate was a shock, it was mitigated by her husband's gift of a fur coat, which she wore for the next fifty years.[31]

Chaos left everyone vulnerable. All countries affected by war had their share of 'DPs' – Displaced Persons. Millions of civilians left rootless and homeless. For them, Christian Dior would be nothing more than a fairytale name. Their aspirations were more modest: to reconstruct the basics of everyday living. A visitor to the ruins of Hamburg in early 1946 was heartened to see evidence of resilience. She described the scenes of devastation in a letter, adding: 'High up on a pile of rubble was a clothes-line, a few bits of washing flapping in the wind.'[32] The need for civilisation, for dignity and for normal life – all this is shown by laundry among the ruins. It was a sign of life. A sign that whatever war threw at them, women would carry on regardless.

Japanese hikers enjoy their freedom post-war, wearing comfortable clothes. What's beyond the horizon? A new decade and new possibilities.

Notes

Chapter 1: EVERYWHERE AT ONCE

1. *Fili Moda,* January 1942
2. Tomita, Mary Kimoto, *Dear Miye: Letters Home from Japan 1939-1946*, Stanford University Press (1995)
3. Hudson-Richards, Julia, 'Shifting Ideologies of Women's Work in Franco's Spain 1939-1962' *Journal of Women's History* 27:2 (2015)
4. Davin, Deliah, *Woman-Work: Women and the Party in Revolutionary China*, Oxford University Press (1976)
5. Broad, Richard & Suzie Fleming, *Nella Last's War, the Second World War Diaries of Housewife, 49*, Profile Books Ltd (2006)
6. Knill, Iby, *The Woman Without a Number*, Scratching Shed Publishing (2010)
7. Beck, Earl R., *Under the Bombs: The German Home Front, 1942-1945*, The University Press of Kentucky (1986)
8. Correspondence with the author
9. Kynaston, David, *Austerity Britain 1945-1951*, Bloomsbury (2007)
10. Grenfell, Joyce, *The Time of My Life*, Hodder & Stoughton (1989)
11. Tec, Nechama, *Defiance: The True Story of the Bielski Partisans*, Oxford University Press (2008)
12. Alexievich, Svetlana, *The Unwomanly Face of War*, Penguin Random House (2017)
13. Anonymous, *A Woman in Berlin*, Virago (2005)
14. *Vogue* April 1945
15. Barbery, Mary Anna ed,. *39-45: les femmes et la Mob*, Editions Zoé (1989)
16. Montgomerie, Deborah, *The Women's War: New Zealand Women 1939-1945*, Auckland University Press (2001)
17. De Quesada, Alehandro, *The US Home Front 1941-45*, Osprey Publishing (2008)
18. Tipton, Elise, *Modern Japan, a Social and Political History*, Routledge (2008)
19. Anon, *Frauenfundgebung Reichsparteitag Grossdeutschland*, 1938
20. Koontz, Claudia, *Mothers in the Fatherland: Women, the Family and Nazi Politics*, Methuen (1988)
21. Graves, Charles, *Women in Green, The Story of the WVS in Wartime*, Windmill Press (1948)
22. Origo, Iris, *War in Val D'Orcia*, Jonathan Cape (1947)

Chapter 2: TAKING AIM

1. Sands, Phillipe, *East West Street: On the Origins of Genocide and Crimes against Humanity*, Weidenfeld & Nicolson (2016)
2. Langford, Liesbeth, *Written by Candlelight*, Ergo Press (2009)
3. Owings, Alison, *Frauen: German Women Recall the Third Reich*, Penguin (2001)
4. Barrett, Duncan, *Hitler's British Isles*, Simon & Schuster UK (2018)
5. Spanier, Ginette, *It Isn't All Mink*, Random House (1960)
6. Koontz, Claudia, *Mothers in the Fatherland: Women, the Family and Nazi Politics,* Methuen (1988)
7. Holden, Wendy, *Born Survivors*, Sphere (2015)

8. Khan, Yasmin, *The Raj at War: A People's History of India's Second World War,* The Bodley Head (2015)
9. Ericsson, Kjersti, Ed., *Women in War: Examples from Norway and Beyond*, Ashgate Publishing Ltd (2015)
10. Peteet, Julia, *Gender in Crisis: Women and the Palestinian Resistance Movement*, Colombia University Press (1991)
11. Lines, Lisa Margaret, *Milicianas: Women in Combat in the Spanish Civil War*, Lexington Books (2012)
12. Aduga, Minale, *Women and War in Ethiopia*, Gender Issues Research Report Series no. 13 (2001)
13. Byfield, Judith A., Carolyn A. Brown, Timothy Parsons, Ahmad Alawad Sikainga, *Africa in World War II*, Cambridge University Press (2015)
14. Hart, Janet, *New Voices in the Nation: Women and the Greek Resistance, 1941-1964*, Cornell University Press (1996)
15. Slaughter, Jane, *Women and the Italian Resistance 1943-45*, Arden Press (1997)
16. Fowler, Will, *Barbarossa, The First Seven Days*, Casemate Publishers (2004)
17. Edwards, Louise, *Women Warriors and Wartime Spies of China*, CUP (2016)
18. Taylor, Sandra C., *Vietnamese Women at War: Fighting for Ho Chi Minh and the Revolution*, University Press of Kansas (1999)
19. Thomas, Vicky, *The Naga Queen*, The History Press (2012)
20. Baldwin, Monica, *I Leap over the Wall*, Hamish Hamilton (1949)
21. Phillips, Winifred, *Mum's Army: Love and Adventure from the NAAFI to Civvy Street*, Simon & Schuster UK Ltd (2013)
22. Barbery, Mary Anna ed., *39-45: les femmes et la Mob*, Editions Zoé (1989)
23. Brayley, Martin, *World War II Allied Women's Services*, Osprey Publishing (2001)
24. 'A WAC speaks to a soldier' and 'I was a Woman at War' quoted in Maureen Honey, *Bitter Fruit. African American Women in World War II*, University of Missouri Press (1999)
25. Bousquest, Ben & Colin Douglas, *West Indian Women at War. British Racism in World War II*, Lawrence & Wishart (1991)
26. Montgomerie, Deborah, *The Women's War: New Zealand Women 1939-1945*, Auckland University Press (2001)
27. Interview with the author
28. Stargardt, Nicholas, *The German War: A Nation Under Arms, 1939-1945*, Vintage (2016)
29. *The German War*
30. *World War II Allied Women's Services*
31. Braithwaite, Rodric, *Moscow 1941, A City and Its People at War*, Profile Books (2007)
32. Settle, Mary Lee, *All the Brave Promises: Memories of Aircraft Woman 2nd Class 2146391*, Charles Scribner Sons (1998)
33. Alexievich, Svetlana, *The Unwomanly Face of War*, Penguin Random House (2017)
34. Earhart, David C., *Certain Victory: Images of World War II in the Japanese Media*, M.E. Sharpe (2009)
35. Tomita, Mary Kimoto, *Dear Miye: Letters Home from Japan 1939-1946*, Stanford University Press (1995)
36. Hastings, Max, *Nemesis, The Battle for Japan 1944-45*, Harper Press (2007)
37. Graves, Charles, *Women in Green, The Story of the WVS in Wartime*, Windmill Press (1948)
38. *Yorkshire Post,* 31 August 1942 and 4 November 1944
39. *Women in Green*

Chapter 3: OUT OF NOTHING

1. White, Shane and Graham White, *Stylin' – African American Expressive Culture from its Beginnings to the Zoot Suit*, Cornell University Press (1998)
2. Osborne, Elizabeth, *Torres Strait Island Women and the Pacific War*, Aboriginal Studies Press (1997)

3. Khan, Yasmin, *The Raj at War: A People's History of India's Second World War*, The Bodley Head (2015)
4. Czocher, Anna and Dobrochna Kałwa, Barbara Klich-Kluczewska, Beata Łabno, *Is War Men's Business? Fates of Women in Occupied Kraków in Twelve Scenes*, Muzeum Historyczne Miasta Krakowa (2011)
5. Stargardt, Nicholas, *The German War: A Nation Under Arms, 1939-1945*, Vintage (2016)
6. Beck, Earl R., *Under the Bombs: The German Home Front, 1942-1945*, The University Press of Kentucky (1986)
7. Wolff-Mönckeberg, Mathilde, *On The Other Side: To My Children: From Germany 1940-1945*, Pan (1979)
8. Sladen, Christopher, The Conscription of Fashion. Utility Cloth, Clothing and Footwear 1941-1952, Scolar Press (1995)
9. Baldwin, Monica, *I Leap over the Wall*, Hamish Hamilton (1949)
10. Roelen-Grant, Janine, ed., *Fighting for Home and Country. Women remember World War II*, Moffit Print Craft Ltd (2004)
11. Settle, Mary Lee, *All the Brave Promises: Memories of Aircraft Woman 2nd Class 2146391*, Charles Scribner Sons (1998)
12. Janie Hampton, *How the Girl Guides Won the War*, Harper Press (2011)
13. Roelen-Grant, *Fighting for Home and Country*

Chapter 4: AT THE MACHINES

1. Interview with the author
2. Davin, Deliah, *Woman-Work: Women and the Party in Revolutionary China*, Oxford University Press (1976)
3. Correspondence with the author
4. Correspondence with the author
5. Montgomerie, Deborah, *The Women's War: New Zealand Women 1939-1945*, Auckland University Press (2001)
6. Ibid
7. Taiyi, Lin, *War Tide*, John Day Company (1943)
8. Davin, *Woman-Work*
9. Khan, Yasmin, *The Raj at War: A People's History of India's Second World War,* The Bodley Head (2015)
10. Turgel, Gena, *I Light a Candle*, Vallentine Mitchel (2006)
11. Howard, Keith ed., *True Stories of the Korean Comfort Women*, Cassell (1995)
12. Correspondence with the author
13. Walford, Jonathon, *Forties Fashion*, Thames & Hudson (2008)
14. Correspondence with the author
15. Earhart, David C., *Certain Victory: Images of World War II in the Japanese Media*, M.E. Sharpe (2009)
16. Howard, Keith ed., *True Stories of the Korean Comfort Women* Cassell (1995)
17. Marglius, Heda, *Under a Cruel Star: A Life in Prague 1941-1968,* Holmes & Meier (1997)
18. Honey, Maureen, *Bitter Fruit: African American Women in World War II*, University of Missouri Press (1999)
19. Roelen-Grant, Janine, ed., *Fighting for Home and Country: Women remember World War II*, Moffit Print Craft Ltd (2004)
20. Hughes, Helga, *War on Words, Memories of the Home Front during the Second World War from the people of the Kirklees area*, Kirklees Cultural Services (1991)
21. '*The Ladies' Bridge*' article in *The People's Friend,* 12 March 2017
22. Major, Susan, *Female Railway Workers in World War II*, Pen & Sword Transport (2018)

23. Bassett, Jan, ed., *As We Wave You Goodbye: Australian Women and War*, Oxford University Press (1998)
24. Enid Ellis, interview with the author

Chapter 5: ALONG THE CATWALK

1. Moorehead, Caroline, *Martha Gellhorn. A Life*, Vintage (2004)
2. Spanier, Ginette, *It Isn't All Mink*, Random House (1960)
3. Uchalova, Eva, *Prague Fashion Houses 1900-1948*, Arbor Vitae (2011)
4. Epstein, Helen, *Where She Came From: A Daughter's Search for her Mother's History*, Holmes & Meier (2005)
5. Veillon, Dominique, trans. Miriam Kochan, *Fashion Under the Occupation*, Berg (2002)
6. Guenther, Irene, *Nazi Chic? Fashioning Women in the Third Reich*, Berg (2004)
7. Haste, Cate, Nazi Women, Channel 4 Books (2001)
8. Junge, Traudl, with Melissa Müller, *Until the Final Hour*, Phoenix (2005)
9. Arnold, Rebecca, *The American Look. Fashion, Sportswear and the Image of Women in 1930s and 1940s New York*, I.B. Tauris & Co. Ltd (2009)
10. Smith, Julia Faye, *Something to Prove: The Biography of Ann Lowe, America's Forgotten Designer*, Julia Faye Smith (2016)
11. Kramer, Clara, *Clara's War*, Ebury Press (2008)
12. Morris, F.R., *Ladies' Garment Cutting and Making*, The New Era Publishing Co Ltd (undated)
13. Spanier, Ginette, *It Isn't All Mink*, Random House (1960)
14. Ballard, Bettina, *In My Fashion*, Secker & Warburg (1960)

Chapter 6: IN THE QUEUE

1. Kynaston, David, *Austerity Britain 1945-1951*, Bloomsbury (2007)
2. Bousquest, Ben & Colin Douglas, *West Indian Women at War: British Racism in World War II*, Lawrence & Wishart (1991)
3. Baldwin, Monica, *I Leap over the Wall*, Hamish Hamilton (1949)
4. Kynaston, David, *Austerity Britain 1945-1951*, Bloomsbury (2007)
5. Barrett, Duncan, *Hitler's British Isles*, Simon & Schuster UK (2018)
6. Graves, Charles, *Women in Green, The Story of the WVS in Wartime*, Windmill Press (1948)
7. Anon, *The Book of Hints and Wrinkles,* Odhams Press Ltd (no date)
8. Cooper, Artemis, *Cairo in the War 1939-1945*, Hamish Hamilton (1989)
9. Grenfell, Joyce, *The Time of My Life*, Hodder & Stoughton (1989)
10. Ibid
11. *The War Illustrated*, 29 October 1943
12. Majewicz, Leokadia T., *Slaves in Paradise*, GraDar (2004)
13. Goode Robeson, Eslanda, *African Journey*, Victor Gollancz Ltd (1946)
14. Underwood, Sharry Traver, *No Daughter of Mine is Going to Be a Dancer!* Sharry Traver Underwood (2012)
15. Morrison Garrett, Caroline, *Short Skirts and Snappy Salutes: A Woman's Memoir of the WWII Years*, Robertson Publishing (2007)
16. 'Justice Wears Dark Glasses', Negro Story, July-August 1944
17. Roelen-Grant, Janine, ed., *Fighting for Home and Country: Women remember World War II*, Moffit Print Craft Ltd (2004)
18. Hart, Janet, *New Voices in the Nation. Women and the Greek Resistance, 1941-1964*, Cornell University Press (1996)
19. Ligocka, Roma, *The Girl in the Red Coat* – Delta (2003)
20. Roelen-Grant, *Fighting for Home and Country*

21. Kramer, Clara, *Clara's War*, Ebury Press (2008)
22. Stargardt, Nicholas, *The German War: A Nation Under Arms, 1939-1945*, Vintage (2016)
23. Schloss, Eva, with Evelyn Julia Kent, *Eva's Story*, Wm B. Eerdman's (1988,2010)
24. Owings, Alison, *Frauen: German Women Recall the Third Reich*, Penguin (2001)
25. Stargardt, *The German War A Nation Under Arms, 1939-1945*, Vintage (2016)
26. Wolff-Mönckeberg, Mathilde, *On The Other Side: To My Children: From Germany 1940-1945*, Pan (1979)
27. Moorehead, Caroline, *A Train in Winter – A Story of Resistance*, Vintage (2012)
28. Stargardt, *The German War A Nation Under Arms, 1939-1945*, Vintage (2016)
29. Veillon, Dominique, trans. Miriam Kochan, *Fashion Under the Occupation*, Berg (2002)
30. Tomita, Mary Kimoto, *Dear Miye: Letters Home from Japan 1939-1946*, Stanford University Press (1995)
31. Taiyi, Lin, *War Tide*, John Day Company (1943)
32. Abkhazi, Peggy, S.W. Jackman ed. *Enemy Subject: Life in a Japanese Internment Camp 1943-45*, Alan Sutton Publishing Ltd (1981
33. Godden, Rumer, *Bengal Journey*, Longmans Green & Co Ltd (1945)
34. Khan, Yasmin, *The Raj at War: A People's History of India's Second World War*, The Bodley Head (2015)
35. Lewis, Norman, *Naples '44: An intelligence officer in the Italian labyrinth*, Eland (2011)

Chapter 7: ON THE LAND

1. Tomita, Mary Kimoto, *Dear Miye: Letters Home from Japan 1939-1946*, Stanford University Press (1995)
2. *Hacksaw Ridge* dir. Mel Gibson, Cross Creek Pictures (2016)
3. Braithwaite, Rodric, *Moscow 1941, A City and Its People at War*, Profile Books (2007)
4. Taylor, Sandra C., *Vietnamese Women at War: Fighting for Ho Chi Minh and the Revolution*, University Press of Kansas (1999)
5. Stark, Freya, *Dust in the Lion's Paw: Autobiography 1939-1946*, Arrow (1985)
6. Eileen Little, correspondence with the author
7. Roelen-Grant, Janine, ed., *Fighting for Home and Country: Women remember World War II*, Moffit Print Craft Ltd (2004)
8. Owings, Alison, *Frauen: German Women Recall the Third Reich*, Penguin (2001)
9. Barbery, Mary Anna ed., *39-45: les femmes et la Mob*, Editions Zoé (1989)
10. Montgomerie, Deborah, *The Women's War: New Zealand Women 1939-1945*, Auckland University Press (2001)
11. Scott, Jean, *Girls With Grit: Memories of the Australian Women's Land Army*, Allen & Unwin (1986)
12. Anon, *Meet the Members, A Record of the Timber Corps of the Women's Land Army*, Bennet Brothers Ltd, 1945
13. Williams, Mavis, *Lumber Jill, Her story of four years in the Women's Timber Corps 1942-45*, Ex Libris Press (1994)
14. *Woman's Fair*, March 1940

Chapter 8: SKIES ABOVE – Aviation

1. Pelletier, Alain, *High-Flying women: A World History of Female Pilots*, Haynes (2012)
2. Escott, Beryl E., *Our Wartime Days, The WAAF*, The History Press (1995)
3. Interview with the author
4. Younghusband, Eileen, *One Woman's War*, Candy Jar Books (2013)
5. Escott, Beryl E., *Our Wartime Days The WAAF*, The History Press (1995)
6. Ibid

7. Ibid
8. Noggle, Anne, *A Dance with Death: Soviet Airwomen in World War II*, Texas A&M University Press (2001)
9. Bousquest, Ben & Colin Douglas, *West Indian Women at War: British Racism in World War II*, Lawrence & Wishart (1991)
10. 'A Woman Warrior' *ERK* magazine March 1943
11. Correspondence with the author
12. Ewing, Elizabeth, *Women in Uniform through the Centuries*, Batsford (1975)
13. Escott, Beryl E., *Our Wartime Days, The WAAF*, The History Press (1995)
14. Settle, Mary Lee, *All the Brave Promises: Memories of Aircraft Woman 2nd Class 2146391*, Charles Scribner Sons (1998)
15. Correspondence with the author
16. Interview with the author
17. Curtiss, Lettice, *The Forgotten Pilots*, G.T.Foulis & Co (1971)
18. Pelletier, Alain, *High-Flying women: A World History of Female Pilots*, Haynes (2012)
19. Ibid
20. Hyams, Jacky, *The Female Few: Spitfire Heroines*, The History Press (2018)
21. Cheeseman, E.C., *Brief Glory, The Story of the Air Transport Auxiliary*, CPI Group (1946)
22. Reitsch, Hanna, trans. Lawrence Wilson, *The Sky My Kingdom*, Bodley Head (1955)
23. Mulley, Clare, *The Women Who Flew for Hitler*, Macmillan (2017)
24. Pennington, Reina, *Wings, Women & War: Soviet Airwomen in World War II Combat*, University Press of Kansas (2001)
25. Alexievich, Svetlana, *The Unwomanly Face of War*, Penguin Random House (2017)
26. Noggle, Anne, *A Dance with Death: Soviet Airwomen in World War II*, Texas A&M University Press (2001)
27. Information from Hilary Dodd and Fiona Tuck; correspondence with the author
28. Bourne, Stephen, *Mother Country: Britain's Black Community on the Home Front 1939-45*, The History Press (2010)

Chapter 9: ALL AT SEA

1. Phillips, Winifred, *Mum's Army: Love and Adventure from the NAAFI to Civvy Street*, Simon & Schuster UK Ltd (2013)
2. Tomita, Mary Kimoto, *Dear Miye: Letters Home from Japan 1939-1946*, Stanford University Press (1995)
3. Howarth, David, *The Shetland Bus*, The Shetland Times Ltd (2017)
4. Janie Hampton, *How the Girl Guides Won the War*, Harper Press (2011)
5. Prince, Cathryn J., *Death in the Baltic: The World War II Sinking of the Wilhelm Gustloff*, Palgrave Macmillan (2013)
6. Janie Hampton, *How the Girl Guides Won the War*, Harper Press (2011)
7. Brittain, Vera, *England's Hour*, Continuum (2005)
8. Stanley, Jo, *Women and the Royal Navy*, I.B.Tauris (2018)
9. Brayley, Martin & Richard Ingram, *World War II British Women's Uniforms in Colour Photographs*, The Crowood Press Ltd (2011)
10. Roelen-Grant, Janine, ed., *Fighting for Home and Country: Women remember World War II*, Moffit Print Craft Ltd (2004)
11. Houston, Roxane, *Changing Course, the Engaging Memoir of a Second World War Wren*, Grub Street (2005)
12. Brayley, Martin, *World War II Allied Women's Services*, Osprey Publishing (2001)
13. Houston, Roxane, *Changing Course, the Engaging Memoir of a Second World War Wren*, Grub Street (2005)

14. Correspondence with the author
15. Miller, Lee, *Wrens in Camera*, Hollis and Carter (1945)
16. Stanley, Jo, *Women and the Royal Navy*, I.B.Tauris (2018)
17. Ibid
18. Miller, Lee, *Wrens in Camera*, Hollis and Carter (1945)
19. *Military History* magazine November 2017
20. Raynes, Rozelle, *Maid Matelot: Adventures of a Wren Stoker in World War Two*, Catweasel Publishing (2004)

Chapter 10: BEHIND CLOSED DOORS

1. Guenther, Irene, *Nazi Chic? Fashioning Women in the Third Reich*, Berg (2004)
2. Baldwin, Monica, *I Leap over the Wall*, Hamish Hamilton (1949)
3. Morrison Garrett, Caroline, *Short Skirts and Snappy Salutes: A Woman's Memoir of the WWII Years*, Robertson Publishing (2007)
4. Lefebure, Molly, *Murder on the Home Front*, Sphere (2013/1954)
5. Souhami, Diana, *Murder at Wrotham Hill*, Quercus (2013)
6. Chase, Joanna, *Sew and Save*, The Literary Press Ltd (undated)
7. Kathleen Wilkie and Joan Bell. Interviews with the author
8. Tec, Nechama, *Defiance: The True Story of the Bielski Partisans*, Oxford University Press (2008)
9. Holden, Wendy, *Born Survivors*, Sphere (2015)
10. *Headrow Herald* magazine December 1948
11. Hughes, Helga, *War on Words, Memories of the Home Front during the Second World War from the people of the Kirklees area*, Kirklees Cultural Services (1991)
12. Lorna Carr. Interview with the author
13. Garrett-Morrison, *Short Skirts and Snappy Salutes*
14. Interview with the author
15. Houston, Roxane, *Changing Course, the Engaging Memoir of a Second World War Wren*, Grub Street (2005)
16. Phillips, Winifred, *Mum's Army: Love and Adventure from the NAAFI to Civvy Street*, Simon & Schuster UK Ltd (2013)
17. Anonymous, *A Woman in Berlin*, Virago (2005)
18. Barbery, Mary Anna ed., *39-45: les femmes et la Mob*, Editions Zoé (1989)
19. Ericsson, Kjersti, Ed., *Women in War: Examples from Norway and Beyond*, Ashgate Publishing Ltd (2015)
20. *Vogue* April 1945
21. Majewicz, Leokadia T., *Slaves in Paradise*, GraDar (2004)
22. Settle, Mary Lee, *All the Brave Promises: Memories of Aircraft Woman 2nd Class 2146391*, Charles Scribner Sons (1998)
23. Escott, Beryl E., *Our Wartime Days, The WAAF*, The History Press (1995)
24. Hughes, Helga, *War on Words, Memories of the Home Front during the Second World War from the people of the Kirklees area*, Kirklees Cultural Services (1991)
25. Majewicz, Leokadia T., *Slaves in Paradise*, GraDar (2004)

Chapter 11: UNDER COVER – Spies, codes and computing

1. McDonald-Rothwell, Gabrielle, *Her Finest Hour: The Heroic Life of Diana Rowden, Wartime Secret Agent*, Amberley Books (2017)
2. Interview with the author
3. Berr, Hélène. Trans. David Bellos, *Le Journal of Hélène Berr*, McClelland & Stewart (2008)
4. Barbery, Mary Anna ed., *39-45: les femmes et la Mob*, Editions Zoé (1989)

5. Etherington, William, *A Quiet Woman's War*, Mousehold Press (2002)

6. Janie Hampton, *How the Girl Guides Won the War*, Harper Press (2011)

7. Howarth, David, *The Shetland Bus*, The Shetland Times Ltd (2017)

8. Mazzeo, Tilar J., *Irena's Children*, Gallery Books (2016)

9. Stargardt, Nicholas, *The German War: A Nation Under Arms, 1939-1945*, Vintage (2016)

10. Roelen-Grant, Janine, ed., *Fighting for Home and Country: Women remember World War II*, Moffit Print Craft Ltd (2004)

11. Slaughter, Jane, *Women and the Italian Resistance 1943-45*, Arden Press (1997)

12. *Ibid*

13. Helm, Sarah, *If This is a Woman: Inside Ravensbrück: Hitler's Concentration Camp for Women*, Abacus (2016)

14. Czocher, Anna and Dobrochna Kałwa, Barbara Klich-Kluczewska, Beata Łabno, *Is War Men's Business? Fates of Women in Occupied Kraków in Twelve Scenes*, Muzeum Historyczne Miasta Krakowa (2011)

15. Ibid

16. Kirschner, Ann, *Sala's Gift*, Free Press (2006)

17. Khan, Yasmin, *The Raj at War: A People's History of India's Second World War*, The Bodley Head (2015)

18. McKay, Sinclair, *The Lost World of Bletchley Park: An Illustrated History of the Wartime Codebreaking Centre*, Aurum Press Ltd (2013)

19. *The Times* obituary 6 March 2015

20. Mulvihill, Mary, ed., *Lab coats and lace: The lives and legacies of inspiring Irish women scientists and pioneers*, WITS Women in Technology and Science (2009)

21. Shetterly, Margot Lee, *Hidden Figures: The Untold Story of the African American Women who Helped Win the Space Race*, William Collins (2016)

22. Mulvihill, Mary, ed., *Lab Coats and Lace*

23. Knill, Iby, *The Woman Without a Number*, Scratching Shed Publishing (2010)

24. Mulley, Clare, *The Spy Who Loved*, Pan (2013)

25. Escott, Beryl E. - *Mission Improbable: A salute to the RAF women of SOE in wartime France*, Patrick Stevens Limited (1991)

26. Ottaway, Susan, *Sisters, Secrets and Sacrifice, the True Stories of WWII Special Agents Eileen and Jacqueline Nearne*, Harper Elemental (2013)

27. Anand, Vidya, *Indian Heroes and Heroines of World War II a Brief History*, Institute for Media Communication (1995)

Chapter 12: ON THE DANCE FLOOR

1. Cooper, Artemis, *Cairo in the War 1939-1945*, Hamish Hamilton (1989)

2. Morris, Mary, ed. Carol Acton, *A Very Private Diary: A Nurse in Wartime*, Wiedenfeld & Nicholson (2014)

3. Stark, Freya, *Dust in the Lion's Paw: Autobiography 1939-1946*, Arrow (1985)

4. Cooper, Artemis, *Cairo in the War*

5. Morrison Garrett, Caroline, *Short Skirts and Snappy Salutes: A Woman's Memoir of the WWII Years*, Robertson Publishing (2007)

6. Graves, Charles, *Women in Green, The Story of the WVS in Wartime*, Windmill Press (1948)

7. *Dancing Times* May 1944

8. Barrett, Duncan, *Hitler's British Isles*, Simon & Schuster UK (2018)

9. Young, Caroline, *Classic Hollywood Style* – Frances Lincoln (2012)

10. Huang, Nicole, *Women, War, Domesticity: Shanghai Literature and Popular Culture of the 1940s*, Brill (2003)

11. Honey, Maureen, *Bitter Fruit: African American Women in World War II*, University of Missouri Press (1999)

12. Lusane, Clarence, *Hitler's Black Victims: The Historical Experience of Afro-Germans, European Blacks, Africans and African Americans in the Nazi Era*, Routledge (2003)
13. Roelen-Grant, Janine, ed., *Fighting for Home and Country: Women remember World War II*, Moffit Print Craft Ltd (2004)
14. Braithwaite, Rodric, *Moscow 1941, A City and Its People at War*, Profile Books (2007)
15. Bourne, Stephen, *Mother Country: Britain's Black Community on the Home Front 1939-45*, The History Press (2010)
16. Houston, Roxane, *Changing Course, the Engaging Memoir of a Second World War Wren*, Grub Street (2005)
17. Flanner, Janet, *Paris Journal 1944-1965*, Atheneum Publishers (1965)
18. Cooper, Artemis, *Cairo in the War*
19. Grenfell, Joyce, *The Time of My Life*, Hodder & Stoughton (1989)
20. Ibid
21. Lynn, Dame Vera, *Some Sunny Day: My Autobiography*, Harper (2010)
22. Grenfell, Joyce, *The Time of My Life*
23. Anonymous, *The Social Half-Hour Handbook*, National Federation of Women's Institutes, University Press (1948)
24. Hunt, Margaret, *Beauty Culture*, Unknown Publisher/Date
25. Bolton, Angela, *The Maturing Sun: An Army Nurse in India 1942-45*, Headline (1985)

Chapter 13: IN THE LOOKING GLASS

1. Hunt, Margaret, *Beauty Culture*, Unknown Publisher/Date
2. Fromm, Bella, *Blood and Banquets: A Berlin Social Diary*, Birch Lane Press (1990)
3. Moorhouse, Roger, *The Third Reich in 100 Objects. A Material History of Nazi Germany*, Greenhill Books (2017)
4. *Illustrated Weekly of India*, November 1945
5. *The Strand* May 1940
6. *Headrow Herald* December 1948
7. *Elle* 8 January 1941
8. Goode Robeson, Eslanda, *African Journey*, Victor Gollancz Ltd (1946)
9. Bolton, Angela, *The Maturing Sun: An Army Nurse in India 1942-45*, Headline (1985)
10. Ostrom, Lizzie, *Perfume, a Century of Scents*, Hutchinson (2015)
11. Godden, Rumer, *Bengal Journey*, Longmans Green & Co Ltd (1945)
12. Morris, Mary, ed. Carol Acton, *A Very Private Diary, A Nurse in Wartime*, Wiedenfeld & Nicholson (2014)
13. Ibid
14. Veillon, Dominique, trans. Miriam Kochan, *Fashion Under the Occupation*, Berg (2002)
15. Ballard, Bettina, *In My Fashion*, Secker & Warburg (1960)
16. Broad, Richard & Suzie Fleming, *Nella Last's War, the Second World War Diaries of Housewife, 49*, Profile Books Ltd (2006)

Chapter 14: UP THE AISLE

1. Kanter, Trudi, *Some Girls, Some Hats and Hitler*, Neville Spearman Ltd (1984); Virago (2012)
2. Cooper, Artemis, *Cairo in the War 1939-1945*, Hamish Hamilton (1989)
3. Knill, Iby, *The Woman Without a Number*, Scratching Shed Publishing (2010)
4. Kornreich, Rena, *Rena's Promise: Two Sisters in Auschwitz*, Weidenfeld & Nicholson (1996)
5. Alexievich, Svetlana, *The Unwomanly Face of War*, Penguin Random House (2017)
6. Settle, Mary Lee, *All the Brave Promises: Memories of Aircraft Woman 2nd Class 2146391*, Charles Scribner Sons (1998)

7. Gun, Nerin E., *Eva Braun, Hitler's Mistress*, Leslie Frewin (1969)
8. Graves, Charles, *Women in Green, The Story of the WVS in Wartime*, Windmill Press (1948)
9. Lynn, Dame Vera, *Some Sunny Day: My Autobiography*, Harper (2010)
10. *The Lady*, 29 August 2014
11. Morris, Mary, ed. Carol Acton, *A Very Private Diary, A Nurse in Wartime*, Wiedenfeld & Nicholson (2014)
12. Interview with the author
13. Correspondence with the author
14. Osborne, Elizabeth, *Torres Strait Island Women and the Pacific War*, Aboriginal Studies Press (1997)
15. Escott, Beryl E., *Our Wartime Days, The WAAF*, The History Press (1995)
16. Correspondence with the author
17. Correspondence with the author
18. Correspondence with the author
19. Stark, Freya, *Dust in the Lion's Paw: Autobiography 1939-1946*, Arrow (1985)
20. Granqvist, Hilma, *Marriage Conditions in a Palestinian Village II*, Societas Scientiarum Fennica (1935)
21. Knill, Iby, *The Woman Without a Number*, Scratching Shed Publishing (2010)
22. Hart, Janet, *New Voices in the Nation: Women and the Greek Resistance, 1941-1964*, Cornell University Press (1996)
23. Correspondence with the author
24. Correspondence with the author
25. Correspondence with the author
26. Flanner, Janet, *Paris Journal 1944-1965*, Atheneum Publishers (1965)

Chapter 15: ROCKING THE CRADLE

1. Alexievich, Svetlana, *The Unwomanly Face of War*, Penguin Random House (2017)
2. De Grazia, Victoria, *How Fascism Ruled Women*, University of California Press (1992)
3. Owings, Alison, *Frauen: German Women Recall the Third Reich*, Penguin (2001)
4. Fromm, Bella, *Blood and Banquets: A Berlin Social Diary*, Birch Lane Press (1990)
5. Moorhouse, Roger, *The Third Reich in 100 Objects. A Material History of Nazi Germany*, Greenhill Books (2017)
6. Sullivan, Jim ed., *Doing Their Bit: New Zealand Women tell their Stories of World War Two*, HarperCollins (2002)
7. Correspondence with the author
8. Aduga, Minale, *Women and War in Ethiopia*, Gender Issues Research Report Series no. 13 (2001)
9. Alexievich, Svetlana, *The Unwomanly Face of War*
10. Roelen-Grant, Janine, ed., *Fighting for Home and Country: Women remember World War II*, Moffit Print Craft Ltd (2004)
11. Holland, James, *Fortress Malta, An Island Under Siege 1940-1943*, Phoenix (2005)
12. Helm, Sarah, *If This is a Woman: Inside Ravensbrück: Hitler's Concentration Camp for Women*, Abacus (2016)
13. *Life* 23 October 1939
14. H.M.S.O., *The First to be Freed: The Record of British Military Administration in Eritrea and Somalia 1941-1943* (1944)
15. Allen, Elaine, *Watkins Household Hints*, Whitman Publishing Co. (1941)
16. Correspondence with the author
17. Origo, Iris, *War in Val D'Orcia*, Jonathan Cape (1947)
18. Interview with the author
19. Storey, Joyce, *Joyce's War 1939-1945*, Virago (1992)
20. Priestley, J.B., *British Women Go To War*, Collins (1943)

Chapter 16: RUNNING FOR COVER

1. Wolff-Mönckeberg, Mathilde, *On The Other Side: To My Children: From Germany 1940-1945*, Pan (1979)
2. Hiroshima Peace Culture Foundation, *Eyewitness Testimonies: Appeals from the A-bomb Survivors* (1990)
3. Moorehead, Caroline, *Martha Gellhorn. A Life*, Vintage (2004)
4. Hughes, Helga, *War on Words, Memories of the Home Front during the Second World War from the people of the Kirklees area*, Kirklees Cultural Services (1991)
5. Wolff-Mönckeberg, *On The Other Side*
6. Osborne, Elizabeth, *Torres Strait Island Women and the Pacific War*, Aboriginal Studies Press (1997)
7. Khan, Yasmin, *The Raj at War: A People's History of India's Second World War*, The Bodley Head (2015)
8. *Heaven and Earth Monthly*, 5 February 1944
9. Correspondence with the author
10. Euphan Todd, Barbara, *Miss Ranskill Comes Home*, Chapman & Hall (1946)
11. Correspondence with the author
12. Ballard, Bettina, *In My Fashion*, Secker & Warburg (1960)
13. Holland, James, *Fortress Malta, An Island Under Siege 1940-1943*, Phoenix (2005)
14. Choudhary, Savitri, *I Made My Home in England*, Grant-West (1960)
15. Houston, Roxane, *Changing Course, the Engaging Memoir of a Second World War Wren*, Grub Street (2005)
16. Origo, Iris, *War in Val D'Orcia*, Jonathan Cape (1947)
17. McGrory, David, *Coventry at War*, The History Press (2009)
18. Beck, Earl R., *Under the Bombs: The German Home Front, 1942-1945*, The University Press of Kentucky (1986)
19. Schneider, Helga, *The Bonfire of Berlin: A lost childhood in wartime Germany*, William Heinemann (2005)
20. Anonymous, *A Woman in Berlin*, Virago (2005)
21. *Our Blitz: Red Skies over Manchester*, Kemsley Newspapers Ltd (1945)
22. Interview with the author
23. Ewing, Elizabeth, *Women in Uniform through the Centuries*, Batsford (1975)
24. Graves, Charles, *Women in Green, The Story of the WVS in Wartime*, Windmill Press (1948)
25. Stargardt, Nicholas, *The German War: A Nation Under Arms, 1939-1945*, Vintage (2016)
26. Interview with the author

Chapter 17: ON CALL

1. Anonymous, *A Woman in Berlin*, Virago (2005)
2. Hart, Janet, *New Voices in the Nation: Women and the Greek Resistance, 1941-1964*, Cornell University Press (1996)
3. Moorehead, Caroline, *Martha Gellhorn. A Life*, Vintage (2004)
4. Fyrth, Jim and Sally Alexander, eds., *Women's Voices from the Spanish Civil War*, Lawrence and Wishart (1991)
5. Ballard, Bettina, *In My Fashion*, Secker & Warburg (1960)
6. De Grazia, Victoria, *How Fascism Ruled Women*, University of California Press (1992)
7. Godden, Rumer, *Bengal Journey*, Longmans Green & Co Ltd (1945)
8. Holman, Dennis, *Lady Louis, Life of the Countess Mountbatten of Burma*, Odhams Press Ltd (1952)
9. Boss, Joan, *Love and War in India: My War Years, 1942-1945*, Brook Bros (2005)
10. Janie Hampton, *How the Girl Guides Won the War*, Harper Press (2011)

11. Morris, Mary, ed. Carol Acton, *A Very Private Diary, A Nurse in Wartime*, Wiedenfeld & Nicholson (2014)
12. Correspondence with the author
13. Interview with the author
14. Bolton, Angela, *The Maturing Sun: An Army Nurse in India 1942-45*, Headline (1985)
15. Madden, Brian, *Hernia Bay, Sydney's Wartime Hospitals at Riverwood*, Canterbury & District Historical Society (2001)
16. Bassett, Jan, ed., *As We Wave You Goodbye: Australian Women and War*, Oxford University Press (1998)
17. Collins, Robert & Han Hogerzeil, *Straight On – Journey to Belsen and the Road Home*, Methuen & Co Ltd. (1947)
18. Interview with the author
19. Aharoni, Ada, *The Woman in White: An Extraordinary Life*, Createspace Independent Publishing Platform (2017)
20. Interview with the author
21. Morris, Mary, ed. Carol Acton, *A Very Private Diary, A Nurse in Wartime*, Wiedenfeld & Nicholson (2014)
22. Braithwaite, Rodric, *Moscow 1941, A City and Its People at War*, Profile Books (2007)
23. Alexievich, Svetlana, *The Unwomanly Face of War*, Penguin Random House (2017)

Chapter 18: BEHIND BARS

1. Flanner, Janet, *Paris Journal 1944-1965*, Atheneum Publishers (1965)
2. Yamaguchi, Precious – *Experiences of Japanese American Women during and after World War II*, Lexington Books (2014)
3. Bassett, Jan, ed., *As We Wave You Goodbye: Australian Women and War*, Oxford University Press (1998)
4. www.changi.redcross.org.uk Retrieved January 2019
5. Abkhazi, Peggy, S.W. Jackman ed., *Enemy Subject: Life in a Japanese Internment Camp 1943-45*, Alan Sutton Publishing Ltd (1981)
6. Holland, Noel & Rosemary Say, *Rosie's War – an Englishwoman's Escape from Occupied France*, Michael O'Mara books (2011)
7. Ginzburg, Eugenia Semyonovna, trans. Paul Stevenson & Max Hayward, *Journey Into the Whirlwind*, Harcourt Brace Jovanovich (1967)
8. Majewicz, Leokadia T., *Slaves in Paradise*, GraDar (2004)
9. Barrett, Duncan, *Hitler's British Isles*, Simon & Schuster UK (2018)
10. Fantlova, Zdenka, *The Tin Ring, How I cheated Death*, Northumbria Press (2010)
11. Sereny, Gitta, *Into That Darkness: From Mercy Killing to Mass Murder*, Pimlico (1995)
12. Steinbacher, Sybille, trans. Shaun Whiteside, *Auschwitz – A History*, Penguin (2004)
13. Schneider, Helga, *The Bonfire of Berlin: A lost childhood in wartime Germany*, William Heinemann (2005)
14. Moorehead, Caroline, *Martha Gellhorn. A Life*, Vintage (2004)
15. Kounio Amariglio, Erika, *From Thessaloniki to Auschwitz and Back*, Valentine Mitchell (2000)
16. Correspondence with the author
17. Koontz, Claudia, *Mothers in the Fatherland: Women, the Family and Nazi Politics*, Methuen (1988)
18. Shelley, Lore ed., *Auschwitz – The Nazi Civilization: Twenty-three Women Prisoners' Accounts*, University Press of America (1992)
19. Kirschner, Ann, *Sala's Gift*, Free Press (2006)
20. Kounio Amariglio, Erika, *From Thessaloniki to Auschwitz and Back*
21. Delbo, Charlotte, *Auschwitz and After*, Yale University Press (1995)
22. Buber-Neumann, Margarete, trans. Ralph Manheim, *Milena*, Collins Harvill (1989)

23. Ginzburg, Eugenia Semyonovna, *Journey into the Whirlwind*
24. Holden, Wendy, *Born Survivors*, Sphere (2015)
25. Collins, Robert & Han Hogerzeil, *Straight On – Journey to Belsen and the Road Home*, Methuen & Co Ltd. (1947)
26. Interview with the author
27. Holman, Dennis, *Lady Louis, Life of the Countess Mountbatten of Burma*, Odhams Press Ltd (1952)

Chapter 19: PICKING UP THE PIECES

1. Spanier, Ginette, *It Isn't All Mink*, Random House (1960)
2. Hunt, Vincent, *Fire and Ice: The Nazis' Scorched Earth Campaign in Norway*, The History Press (2018)
3. Kanter, Trudi, *Some Girls, Some Hats and Hitler*, Neville Spearman Ltd (1984); Virago (2012)
4. Correspondence with the author
5. Barrett, Duncan, *Hitler's British Isles*, Simon & Schuster UK (2018)
6. Interview with the author
7. Alexievich, Svetlana, *The Unwomanly Face of War*, Penguin Random House (2017)
8. Morrison Garrett, Caroline, *Short Skirts and Snappy Salutes: A Woman's Memoir of the WWII Years*, Robertson Publishing (2007)
9. Panter-Downes, Mollie, *Good Evening Mrs Craven – the Wartime Stories of Mollie Panter-Downes*, Persephone Classics (2008)
10. Escott, Beryl E., *Our Wartime Days, The WAAF*, The History Press (1995)
11. Anonymous, *A Woman in Berlin*, Virago (2005)
12. Morris, Mary, ed. Carol Acton, *A Very Private Diary, A Nurse in Wartime*, Wiedenfeld & Nicholson (2014)
13. Barrett, Duncan, *Hitler's British Isles*
14. Marglius, Heda, *Under a Cruel Star, A Life in Prague 1941-1968*, Holmes & Meier (1997)
15. Ballard, Bettina, *In My Fashion*, Secker & Warburg (1960)
16. *Yorkshire Evening News*, 1 January 1947
17. Ballard, *In My Fashion*
18. Pick, Michael, *Hardy Amies*, ACC (2012)
19. Fields, Jill, *An Intimate Affair. Women: Lingerie and Sexuality*, University of California Press (2007)
20. Sladen, Christopher, The Conscription of Fashion. Utility Cloth, Clothing and Footwear 1941-1952, Scolar Press (1995)
21. *Picture Post*, 27 September 1947
22. *Headrow Herald*, Christmas 1948
23. Correspondence with the author
24. Correspondence with the author
25. Ericsson, Kjersti, Ed., *Women in War: Examples from Norway and Beyond*, Ashgate Publishing Ltd (2015)
26. Hart, Janet, *New Voices in the Nation: Women and the Greek Resistance, 1941-1964*, Cornell University Press (1996)
27. Parks, Rosa, *Rosa Parks. My Story*, Puffin Books (1999)
28. Hart, Janet, *New Voices in the Nation: Women and the Greek Resistance, 1941-1964*, Cornell University Press (1996)
29. Fleishchmann, Ellen, *The Emergence of the Palestinian Women's movement 1929-1938*, Insititue for Palestine Studies vol 29 no 3 1999/2000
30. *The Daily Gleaner*, 5 August 1948
31. https://windrushfoundation.com Retrieved January 2019
32. Wolff-Mönckeberg, Mathilde, *On The Other Side: To My Children: From Germany 1940-1945*, Pan (1979)

Bibliography

Autobiographies

Abkhazi, Peggy, S.W. Jackman ed., *Enemy Subject: Life in a Japanese Internment Camp 1943-45*, Alan Sutton Publishing Ltd (1981)

Adams Earley, Charity, *One Woman's Army: A Black Officer Remembers the WAC*, Texas A&M University Military History (2009)

Anonymous, *A Woman in Berlin*, Virago (2005)

Aubrac, Lucie, *Outwitting the Gestapo*, (Kindle edition) (2015)

Bagnall, Audrey, *When Grandma Wore Breeches*, Amberley (2009)

Baldwin, Monica, *I Leap over the Wall*, Hamish Hamilton (1949)

Ballard, Bettina, *In My Fashion*, Secker & Warburg (1960)

Bernstein, Sara Tuvel, *The Seamstress: A Memoir of Survival*, Penguin Putnam Inc (1999)

Berr, Hélène. Trans. David Bellos, *Le Journal of Hélène Berr*, McClelland & Stewart (2008)

Bolton, Angela, *The Maturing Sun: An Army Nurse in India 1942-45*, Headline (1985)

Boss, Joan, *Love and War in India: My War Years, 1942-1945*, Brook Bros (2005)

Bourne, Stephen and Esther Bruce, *Aunt Esther's Story*, Ethnic Communities Oral History Project (2001)

Brittain, Vera, *England's Hour*, Continuum (2005)

Broad, Richard & Suzie Fleming, *Nella Last's War, the Second World War Diaries of Housewife, 49*, Profile Books Ltd (2006)

Buch, Mary Hawkins, *Props On Her Sleeve: The Wartime Letters of a Canadian Airwoman*, Dundern (1997)

Choudhary, Savitri, *I Made My Home in England*, Grant-West (1960)

Curtiss, Lettice, *The Forgotten Pilots*, G.T.Foulis & Co (1971)

Delbo, Charlotte, *Auschwitz and After*, Yale University Press (1995)

Dickens, Monica, *One Pair of Feet*, Michael Joseph Ltd (1942)

Fantlova, Zdenka, *The Tin Ring, How I cheated Death*, Northumbria Press (2010)

Flanner, Janet, *Paris Journal 1944-1965*, Atheneum Publishers (1965)

Fromm, Bella, *Blood & Banquets: A Berlin Social Diary*, Birch Lane Press (1990)

Ginzburg, Eugenia Semyonovna, trans. Paul Stevenson & Max Hayward, *Journey Into the Whirlwind*, Harcourt Brace Jovanovich (1967)

Goering, Emmy, *My Life with Goering*, David Bruce & Watson Ltd (1972)

Goode Robeson, Eslanda, *African Journey*, Victor Gollancz Ltd (1946)

Grenfell, Joyce, *The Time of My Life*, Hodder & Stoughton (1989)

Guttman, Ester, *'Thank God for England': Escape from Nazi Germany*, Barney books (date unknown)

Hahn, Lili, *White Flags of Surrender*, Robert B. Luce Inc. (1974)

Hart-Moxon, Kitty, *Return to Auschwitz*, The Holocaust Memorial Centre (2007)

Holland, Noel & Rosemary Say, *Rosie's War – an Englishwoman's Escape from Occupied France*, Michael O'Mara books (2011)

Houston, Roxane, *Changing Course, the Engaging Memoir of a Second World War Wren*, Grub Street (2005)

Howarth, David, *The Shetland Bus*, The Shetland Times Ltd (2017)

Bibliography

Hughes, Helga, *War on Words: Memories of the Home Front during the Second World War from the people of the Kirklees area*, Kirklees Cultural Services (1991)

Jalowicz-Simon, Marie, *Gone to Ground: One Woman's extraordinary account of survival in the heart of Nazi Germany*, Clerkenwell Press (2015)

Junge, Traudl, with Melissa Müller, *Until the Final Hour*, Phoenix (2005)

Kanter, Trudi, *Some Girls, Some Hats and Hitler*, Neville Spearman Ltd (1984); Virago (2012)

Kerr, Judith, *Bombs on Aunt Dainty*, HarperCollins Children's Books (2012)

Kitagawa, Muriel, *This is My Own: Letters to Wes & Other Writings on Japanese Canadians, 1941-1948*, Talonbooks (1985)

Knill, Iby, *The Woman Without a Number*, Scratching Shed Publishing (2010)

Kornreich, Rena, *Rena's Promise: Two Sisters in Auschwitz*, Weidenfeld & Nicholson (1996)

Kounio Amariglio, Erika, *From Thessaloniki to Auschwitz and Back*, Valentine Mitchell (2000)

Kovaly, Heda Margolius – *Under a Cruel Star: A Life in Prague 1941-68*, Granta Books (2012)

Kramer, Clara, *Clara's War* Ebury Press (2008)

Lack, Katherine, *Frontstalag 142: The Internment Diary of an English Lady*, Amberley (2010)

Lanckoronkska, Countess Karolina, *Those Who Trespass Against Us. One Woman's War Against the Nazis*, Pimlico (2005)

Langford, Liesbeth, *Written by Candlelight*, Ergo Press (2009)

Lasker-Wallfisch, Anita, *Inherit the Truth 1939-1945*, Giles de la Mare Publishers Ltd (1996)

Lefebure, Molly, *Murder on the Home Front*, Sphere (2013/1954)

Leipman, Flora, *The Long Journey Home: The Memoirs of Flora Leipman*, Bantam Press (1987)

Leslie, Anita, *A Story Half Told: A Wartime Autobiography*, Hutchinson (1983)

Lewis, Norman, *Naples '44: An intelligence officer in the Italian labyrinth,* Eland (2011)

Ligocka, Roma, *The Girl in the Red Coat*, Delta (2003)

Lipszyce, Rywka, *Rywka's Diary*, HarperCollins (2015)

Loridan-Ivens Marceline, *But You Did Not Come Back*, Faber & Faber Ltd (2017)

Lum, Lucy, *The Thorn of Lion City, A Memoir*, Harper Perennial (2008)

Lynn, Dame Vera, *Some Sunny Day: My Autobiography*, Harper (2010)

Majewicz, Leokadia T., *Slaves in Paradise*, GraDar (2004)

Marglius, Heda, *Under a Cruel Star, A Life in Prague 1941-1968,* Holmes & Meier (1997)

Meggison, Irene, *Mud on My Doorstep: Reminiscences of a Yorkshire Farmwife*, Hutton Press Ltd (1987)

Morris, Mary, ed. Carol Acton, *A Very Private Diary, A Nurse in Wartime*, Wiedenfeld & Nicholson (2014)

Morrison Garrett, Caroline, *Short Skirts and Snappy Salutes: A Woman's Memoir of the WWII Years*, Robertson Publishing (2007)

Moyle, Anwyn, *Her Ladyship's Girl: A Maid's Life in London*, Simon & Schuster (2014)

Origo, Iris, *War in Val D'Orcia*, Jonathan Cape (1947)

Parks, Rosa, *Rosa Parks: My Story*, Puffin Books (1999)

Peron, Eva, trans. Laura Dail, *In My Own Words: Evita*, Mainstream Publishing (1996)

Phillips, Winifred, *Mum's Army: Love and Adventure from the NAAFI to Civvy Street*, Simon & Schuster UK Ltd (2013)

Raynes, Rozelle, *Maid Matelot: Adventures of a Wren Stoker in World War Two*, Catweasel Publishing (2004)

Reitsch, Hanna, trans. Lawrence Wilson, *The Sky My Kingdom*, Bodley Head (1955)

Rougier-Lecoq, Violette, *Témoinages 36 Dessins à la plume Ravensbrück*, Imprimerie Auclerc (1982)

Say, Rosemary, *Rosie's War: An Englishwoman's Escape from Occupied France*, Michael O'Mara Books (2011)

Schloss, Eva, with Evelyn Julia Kent, *Eva's Story*, Wm B. Eerdman's (1988, 2010)

Schloss, Eva, with Karen Bartlett, *After Auschwitz: A Story of Heartbreak and Survival by the Stepsister of Anne Frank*, Hodder (2013)

Schneider, Helga, *Let Me Go: My Mother and the SS*, Vintage (2005)

Schneider, Helga, *The Bonfire of Berlin: A lost childhood in wartime Germany*, William Heinemann (2005)

Settle, Mary Lee, *All the Brave Promises: Memories of Aircraft Woman 2nd Class 2146391*, Charles Scribner Sons (1998)

Shelley, Lore ed., *Auschwitz – The Nazi Civilization: Twenty-three Women Prisoner's Accounts* (University Press of America (1992)

Smith, Emma, *As Green as Grass: Growing Up Before, During & After the Second World War*, Bloomsbury (2013)

Somerset Country Federation of Women's Institutes, *What Did You Do In the War, Grandma?,* Countryside Books (2005)

Sone, Monica, *Nisei Daughter*, University of Washington Press (1979)

Spanier, Ginette, *It Isn't All Mink*, Random House (1960)

Stark, Freya, *Dust in the Lion's Paw: Autobiography 1939-1946*, Arrow (1985)

Steel, Dyne, *A 'One and Only' Looks Back*, The Pentland Press Ltd (1992)

Storey, Joyce, *Joyce's War 1939-1945*, Virago (1992)

Tomita, Mary Kimoto, *Dear Miye: Letters Home from Japan 1939-1946*, Stanford University Press (1995)

Turgel, Gena, *I Light a Candle*, Vallentine Mitchel (2006)

Tyrer, Nicola, *Sisters in Arms: British Army Nurses Tell Their Story*, Weidenfeld & Nicholson (2008)

Underwood, Sharry Traver, *No Daughter of Mine is Going to Be a Dancer!* Sharry Traver Underwood (2012)

Vassilieva, Tatiana, trans. Anna Trenter, *A Hostage to War*, Hamish Hamilton (1996)

Vassiltchikov, Marie, *Berlin Diaries 1940-1945*, Vintage (1988)

Verrill-Rhys & Deirdre Beddoe eds., *Parachutes and Petticoats: Welsh women writing on the Second World War*, Honno (1992)

Wells, Irene, *My Life in the Land Army, Work and Play in the WLA*, Bidford Printers (1984)

Wendel, Else, *Hausfrau at War (1939-1945) A German Woman's Account of Life in Hitler's Reich*, The Pentland Press Ltd

Wild, Sylvia, *Woman at the Front: Memoirs of an ATS Girl D-Day to 1946*, Amberley (2012)

Wildgoose, Doreen, *What did you do in the War, Grandma? Doreen Wildgoose remembers her childhood in wartime Sheffield*, Sheaf Publishing (1995)

Williams, Mavis, *Lumber Jill: Her story of four years in the Women's Timber Corps 1942-45*, Ex Libris Press (1994)

Witherington Cornioley, Pearl, *Code Name Pauline: Memoirs of a World War II Special Agent*, Chicago Review Press (2015)

Wolff-Mönckeberg, Mathilde, *On The Other Side: To My Children: From Germany 1940-1945*, Pan (1979)

Women's Institute Memoir Writers, *Crocodiles, Cakes and the Queen's Petticoats*, Queenbee Press (2011)

Yeadon, Hazel, *What Did You Do In the War, Granny? Stories from women now living in the Teesdale area who played their part in WW2*, self-published (2006)

Younghusband, Eileen, *One Woman's War*, Candy Jar Books (2013)

Biographies

Aharoni, Ada, *The Woman in White: An Extraordinary Life*, Createspace Independent Publishing Platform (2017)

Anand, Vidya, *Indian Heroes and Heroines of World War II a Brief History*, Institute for Media Communication (1995)

Braddon, Russell, *Nancy Wake*, The Book Club (1956)

Bruley, Sue, ed., *Working for Victory: A Diary of Life in a Second World War Factory*, The History Press (2001)

Bibliography

Buber-Neumann, Margarete, trans. Ralph Manheim, *Milena*, Collins Harvill (1989)

Burke, Carolyn, *Lee Miller: On Both Sides of the Camera*, Bloomsbury Publishing (2005)

Coatts, Margot, *A Weaver's Life: Ethel Mairet 1872 – 1952*, Crafts Council (1983)

Epstein, Helen, *Where She Came From: A Daughter's Search for her Mother's History*, Holmes & Meier (2005)

Fraser, Nicholas & Marysa Navarro, *Evita: The Real Lives of Eva Peron*, André Deutsch (2003)

Glaser, Paul, *Dancing with the Enemy: My Family's Holocaust Secret*, Oneworld Publications (2015)

Gun, Nerin E., *Eva Braun, Hitler's Mistress*, Leslie Frewin (1969)

Gwizdak Greenwood, CM., *The Whistler*, Marilyn Greenwood (2014)

Holman, Dennis, *Lady Louis, Life of the Countess Mountbatten of Burma*, Odhams Press Ltd (1952)

Kirschner, Ann, *Sala's Gift*, Free Press (2006)

Klabunde, Anja, *Magda Goebbels*, Sphere (2001/7)

Mazzeo, Tilar J., *Irena's Children*, Gallery Books (2016)

McDonald-Rothwell, Gabrielle, *Her Finest Hour: The Heroic Life of Diana Rowden, Wartime Secret Agent*, Amberley Books (2017)

Moorehead, Caroline, *Martha Gellhorn. A Life*, Vintage (2004)

Mulley, Clare, *The Spy Who Loved*, Pan (2013)

Philipponnat, Oliver & Patrick Lienhardt, *The Life of Irène Némirovsky*, Chatto & Windus (2010)

Purnell, Sonia, *First Lady, the Life and Wars of Clementine Churchill*, Aurum Press Ltd (2015)

Smith, Julia Faye, *Something to Prove: The Biography of Ann Lowe, America's Forgotten Designer*, Julia Faye Smith 2016)

Sands, Phillipe, *East West Street: On the Origins of Genocide and Crimes against Humanity*, Weidenfeld & Nicolson (2016)

Starns, Penny, *Surviving Tenko, the Story of Margot Turner*, The History Press (2010)

Thomas, Vicky, *The Naga Queen*, The History Press (2012)

Social and Military History

Adam-Smith, Patsy, *Australian Women at War*, Nelson (1984)

Aduga, Minale, *Women and War in Ethiopia*, Gender Issues Research Report Series no. 13 (2001)

Aldrich, Richard J., *Witness to War: Diaries of the Second World War in Europe and the Middle East*, Corgi Books (2005)

Alexievich, Svetlana, *The Unwomanly Face of War*, Penguin Random House (2017)

Aly, Gotz & Susanne Heim, *Architects of Annihilation, Auschwitz and the logic of destruction*, Phoenix (2003)

Anderson, Janice, *Thrifty Tips from the War Years*, Futura (2010)

Baade, Christina, 'Between Factory and Home. *Music while you work and women listeners at the wartime BBC*', Feminist Media Studies vol 7 no 3 September 2007

Barker, Stacey and Molly McCullough, *World War Women*, Canadian Museum of History (2015)

Bassett, Jan, ed., *As We Wave You Goodbye: Australian Women and War*, Oxford University Press (1998)

Barbery, Mary Anna ed., *39-45: les femmes et la Mob*, Editions Zoé (1989)

Barrett, Duncan, *Hitler's British Isles*, Simon & Schuster UK (2018)

Beck, Earl R., *Under the Bombs: The German Home Front, 1942-1945*, The University Press of Kentucky (1986)

Beevie, Mariam, '*The Passing of Literary Tradition. The Figure of the Woman from Vietnamese Nationalism to Vietnamese American Transnationalism*' Amerasia Journal 23:2 (1997)

Beevor, Anthony, *Berlin, the Downfall 1945*, Viking (2002)

Beevor, Anthony & Luba Vinogradova eds & trans., *A Writer At War: Vasily Grossman with the Red Army 1941-1945*, Pimlico (2006)

Bourne, Stephen, *Mother Country: Britain's Black Community on the Home Front 1939-45*, The History Press (2010)

Bousquest, Ben & Colin Douglas, *West Indian Women at War. British Racism in World War II*, Lawrence & Wishart (1991)

Braithwaite, Rodric, *Moscow 1941, A City and Its People at War*, Profile Books (2007)

Brayley, Martin, *World War II Allied Women's Services*, Osprey Publishing (2001)

Brayley, Martin & Richard Ingram, *World War Two British Women's Uniforms*, Crowood (2011)

Bryan, Tim, *The Great Western at War 1939-1945,* Patrick Stephens Ltd (1995)

Byfield, Judith A., Carolyn A. Brown, Timothy Parsons, Ahmad Alawad Sikainga, *Africa in World War II*, Cambridge University Press (2015)

Cheeseman, E.C., *Brief Glory, The Story of the Air Transport Auxiliary*, CPI Group (1946)

Collins, Robert & Han Hogerzeil, *Straight On – Journey to Belsen and the Road Home*, Methuen & Co Ltd. (1947)

Costello, John, *Love, Sex & War. Changing Values 1939-45*, Guild Publishing (1985)

Cooper, Artemis – *Cairo in the War 1939-1945*, Hamish Hamilton (1989)

Czocher, Anna and Dobrochna Kałwa, Barbara Klich-Kluczewska, Beata Łabno, *Is War Men's Business? Fates of Women in Occupied Kraków in Twelve Scenes*, Muzeum Historyczne Miasta Krakowa (2011)

Davin, Deliah, *Woman-Work: Women and the Party in Revolutionary China*, Oxford University Press (1976)

De Grazia, Victoria, *How Fascism Ruled Women*, University of California Press (1992)

De Quesada, Alehandro, *The US Home Front 1941-45*, Osprey Publishing (2008)

Earhart, David C., *Certain Victory: Images of World War II in the Japanese Media*, M.E. Sharpe (2009)

Edwards, Louise, *Women Warriors and Wartime Spies of China*, CUP (2016)

Ericsson, Kjersti, ed., *Women in War: Examples from Norway and Beyond*, Ashgate Publishing Ltd (2015)

Escott, Beryl E., *Mission Improbable: A salute to the RAF women of SOE in wartime France*, Patrick Stevens Limited (1991)

Escott, Beryl E., *Our Wartime Days, The WAAF*, The History Press (1995)

Etherington, William, *A Quiet Woman's War*, Mousehold Press (2002)

Evans, Paul & Peter Doyle, *The 1940s Home*, Shire Publications (2010)

Ewing, Elizabeth, *Women in Uniform Through the Centuries*, Batsford (1975)

FitzGibbon, Constantine, *London's Burning*, Ballantine Books (1970)

FitzGibbon, Constantine, *The Blitz*, Macdonald (1970)

Fowler, Will, *Barbarossa, The First Seven Days*, Casemate Publishers (2004)

Fryer, Peter, *Staying Power, The History of Black People in Britain*, Pluto Press (2010)

Fyrth, Jim and Sally Alexander, eds., *Women's Voices from the Spanish Civil War*, Lawrence and Wishart (1991)

Gilroy, Paul, *Black Britain: A Photographic History*, Saqi (2007)

Godden, Rumer, *Bengal Journey,* Longmans Green & Co Ltd (1945)

Goldberg, Myrna & Amy H. Shapiro, eds., *Different Horrors, Same Hell: Gender and the Holocaust*, University of Washington Press (2013)

González-Ruibal, Alfredo, Yonatan Sahle, Xurxo Ayán Vila, *'A social archaeology of colonial war in Ethiopia'* World Archaeology, vol 43, issue 1 (2011)

Goodpaster-Strebe, Amy, *Flying for Her Country: The American and Soviet Women Military Pilots of World War II*, Praeger Security International (2007)

Gossage, Carolyn, *Greatcoats and Glamour Boots*, Dundern (2001)

Graf, Mercedes, *To Heal and To Serve: Women Army Doctors in World War Two*, Hellgate Press (2014)

Graves, Charles, *Women in Green, The Story of the WVS in Wartime,* Windmill Press (1948)

Halson, Penrose, *Marriages Are Made in Bond Street: True Stories from a 1940s Marriage Bureau*, Macmillan (2016)

Hampton, Ellen, *Women of Valor: The Rochambelles on the WWII Front*, Palgrave Macmillan (2006)

Janie Hampton, *How the Girl Guides Won the War*, Harper Press (2011)

Hart, Janet, *New Voices in the Nation: Women and the Greek Resistance, 1941-1964,* Cornell University Press (1996)

Bibliography

Haste, Cate, *Nazi Women,* Channel 4 Books (2001)

Hastings, Max, *Nemesis, The Battle for Japan 1944-45*, Harper Press (2007)

Hawkins-Buch, Mary, *Props on Her Sleeve: The Wartime Letters of a Canadian Airwoman*, Dundum (1997)

Helm, Sarah, *If This is a Woman: Inside Ravensbrück: Hitler's Concentration Camp for Women*, Abacus (2016)

Hershey, John, *Hiroshima*, Penguin (1946)

Hindus, Maurice, *Mother Russia*, William Collins (1944)

Hiroshima Peace Culture Foundation, *Eyewitness Testimonies: Appeals from the A-bomb Survivors*, (1990)

Hiroshima Publishing Committee, *Days to Remember: An Account of the Bombings of Hiroshima and Nagasaki* (1981)

Holden, Wendy, *Born Survivors*, Sphere (2015)

Holland, James, *Fortress Malta, An Island Under Siege 1940-1943*, Phoenix (2005)

Honey, Maureen, *Bitter Fruit: African American Women in World War II*, University of Missouri Press (1999)

Howard, Keith ed., *True Stories of the Korean Comfort Women*, Cassell (1995)

Huang, Nicole, *Women, War, Domesticity: Shanghai Literature and Popular Culture of the 1940s*, Brill (2003)

Hudson-Richards, Julia, *'Shifting Ideologies of Women's Work in Franco's Spain 1939-1962'* Journal of Women's History 27:2 (2015)

Hunt, Vincent, *Fire and Ice: The Nazis' Scorched Earth Campaign in Norway*, The History Press (2018)

Hyams, Jacky, *Bomb Girls: Britain's Secret Army: the Munitions Women of World War II*, John Blake Publishing Ltd (2014)

Hyams, Jacky, *The Female Few: Spitfire Heroines*, The History Press (2018)

Jenkins, Alan, *The Forties*, Heinemann (1977)

Jones, Michael, *Leningrad, State of Seige*, John Murray (2008)

Khan, Yasmin, *The Raj at War: A People's History of India's Second World War,* The Bodley Head (2015)

Kee, Robert & Joanna Smith, *We'll Meet Again: Photographs of Daily Life in Britain during World War II*, Dent (1984)

Kiernan, Denise, *The Girls of Atomic City: The Untold Story of the Women who Helped Win World War II*, Touchstone (2013)

Knopp, Guido, trans. Angus McGeoch, *Hitler's Women,* Sutton Publishing (2006)

Koontz, Claudia, *Mothers in the Fatherland: Women, the Family and Nazi Politics*, Methuen (1988)

Kynaston, David, *Austerity Britain 1945-1951*, Bloomsbury (2007)

Lines, Lisa Margaret, *Milicianas: Women in Combat in the Spanish Civil War*, Lexington Books (2012)

Longmate, Norman, *How We Lived Then: A history of everyday life during the Second World War*, Arrow Books Ltd (1977)

Lower, Wendy, *Hitler's Furies, German Women in the Nazi Killing Fields*, Chatto & Windus (2013)

Lusane, Clarence, *Hitler's Black Victims: The Historical Experience of Afro-Germans, European Blacks, Africans and African Americans in the Nazi Era*, Routledge (2003)

Lynn, Vera, *Unsung Heroines: The Women Who Won the War*, Sidgwick & Jackson (1990)

MacDonogh, Giles, *After the Reich: From the Liberation of Vienna to the Berlin Airlift*, John Murray (2007)

Madden, Brian, *Hernia Bay, Sydney's Wartime Hospitals at Riverwood*, Canterbury & District Historical Society (2001)

Major, Susan, *Female Railway Workers in World War II,* Pen & Sword Transport (2018)

Malcolmson, Patricia & Robert, *Women at the Ready: The Remarkable Story of the Women's Voluntary Services on the Home Front*, Little, Brown (2013)

Mant, Joan, *All Muck, Now Medals: Landgirls by Landgirls,* Amberley Publishing (2009)

McBryde, Brenda, *Quiet Heroines: Nurses of the Second World War*, Chatto & Windus (1985)

McGrory, David, *Coventry at War*, The History Press (2009)

McKay, Sinclair, *The Lost World of Bletchley Park: An Illustrated History of the Wartime Codebreaking Centre*, Aurum Press Ltd (2013)

McKay, Sinclair, *The Secret Life of Bletchley Park: The WWII Codebreaking Centre and the Men and Women Who Worked There,* Aurum Press Ltd (2010)

McKay, Sinclair, *The Secret Listeners: The Men and Women Posted Across the World to Intercept the German Codes for Bletchley Park*, Aurum Press Ltd (2012)

Miller, Lee, *Wrens in Camera,* Hollis and Carter (1945)

Montgomerie, Deborah, *The Women's War: New Zealand Women 1939-1945*, Auckland University Press (2001)

Moore, Brenda L., *To Serve My Country, To Serve My Race: The Story of the Only African American WACs Stationed Overseas during World War II*, New York University Press (1996)

Moorehead, Caroline, *A Train in Winter – A Story of Resistance*, Vintage (2012)

Moorhouse, Roger, *The Third Reich in 100 Objects: A Material History of Nazi Germany*, Greenhill Books (2017)

Mulley, Clare, *The Women Who Flew for Hitler*, Macmillan (2017)

Mulvihill, Mary, *Lab Coats and Lace: The Lives and Legacies of Inspiring Irish Women Scientists and Pioneers*, WITS (2009)

National Museum of African American History & Culture – *Double Exposure: African American Women*, GILES (2015)

Nicholson, Virginia, *Millions Like Us: Women's Lives During the Second World War*, Penguin (2012)

Noggle, Anne, *A Dance with Death: Soviet Airwomen in World War II*, Texas A&M University Press (2001)

Norma, Caroline, *The Japanese Comfort Women and Sexual Slavery during the China and Pacific Wars*, Bloomsbury Academic (2016)

Oppenheimer, Melanie, *Australian Women and War*, Department of Veteran's Affairs (2008)

Osborne, Elizabeth – *Torres Strait Island Women and the Pacific War*, Aboriginal Studies Press (1997)

Ostrom, Lizzie, *Perfume, a Century of Scents,* Hutchinson (2015)

Ottaway, Susan, *Sisters, Secrets and Sacrifice, the True Stories of WWII Special Agents Eileen and Jacqueline Nearne*, Harper Elemental (2013)

Owings, Alison, *Frauen: German Women Recall the Third Reich,* Penguin (2001)

Patten, Marguerite, *Victory Cookbook: Nostalgic Food and Facts from 1940-1954*, Chancellor Press (2002)

Pelletier, Alain, *High-Flying women: A World History of Female Pilots*, Haynes (2012)

Pennington, Reina, *Wings, Women & War: Soviet Airwomen in World War II Combat*, University Press of Kansas (2001)

Penrose, Antony, ed., *Lee Miller's War*, Thames & Hudson (2008)

Peteet, Julia, *Gender in Crisis: Women and the Palestinian Resistance Movement*, Colombia University Press (1991)

Powell, Bob & Nigel Westacott, *The Women's Land Army*, The History Press (2009)

Priestley, J.B., *British Women Go To War*, Collins (1943)

Prince, Cathryn J., *Death in the Baltic: The World War II Sinking of the Wilhelm Gustloff*, Palgrave Macmillan (2013)

Ridd, Rosemarry, and Helen Callaway eds., *Caught up in Conflict – Women's Responses to Political Strife*, Macmillan Education (1986)

Roelens-Grant, Janine ed., *Fighting for Home & Country: Women Remember World War II*, Moffit Print Craft Ltd (2004)

Rothnie, Niall, *The Baedeker Blitz: Hitler's Attack on Britain's Historic Cities*, Ian Allan Publishing (1992)

Rotondaro, Anna, *Women at Work on London's Transport 1905-1978*, Tempus Publishing Ltd (2004)

Russell, Lynn & Neil Hanson, *The Sweethearts: Tales of Love, Laughter and Hardship from the Yorkshire Rowntree's girls*, HarperCollins (2013)

Sakaida, Henry, *Heroines of the Soviet Union*, Osprey Publishing (2003)

Scott, Jean, *Girls With Grit: Memories of the Australian Women's Land Army*, Allen & Unwin (1986)

Sebba, Anne, *Les Parisiennes: How the Women of Paris Lived, Loved and Died in the 1940s*, Weidenfeld & Nicolson (2016)

Sereny, Gita, *Into That Darkness: From Mercy Killing to Mass Murder*, Pimlico (1995)

Shaw, Maureen & Helen D. Millgate, *War's Forgotten Women. British Widows of the Second World War*, The History Press (2011)

Sheridan, Dorothy, ed., *Wartime Women: A Mass-Observation Anthology 1937-45*, Phoenix Press (2000)

Shetterly, Margot Lee, *Hidden Figures: The Untold Story of the African American Women who Helped Win the Space Race*, William Collins (2016)

Snyder, Louis L., *Encyclopaedia of the Third Reich*, Wordsworth Editions Ltd (1998)

Slaughter, Jane, *Women and the Italian Resistance 1943-45*, Arden Press (1997)

Souhami, Diana, *Murder at Wrotham Hill*, Quercus (2013)

Stanley, Jo, *Women and the Royal Navy*, I.B. Tauris (2018)

Stargardt, Nicholas, *The German War: A Nation Under Arms, 1939-1945*, Vintage (2016)

Steinbacher, Sybille, trans Shaun Whiteside, *Auschwitz – A History* Penguin (2004)

Sullivan, Jim ed., *Doing Their Bit: New Zealand Women tell their Stories of World War Two*, HarperCollins (2002)

Taylor, Sandra C., *Vietnamese Women at War: Fighting for Ho Chi Minh and the Revolution*, University Press of Kansas (1999)

Tec, Nechama, *Defiance: The True Story of the Bielski Partisans*, Oxford University Press (2008)

Thistlethwaite, June, *Cumbria The War Years: Lake District Life during the 1940s*, Thyme Press (1997)

Tipton, Elise, *Modern Japan, a Social and Political History,* Routledge (2008)

Turner, Des, *Station 12: SOE's Secret Weapons Centre*, The History Press (2006)

Visram, Rozina, *Asians in Britain, 400 Years of History*, Pluto Press (2002)

Von Wormer, Katherine, David W. Jackson III and Charletta Sudduth, *The Maid Narratives. Black domestics and white families in the Jim Crow South,* Louisiana State University Press (2012)

Waller, Jane & Michael Vaughan-Rees, *Women in Wartime: The Role of Women's Magazine 1939-1945*, Macdonald & Co (1987)

Whittell, Giles, *Spitfire Women of World War II*, Harper Perennial (2008)

Wicks, Ben, *Waiting for the All Clear: True Stories from Survivors of the Blitz*, Guild Publishing (1990)

Yamaguchi, Precious, *Experiences of Japanese American Women during and after World War II*, Lexington Books (2014)

Zaki, Omar, 'How did Japanese wars of aggression impact women in Japanese society between 1937 & 1945', School of Oriental and African Studies, BA History paper (2012)

Costume and Textile History

Arnold, Rebecca, *The American Look: Fashion, Sportswear and the Image of Women in 1930s and 1940s New York*, I.B. Tauris & Co. Ltd (2009)

Barth, Nadine ed., *German Fashion Design 1946 – 2012*, Distanz (2011)

Baxter-Wright, Emma, *The Little Book of Schiaparelli* – Carlton Books (2012)

Boydell, Christine, *Horrockses Fashions: Off-the-Peg Style in the '40s and '50s*, V&A Publishing (2010)

Brayley, Martin, *World War II Allied Women's Services*, Osprey Publishing Ltd (2001)

Brayley, Martin & Richard Ingram, *World War II British Women's Uniforms in Colour Photographs*, The Crowood Press Ltd (2011)

Burke, Sue, *West African Adire*, Birmingham Polytechnic (1986)

Byers, Margaretta, *Designing Women: The Art, Technique, and Cost of Being Beautiful*, John Miles (1939)

Caillard, Sylvie, *L'Elégance: Comment être coquette sous l'occupation 1940-1945*, Histoire & Collections (2015)

Carter, Ernestine, *Magic Names of Fashion*, Weidenfeld and Nicolson (1980)

Cawthorne, Nigel, *The New Look: The Dior Revolution*, Hamlyn (1996)

Chase, Joanna, *Sew and Save*, The Literary Press Ltd (1941)

Connell, Linda, *Textile Treasures of the WI*, The National Needlework Archive (2007)

De La Haye, Amy, *The Cutting Edge: 50 Years of British Fashion 1947-1997*, V&A Publications (1997)

Ewing, Elizabeth, *Women in Uniform through the Centuries*, Batsford (1975)

Fields, Jill, *An Intimate Affair: Women, Lingerie and Sexuality*, University of California Press (2007)

Garret, Valery M., *Traditional Chinese Clothing* – Oxford University Press (1994)

Guenther, Irene, *Nazi Chic? Fashioning Women in the Third Reich*, Berg (2004)

Guilfoyle Williams, J., *The Wear and Care of Clothing*, The National Trade Press (1945)

Hopkins, Alan and Vanessa, *Footwear: Shoes and Boots from the Hopkins Collection*, The School of Historical Dress (2015)

Laboissonniere, Wade, *Blueprints of Fashion: Home Sewing Patterns of the 1940s*, Schiffer Publishing Ltd (1997)

Lansdell, Avril, *Wedding Fashions 1860-1980*, History in Camera (1983)

Laver, James, *Letter to a Girl on the Future of Clothes*, Home & Van Thal Ltd (1946)

Lundbäck, Maja, *Hemslöjdens Handarbeten*, Victor Pettersons (1948)

Lupano, Mario and Alessandra Vaccari eds., *Fashion at the Time of Fascism: Italian Modernist Lifestyle 1922-1943,* Damiani (2009)

McDowell, Colin, *Forties Fashion and the New Look*, Bloomsbury (1997)

Museo Poldi Pezzoli, *1922-1943 Vent'anni Di Moda Italiana*, Centro Di (1980)

Nahshon, Edna, *Jews and Shoes* Berg (2008)

Newark, Tim, *Camouflage*, Thames & Hudson (2007)

Olian, JoAnne, *Everyday Fashions of the Forties As Pictured in Sears Catalogs*, Dover Publications (1992)

Page, Christopher, *Foundations of Fashion: The Symington Collection. Corsetry from 1856 to the Present Day*, Leicestershire Museums (1981)

Pick, Michael, *Hardy Amies*, ACC (2012)

Ribeiro, Aileen, with Cally Blackman, *A Portrait of Fashion: Six Centuries of Dress at the National Portrait Gallery*, NPG (2015)

Sladen, Christopher, *The Conscription of Fashion: Utility Cloth, Clothing and Footwear 1941-1952*, Scolar Press (1995)

Summers, Julie, *Fashion on the Ration: Style in the Second World War*, Profile Books Ltd (2015)

The Royal Pavilion, Art Gallery & Museums Brighton, *Norman Hartnell*, Bath City Council (1985)

Torrens, Deborah, *Fashion Illustrated: A Review of Women's Dress 1920-1950*, Studio Vista (1974)

Uchalova, Eva, *Czech Fashion 1918-1939*, Olympia (1996)

Uchalova, Eva, *Prague Fashion Houses 1900-1948,* Arbor Vitae (2011)

Veillon, Dominique, trans. Miriam Kochan, *Fashion Under the Occupation*, Berg (2002)

Walford, Jonathon, *Forties Fashion*, Thames & Hudson (2008)

Weir, Shelagh, *Palestinian Costume*, British Museum Publications Ltd (1990)

White, Shane and Graham White, *Stylin' – African American Expressive Culture from its Beginnings to the Zoot Suit*, Cornell University Press (1998)

Williamson, Gordon, *World War II German Women's Auxiliary Services*, Osprey Publishing Ltd (2003)

Wood, Maggie, *We Wore What We'd Got: Women's Clothes in World War II*, Warwickshire Books (1989)

Wray, Margaret, *The Women's Outerwear Industry*, Duckworth & Co Ltd (1957)

Young, Caroline, *Classic Hollywood Style*, Frances Lincoln (2012)

Contemporary magazines, catalogues, pattern books, leaflets

Album du Figaro, France

BIOS report I.G. Farben 1946 Germany

BIOS report Japanese Textiles 1947 Japan

Bibliography

By Jantzen, Britain

Carson, Mary A., *The Girl's Companion*, Blackie & Son Ltd (1947)

Catalogo di Moda, Italy

Craig, Elizabeth, *Needlecraft*, Collins (1947)

Crisis magazine, USA

Dancing Times Britain

Das Blatt der Hausfrau, Germany

De Haardvriend, Germany

Die Hausfrau, Germany

Elle, France

E.R.K. magazine, South Africa

Farmer's Weekly, Britain

Fili Moda, Italy

Franks, Catherine, *The Pictorial Guide to Modern Home Knitting*, Odhams Press Ltd (undated)

Frauenfundgebung Reichsparteitag Grosdeutchland 1938 (Women's Rally, Reich Party Convention) Germany

Frauen Helfen Siegen, Berlin 1941

Fürs Haus, Germany

Good Housekeeping, *A War Bride's Guide to the USA*, 1945, reprinted Collins & Brown (2006)

Gut Flicken! Gut Stopfen! A.D.A. Germany

H.M.S.O., Frontline 1940-1941 (1941) GB

H.M.S.O., It All Depends On Me series of propaganda cards, undated

H.M.S.O., Join the WAAF – Help the RAF recruitment leaflet, undated

H.M.S.O., Roof Over Britain: The Official Story of the A.A. Defences, 1939-1942 (1943) GB

H.M.S.O., Textile Auxiliary Products Manufactured by I.G. Farbenindustrie Hainkur Works July 1946 Germany

H.M.S.O., Textile Industries of Japan February 1947 Japan

H.M.S.O., The First to be Freed: The Record of British Military Administration in Eritrea and Somalia 1941 -1943 (1944) Somalia

Home Companion, Britain

Huldt, Åke H. Huldt and Eva Benedicks – *Design in Sweden Today*, Swedish Institute for Cultural Relations, Forum (1948) Sweden

Hulme, W.H., *Women's and Children's Garment Design*, The National Trade Press Ltd (1948)

Hunt, Margaret H., *Charm*, publication unknown, undated

Illustrated, Britain

Illustrated Weekly of India

John Bull, Britain

Labores Realces, España

La Petit Echo de la Mode, France

Leach-Way Catalogue of Fashions, Britain

Le Jardin des Modes, France

Les Patrons Universelles, France

Life, USA

Life in the W.R.N.S., anon, Raphael Tuck & Sons Ltd London, undated

LNER Staff magazines 1943-45

L'Officiel, France

London Off Duty, Britain

Make Do And Mend, Board of Trade, Britain

Maudella Fashions and Useful Patterns, Britain

Meet the Members, A Record of the Timber Corps of the Women's Land Army, Bennet Brothers Ltd, 1945

Modes et Travaux, France

Morris, F.R. – *Ladies' Garment Cutting and Making*, The New Era Publishing Co Ltd (undated)
Murray, Margaret & Jane Koster, *Knitting For All,* Odhams Press Ltd (1942)
Murray, Margaret & Jane Koster, Practical Knitting Illustrated, Odhams Press Ltd (1947)
Negro y Blanco Labores, Mexico
Oasis pocket magazine India
Opportunities magazine, USA
Our Blitz: Red Skies over Manchester, Kemsley Newspapers Ltd (1945) GB
Personality Clothes, Britain
Picturegoer, Britain
Picture Show and Film Pictorial, Britain
Picture Show, Britain
Picture Post, USA
Pour Elle, France
Punch, or the London Charivari, Britain
Quick Change Siren Woollies – Weldon's Knitting Series no. 29, Britain
Royal Moden, Germany
Sharp Perrin & Co Ltd, Britain
Simplicity patterns, USA
Société des Nouveautés Textiles Summer 1941
Société des Nouveautés Textiles Winter 1948
Speed, F. Maurice, *Film Review 1945-6*, Macdonald & Co Ltd (1945)
Staite, Frances A. – Glove Making At Home, J.H. Lake & Co. (1948)
Stitchcraft magazine
Swimming Times, Britain
Talbot, Constance, *The Complete Book of Sewing, Book Presentations NY* (1943)
Theatre World, Britain
The Book of Hints and Wrinkles, Odhams Press Ltd (no date)
The Strand Magazine, Britain
The Pictorial guide to Modern Home Needlecraft, Odhams Press (1946)
The War Illustrated, Britain
Union Schnitt, Germany
Vogue, Britain; USA; France
Vogue Book of Smart Dressmaking, USA
Vogue-Knit series, Britain
Vogue Pattern Book, Britain
Votre Amie Marie-France, France
Votre Mode, France
Weldon's Ladies Journal, Britain
Woman, Britain
Woman's Fair, Britain
Woman's Journal, Britain
Woman's Magazine, Britain
Women's Timber Corps Notes for 1943, Home Timber Production Department, Ministry of Supply GB
Wyeth Spears, Ruth – *Better Dressmaking*, The World's Work Ltd (1948)
Yorkshire Evening Post, Britain

Contemporary Fiction and Film

Angelou, May, *I Know Why the Caged Bird Sings*, Virago Press (1984)
Euphan Todd, Barbara, *Miss Ranskill Comes Home*, Chapman & Hall (1946)
Falluda, Hans, *Alone in Berlin*, 1947, trans. Michael Hofmann Penguin (2007)

Bibliography

Hershey, John, *Hiroshima,* Penguin Books (1946)

Huxley, Aldous, *Brave New World*, Chatto & Windus Ltd (1932)

Ibuse, Masuji, trans. John Bester – *Black Rain*, Kodansha International (1969)

Johns, Captain W.E, *Worrals Of the* WAAF and *Worrals* Carries *On*, Lutterworth Press (1942)

Marsh, Ngaio, *Colour Scheme*, Collins (1943)

Némirovsky, Irène, trans. Sandra Smith, *Suite Française*, Chatto & Windus (2006)

Orwell, George, *1984*, Martin Secker & Warburg (1949)

Panter-Downes, Mollie, *Good Evening Mrs Craven – the Wartime Stories of Mollie Panter-Downes,* Persephone Classics (2008)

Petry, Anne, *The Street*, Mariner Books (2013) (original publication 1946)

Powell, Anne, ed., *Shadows of War: British Women's Poetry of the Second World War*, Sutton Publishing (1999)

Priestley, J.B., *Three Men in New Suits,* The Hollen Street Press Ltd (1945)

Shute, Nevil, *A Town Like Alice*, William Heinemann Ltd (1950)

Taiyi, Lin, *War Tide*, John Day Company (1943)

Film/television

Night Will Fall, Channel 4 documentary (2015)

Fabulous Fashions of the 1940s, The British Pathè Cinemagazines, Cherry Red films (2010)

Now It Can Be Told. Top secret wartime missions recreated by real life secret agents, IWM (1946)

Women and Children at War. The role of women in Britain's war effort and tales of evacuee children, IWM

Index